Basic Business Studies
Swift and Stanwell

Commerc

Fifth Edition

Moira K. Swift, LL B

Barrister-at-Law

Thelma B Holden, FSCT,
Senior Lecturer, Business and Management Studies
Department, North Lindsey College of Technology,
Formerly Head of Commerce Department,
Frederick Gough Comprehensive School.

Ronald Warson, FCIS, FCBI

Edward Arnold

© Moira K. Swift, Ronald Warson and Thelma B. Holden 1981

First published 1963
by Edward Arnold (Publishers) Ltd.,
42 Bedford Square,
London WC1B 3DQ

Reprinted 1963, 1964, 1965, 1966
Second Edition 1967
Third Edition 1970
Reprinted 1971, 1972 (with Addendum)
Fourth Edition 1973
Reprinted 1975 (with Addendum)
Reprinted 1977
Fifth Edition 1980
Reprinted 1982
Swift, Moira Kathleen
    Commerce.—5th ed.—(Basic business studies).
    1. Great Britain—Commerce
    I. Title   II. Holden, Thelma Bette   III. Warson,
    Ronald   IV. Series
    380'.0941   HF3504

    ISBN 0-7131-0491-0

The Basic Business Studies series comprises:
Commerce (5th edition)
Office Practice (4th edition)
English in the Office (Book I)
Office Practice Assignments
Spirit Master Documents:
Book 1 General Office Work
Book 2 Post Office and Bank

Typeset by Reproduction Drawings Ltd.
Sutton, Surrey
Printed in Hong Kong by
Wing King Tong Co Ltd

Contents

Preface

In the sixteen years since the first edition of this book was written, there have been enormous changes in the teaching of Commerce. There are wide-ranging changes in the basic background of industry, trade and commerce, and also much greater emphasis on the influence and involvement of the State, especially in the field of finance, in the protection of the individual and the environment, and in intervention in industry by the Government.

Britain is following the United States in becoming a 'cashless society', and a new era of credit has dawned. The Government is assisting first-time home buyers. Equal opportunity for all has evoked still more legislation. So much today is geared towards the 'consumer society' that there is considerable competition for custom, together with changes in the pattern of living and spending over the last decade. These changes are having an ever-widening effect.

Britain's entry into the Common Market, with all its subsequent developments in terms of finance, trade, agriculture and standardisation has also opened a whole new horizon.

This book, then has been rewritten bearing in mind these changes, which include a great many new Acts of Parliament, and the need for basic information on all these things. The need to introduce students to an understanding of the modern business world, and to see their place in their economic environment is being widely recognised. Even the subject title 'Commerce' is being altered by some examining bodies to indicate a broader base and more modern outlook; 'Background to Business' for example.

The book is designed for examinations at elementary and intermediate level, which have Commerce, in its broadest sense, as their basis. The syllabuses of CSE regional examining bodies and of the Royal Society of Arts have been consulted in particular as being typical at this level. Each chapter is followed by examination questions.

Learning can often prove more effective through doing, and practical exercises involving commercial, wages, banking and post office documents can be found in *Office Practice Assignments*, with the documents themselves being produced as *Spirit Master Document* books, by the same publisher.

We hope that this book will appeal to both teachers and students alike and that, not only will it prove invaluable for examination success, but also that it will be a springboard for students to a wider understanding and appreciation of the modern world.

TH

Acknowledgements

I should like to thank the many organisations which have helped in the preparation of this edition, including the banks (Barclays, Lloyds, Midland, National Westminster, TSB and National Giro-bank), the Bank of Education, the building societies (Halifax and Abbey National), the insurance companies (Sun Life and Sun Assurance and Donald McKrae and Janet Berry in particular), the Bonds and Stock Office, the Post Office, the Department of National Savings, the Co-operative Retail Society, British Airways, British Rail, Freightliners Ltd, the Inland Revenue, the DHSS, the Consumers' Association, and my local Citizen's Advice Bureau, Consumer Advice Centre, Customs and Excise Department and Weights and Measures Department.

In addition, my grateful thanks are due to my colleagues for their sympathy, help and co-operation and last, but not least, to my husband without whose active participation and resolve this book would not have been completed.

The Publisher would also like to thank the following examining bodies for permission to reproduce questions from their past examinations.

Associated Lancashire School Examinations Board	(AL)
East Anglian Regional Examinations Board	(EA)
East Midland Regional Examinations Board	(EM)
Metropolitan Regional Examinations Board	(Metro)
Middlesex Regional Examinations Board	(MR)
North Regional Examinations Board	(NR)
North West Regional Examinations Board	(NW)
The Royal Society of Arts	(RSA)
South East Regional Examinations Board	(SE)
Southern Regional Examinations Board	(SR)
South West Regional Examinations Board	(SW)
West Yorkshire and Lindsey Regional Examinations Board	(YE)
Northern Ireland CSE Board	(NI)

1

From producer to consumer

At one time, man had to satisfy his basic needs by his own efforts. If he wanted food, he hunted it or grew it. If he wanted clothes, he made them. If he wanted a house, he built it. If he wanted entertainment he sang, danced, or made and played a musical instrument. From this self-sufficiency a system of barter developed and this is discussed in Chapter 11, Means of payment.

Today, all of these needs, food, clothing and shelter, and many other goods and services, can be bought. They are all produced and made available to us, in shops, at our homes, or wherever we require them by the efforts of other people. These other people are the **producers**. When we buy the goods or services, we are the **consumers**. Almost everybody is both a producer and a consumer.

The total working population of Great Britain is over twenty-six million, which is almost half the total population. Over nine million are engaged in the production of raw materials, in manufacturing, and in construction work. Over four million are engaged in transport and distribution. The rest of the work-force is concerned with essential supplies, such as water, gas and electricity, with professional, scientific or other services, and with government. In addition there are a number of self-employed people in many industries and services.

To employ all these people who contribute so much to our way of life and standard of living, we use all the resources of nature; land, water, natural power and climate. There is a third contribution needed to add to those of **natural resources** and **labour**, and that is **capital**. This is the money required to provide the tools machinery, factories, roads, etc—used by the workers to develop the resources.

When we stand at a shop counter or market stall, or sit in a doctor's surgery, or watch television, we are the last link in a long chain. This is the **chain of distribution** (see page 34). Each link in this chain has a part to play for required goods or services to reach the customer, and the entire chain results in Production.

Production is the satisfaction of an economic need, which means making goods and services available for man where and when he wants them.

Branches of production

Production consists of three main divisions, **industry, commerce** and **direct services.**

Industry

Industry may be sub-divided into three branches, extraction (or primary industry), manufacturing and assembly, and construction (secondary production).

Extraction Extraction takes raw materials from land and sea. It may be sub-divided into exhaustive extraction, in which materials are extracted which cannot be replaced (oil, coal, the fur of an animal becoming extinct); and non-exhaustive extraction, where the raw materials are renewed (agriculture, forestry). In some cases, such as fishing, it is difficult to know whether it is exhaustive or non-exhaustive.

Manufacturing Manufacturing takes the raw materials and through a variety of processes turns them into finished goods, eg, wood into furniture, iron into ships and trains, cod into fish fingers.

Construction Construction is concerned with taking manufactured goods and using them for constructing buildings, roads, tunnels, bridges, etc.

Commerce

Commerce (tertiary services) may be sub-divided into Trade and Commercial Services (the aids to trade).

Trade Trade is made up of wholesale and retail businesses in this country, and of imports and exports in trade with other countries.

Commercial Services Commercial Services include insurance, banking and finance, advertising and distribution, which involves both transport and storage.

2

Direct services

Direct services (tertiary services) are those provided by specialists direct to the rest of the working population, enabling them to continue with their own production. A factory worker with toothache becomes less productive, but returns to full production after receiving the direct services of a dentist. Other direct services are provided by teachers, the armed forces, the police, doctors, lawyers and various entertainers.

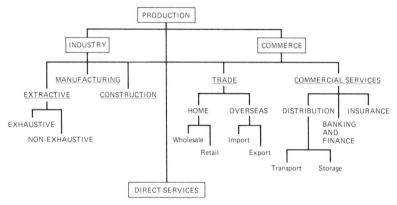

This chart shows the divisions into which PRODUCTION is divided, and each is essential. The chain must be complete if everybody's "wants" are to be satisfied.

The chain of production.

Divisions of labour

Workers are sometimes divided according to the type of work in which they specialise. Thus, those in **Primary Production** (extractive industries) include miners, fishermen, farmers, oil rig workers, foresters and fur trappers. **Secondary Production** (manufacturing, assembly and construction) includes steel-workers, shipbuilders, carpenters, tailors, roadmakers and brewers. **Tertiary Production**, which includes both commerce and direct services, includes wholesalers and retailers, bankers and insurance brokers, shop assistants, hairdressers, locomotive drivers, warehousemen, and doctors, teachers, policemen, radio and television announcers, writers and entertainers.

3

All of this means that workers tend to specialise. This allows training to be cut down to the essentials, and high efficiency can be achieved quickly and maintained.

Mass production and the standard of living

For centuries, everything that Man needed—tools, clothing, weapons, ornaments—was made by hand. It was time-consuming, but time was not important. **Specialisation** began when people with special skills chose to do one kind of work, bartering the results for the products of other workers.

As the population grew, this slow method became less and less satisfactory. There was no longer enough time to produce for the needs of everybody, and only the rich were able to satisfy all their wants. The majority had to decide on their priorities, and use their limited purchasing power on the essentials—bread, boots, coal.

The Industrial Revolution saw the beginning of the use of machinery on an extensive scale, particularly in the fields of transport, clothmaking, steam engines and printing. Unfortunately, however, the population also increased sharply. There was a need for a very large supply of cheap goods for the people of the growing factory towns, and these could only be provided by **mass production.**

Many people think that Henry Ford introduced the means of mass production. This turns away from the idea of a worker doing all the processes leading to the completion of a finished article. Instead, production is divided into a number of single small jobs, each of which can be done by one man.

In fact Sir Marc Brunel (father of I. K. Brunel) started the first **production line** in 1805, in the Royal Dockyards at Portsmouth. The Royal Navy used 100 000 pulley blocks a year, and each was made by hand, slowly and expensively. Brunel devised forty-three machines, each doing a single operation, to make the blocks. The result was that ten men working the machines, instead of 100 handworkers, produced the blocks in one-tenth of the time at a fraction of the cost.

Henry Ford's contribution in 1913 was to carry the idea to its logical conclusion, saying

Everything must be kept moving: the work must come to the man instead of the man going to the work; no man uses more than one tool; all work comes at waist height, so that no man need stoop or move his feet.

By this method of **automation**, Ford could produce a standardised car for £100, compared with thousands of pounds for the handmade models of Daimler, Benz and Rolls-Royce.

'Handmade' became synonymous with luxury goods, because highly-paid craftsmen needed hours, or days, to produce a finished article. At the same time, automated machinery produced cheap goods by the hundred-thousand. With vast quantities produced, prices dropped dramatically, and came within reach of the poorer paid. First clothing, furniture and household goods, then cars and radios, and then televisions and stereo equipment became available at prices which could be afforded by almost everybody. Things which had been luxuries became first everyday equipment, and then were regarded as necessities. This meant that the whole population lived in a greater degree of comfort, and this indicated a rise in the **standard of living.**

Consider this list (which you can probably add to) of things which have only become available to ordinary people since 1950—the mid-point of the century:

refrigerators, automatic washing machines, colour television, deep freezers, stereo equipment.

Since that time, too, many things have come on to the market because of mass production which we take for granted:

tights, transistors, fish fingers, non-stick pans, tea-bags, Japanese motor cycles, pocket calculators, electric mixers and blenders, terylene, orlon and crimplene, throw-away ball point pens and razors.

Henry Ford's requirements for mass production included:

continuity, speed, repetition, simplification, standardisation and specialisation.

As already seen these produce a continuous flow of production, using specially designed machinery and a work force of specialists, each of whom is limited to a single standardised operation which is continuously repeated at great speed.

This specialisation has a number of advantages and disadvantages.

Advantages

- High production can be achieved by comparatively unskilled workers.
- Only a minimum of training is required.
- Continuous repetition leads to expertise and efficiency.

- Time is saved by continuous production.
- Costs are reduced, and this means cheaper goods in the shops.
- Extensive use of machinery cuts the labour force.
- Men are released to other industries, thereby widening the commodities available.

Disadvantages

- Work is often monotonous and boring.
- Workers can have little pride in their work.
- Speed of production may affect quality.
- Absence of key workers can halt or delay production.
- There may be resistance to change by workers.
- Installation of modern machinery may be delayed.
- Boredom and monotony may cause workers' unrest and absenteeism.
- Mechanisation leads to unemployment.

Manufacturers are conscious of the need to compensate workers for the boredom of repetitive jobs and some firms have introduced job rotation to avoid monotony. Generally, there are good working conditions, social facilities and good pay.

Although specialisation is often considered in respect of automation, it is obvious that the administrators—accountants, personnel officers, advertising managers, etc—are certainly specialists, as are skilled craftsmen such as toolmakers.

The goods which we, the consumers require for our day-to-day living, whether necessities or luxuries, are brought to us through the efforts of all these people who are engaged in production. Each of them works for one of a wide variety of employers, private or public, and it is these which we shall examine in the next two chapters.

Questions

1. Commerce has been described as 'Trade and aids to trade'.
   - (a) Describe the branches of *trade*.
   - (b) Say how it is helped by transport, insurance, advertising and banking.
   - (c) Name any other aid to trade.

   (EM)

2. (a) Draw a diagram to show the 'Chain of Production' and add a few explanatory notes. Emphasise the part played by Commerce.
   - (b) Show how people engaged in commercial occupations

help to bring you either wool from Australia or wheat from Canada.

(WY)

3. (a) Explain the meaning of the term 'specialisation' as applied to industry.
   (b) Explain how our society has benefited from the application of specialisation to industry.

(RSA)

4. Explain what is meant by the following and show why they are important to our modern way of life:
   (a) Division of labour
   (b) Mass production
   (c) Capital

(YR)

5. Complete the following sentences with the appropriate words.
   (a) The distribution and exchange of goods is known as
   . . . .
   (b) The police, teachers, nurses and the armed forces are all examples of . . . .
   (c) The final link in the chain of distribution is the . . . . . .
   (d) The exchange of one commodity for another is called

(SR)

. . . .

6. In each of the following lists there is one odd-man-out. In each case you are required to:
   (a) name the odd-man-out, and
   (b) give a short reason in explanation of your answer.

   (i) coal miner; construction worker; train driver; farmer; fisherman; lumberjack.
   (ii) schoolteacher; nurse; vicar; actor; professional footballer; bank manager.

(SW)

2

Ownership—the private sector

Every business must have an owner or owners. There is no form of business organisation which does not belong to some person or group of persons, even though this may not at first be apparent.

This country has what is known as a **mixed economy**, which means that some of the businesses which produce goods or provide services are owned by the state—**the public sector**—and the remainder are owned by private members of the public—**the private sector**. It should be remembered that today there is a limited but growing number of organisations, formerly functioning on their own, where the state now has a shareholding. The public sector is discussed in Chapter 3.

The sole owner

The best known and most common type of personal ownership is the 'one-man business', known as the sole owner, proprietor, or trader. The last name can be confusing, since it implies a retail trader with a single shop. However, a person who owned a whole chain of retail outlets employing many workers would still be a sole trader. A sole proprietor may also be an accountant, architect or insurance broker; or be a plumber, a painter and decorator or a second-hand car dealer.

The first requirement of a person wishing to start a business as a sole owner is capital, in order to obtain premises, equipment and stock. If he has insufficient money of his own for this, he can approach a bank or a friend for a loan, or can obtain equipment on hire purchase or by leasing, can mortgage property or, in many cases can approach government agencies and departments (see Chapter 9). He may also be able to obtain stock on credit.

The sole owner will enjoy all the profits of his business. Other advantages are that he has no-one to consult, so he can make quick decisions; that he is in close contact with his custo-

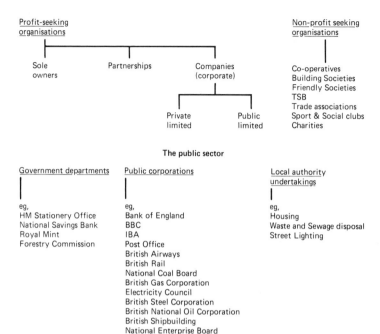

The private sector

Profit-seeking organisations	Non-profit seeking organisations

Profit-seeking organisations:
- Sole owners
- Partnerships
- Companies (corporate)
  - Private limited
  - Public limited

Non-profit seeking organisations:
- Co-operatives
- Building Societies
- Friendly Societies
- TSB
- Trade associations
- Sport & Social clubs
- Charities

The public sector

Government departments	Public corporations	Local authority undertakings
eg,	eg,	eg,
HM Stationery Office	Bank of England	Housing
National Savings Bank	BBC	Waste and Sewage disposal
Royal Mint	IBA	Street Lighting
Forestry Commission	Post Office	
	British Airways	
	British Rail	
	National Coal Board	
	British Gas Corporation	
	Electricity Council	
	British Steel Corporation	
	British National Oil Corporation	
	British Shipbuilding	
	National Enterprise Board	

The mixed economy—owners of business enterprises.

mers, and his employees, if any; and that in his own interest, he will work hard to make his business a success. Finally, once sufficient finance has been obtained there are usually very few difficulties in setting up a one-man business, although licences may be needed for certain types of business. The Registrar of Business Names was informed if the business was to have a name different from that of its owner until 1982.

The chief disadvantage of sole ownership is that the proprietor has **unlimited liability** for the debts of his business. This means that if necessary he must pay these debts by selling the business, and also his personal property, including his home. Other disadvantages include a general reluctance to risk experiments; a

9

limited amount of capital; difficulty in competing with larger companies which can often offer lower prices, discounts, greater choice, etc; difficulty in leaving the business in case of illness or the need for a holiday; the danger that the proprietor may lack the business ability or ideas necessary for success.

However, many small businesses of this kind survive and make profits, especially in a limited locality where goodwill can be generated among customers and clients by the personal service provided.

Partnerships

To overcome some of the difficulties which face a sole owner, he may find it convenient to form a partnership under the Partnership Act of 1890. This limits the total possible number of partners in one business, with certain exceptions, to twenty. The exceptions include bankers (a limit of ten), and stock-brokers, solicitors and accountants who may exceed the figure of twenty with the permission of the Department of Industry. The Act also lays down certain regulations, including the right of all partners to inspect the books and records of the business; that any agreement made by one partner is binding on the others; and that all partners are liable for any debts of the business.

It should be obvious that anyone entering into a partnership should obtain legal help in drawing up an agreement (the *articles* of partnership) to be signed by all partners. This should contain the names of the partners; the amount of capital each contributes to the business; the way in which profits and losses will be shared; and details of any salary paid to an active partner.

The advantages of a partnership are that it can provide more capital and may also provide more skill or expertise in one or other of the aspects of the business. At the same time it spreads the load of responsibility.

The disadvantages of the ordinary partnership include the continuance of **unlimited liability**. Others are the time required for consulting all partners before decisions may be made; and the difficulties which may arise on the death, retirement or bankruptcy of a partner, since these dissolve the partnership and the business has to repay that partner's share in the business. This may result in the business closing down. Problems may also arise should the partners disagree. Partnerships need careful consideration, since one partner may suffer because of another's inefficiency or dishonesty.

A **sleeping partner** is one who provides money, but takes no part in the management of the firm. He still has to share the unlimited liability arising from the business falling into debt, unless he is a limited partner.

Limited partnerships, under the Limited Partnership Act of 1907, are today unusual. They still enable a sleeping partner who has brought in more money than the others, and who feels that his personal property should not be in danger, to limit his liability to the amount of money he has invested. There must be at least one other partner with unlimited liability (ie, someone with full responsibility and liability).

Sole Trader

Partners active & sleeping

Company — Shareholders or members have limited liability

The public trades with an artificial person, the 'company'. It is controlled by a Board of Directors, and usually managed as far as day to day working is concerned by a Managing Director. Both the Board of Directors and the Managing Director act on behalf of the shareholders.

The 'company' means
i) all the shareholders
ii) the Board
iii) the Managing Director.

Limited companies or joint stock companies

Many sole owners and partnerships find it advantageous to seek what is known as 'corporate' ownership and form a **limited liability** company. As its name implies, the liability of its members is limited, which means that the shareholders are not liable for the debts of the business beyond the amount they have invested. This is because a company formed and registered is *incorporated* and becomes a separate legal entity, separate from that of the members forming it. This has the further advantage that it is the company, not its members which may sue or be sued, and that the company has continuity, since the loss of a member results only in that person's shares being transferred. Other advantages are that a greater amount of capital is likely to be available from the greater number of members, so that larger operating economies can be secured, and larger operations carried out.

11

Its disadvantages are the legal formalities required and lack of privacy. To form a limited company, it must first be registered with the Registrar of Companies in accordance with the Company Acts. The documents required are:

1. **the Memorandum of Association** (which governs its relationship with other firms or persons outside the company). This includes:

- the name of the company, including the word 'public limited company' (PLC) if applicable.
- the address of the registered office;
- the objects of the company. These are necessary because if a company acts outside its objects as set out, the doctrine of *ultra vires* (beyond one's power or authority) applies, and any contract is void and cannot be enforced.
- A statement regarding the limitation of liability of the members. (This is normally the amount, if any, unpaid on their shares.)
- The amount of authorised capital; that is, the amount the company wishes to raise;
- The issued share capital which, in the cast of a PLC (public limited company) must be in excess of £50 000. (1980 Companies Act.)

2. **the Articles of Association** (which are the regulations on the internal management of the company). They include:

- the appointment of directors and their powers;
- arrangements for meetings of shareholders;
- the rights and responsibilities attached to various kinds of shares;
- the signatures of the members who signed the Memorandum.

3. A list of persons who have agreed to become directors, together with their written consent and promise to take up shares (except in a private company)

4. A statement of nominal share capital

5. A statutory declaration of compliance with the Company Acts, signed by a solicitor, or a director or secretary

A **Certificate of Incorporation** will be issued by the Registrar

12

of Companies (the company's 'birth certificate') on receipt of the above documents, and this gives the company its legal entity, with perpetual succession (ie, even if the members of the company die, the company itself continues its legal life until it is terminated by a legal act).

The new company may now, if it is a public company, issue a **Prospectus**, offering its shares to the general public. It is intended to inform and interest those members of the public likely to become shareholders. It must be registered with the Registar of Companies, and it is the duty of the directors to ensure that it complies with the fourth Schedule of the Act. It must contain full information about the directors; its auditors; its business, and any other information likely to be of interest to possible buyers, including a **Statement of Minimum Subscription**, which is the sum required to cover the costs of forming the company and provide sufficient working capital.

A public company must also obtain a **Certificate of Trading** before it can start business. The Registrar will issue this when he is satisfied that the initial capital has been raised.

The newly-formed company is required to hold a statutory meeting of shareholders within three months, and every company must thereafter hold an **Annual General Meeting (AGM)**, and send out notice of it to all shareholders. The meeting must:

- declare a dividend;
- consider the accounts, balance sheets and reports of the auditors and directors;
- elect directors;
- appoint auditors.

These four items are the ordinary business of an AGM.

Under the **1981 Companies Act** a business which does not trade under the name(s) of its owner(s) must disclose on its stationery and business premises the names of the owner(s).

Private limited companies

The majority of all registered companies in this country are private companies, many of which originated as a family business which required the protection of being a company. If often remains a family business because:

- a maximum of fifty members (in addition to their employees) is permitted under the Company Acts;
- the company cannot offer its shares for sale to the public, and so trading on the stock exchange is not possible, and
- transfer of shares can be subject to the permission of the directors, who make all decisions in the business.

This usually restricts shareholders to family members and approved friends or business associates.

One disadvantage is a loss of privacy in that, unlike the sole owner or partnership, the private company must file annual accounts with the Registrar of Companies. This, for many small professional businesses, such as accountants and solicitors, would be an embarrassment and a breach of confidentiality.

The private company is usually regarded as ideal for the small business, and the majority of private companies are limited in size and scope. They often operate, too, in a limited area, and include contractors and local industries. However, some private companies become very large, including for example Littlewoods, which deals in a football pool business, mail order, and nation-wide variety chain stores to a value of over £400 million.

Public limited companies

Although there must be a minimum of two members of a public company, there is no upper limit on the number. This means that capital may be raised from any member of the public willing to buy a share or shares. These shareholders own the company (the bigger the share-holding the bigger the voting power), elect the directors, and are able to sell their shares at any time and to anybody. This will usually depend on whether the shareholder feels that he is getting a fair return for his money, or whether his shares are growing in value as the business becomes prosperous, or the reverse.

The great advantage of a public company is that it can raise a large amount of capital, often making use, for its business, of the small savings of many people. Other monies may be obtained from such institutions as pension funds or from other companies. This widens the scope of the business and the scale of project it can undertake, and yet enables it to obtain economies by large-scale trading.

One disadvantage of the public company is that, in order to protect the shareholders, the Companies Acts enforce strict legal requirements and documentation, which is usually costly. Again, shareholders tend to be interested only in the return on their investment, and are unconcerned with the running of the company, leaving it in the hands of the specialist directors and managers. In addition, possession of 51 per cent of a company's voting shares enables the owner to exercise complete control when voting at meetings. As already seen, directors are elected at Annual General Meetings. Thus, the buying of shares enables one company to 'take-over' another. However, the Companies

Acts enable some control to be exercised by the Department of Trade and Industry, and the Registrar of Companies must be supplied with the annual accounts, the auditors' report and the directors' report, as submitted at the company's AGM. Special rules to protect the public from gross dishonesty or inefficiency are in force for some types of companies, including insurance companies.

The shareholders' only control on policy is through the election of directors, who are then responsible for the day-to-day running of the company. The directors are likely to appoint a Managing Director, who will be professionally qualified to ensure that the company runs smoothly. He may be responsible for the appointment of other senior managers, such as a Chief Accountant, each with an area of responsibility.

For a variety of reasons, some public companies find themselves in difficulties. This may be because of inefficient management. resulting in failure to replace out-of-date machinery; to streamline old-fashioned methods of production; to change products to meet modern demands; or an ill-advised venture which fails, such as over-production of skate-boards in the short-lived craze of 1977–78. Other factors contributing to failure include industrial disputes, rising costs and foreign competition.

However, many public limited companies are household names and are regarded as models of good management. They cover a wide field, including department stores (House of Fraser), variety chain stores (Marks & Spencer), food (Sainsbury's and Cadbury–Schweppes), drink (Bass Charrington), tobacco (Imperial Tobacco) and chemicals (ICI) as well as many other industrial and financial companies.

Profit-sharing

Under Government legislation following the April 1978 Budget, a company may give an annual taxable sum of up to £500 to each employee with a qualifying period of service, with which to buy company shares. He may sell the shares after a period of five years, but the dividends become tax-free if he keeps them for fifteen years.

Profit-sharing is not a new thing, John Lewis first introduced it in 1928. It is interesting to note that some of the most successful public limited companies introduced it before the Government intervened. ICI have benefited nearly 90 000 of their staff since the scheme was introduced in 1954. Others include Lloyds Bank, British Home Stores and the House of Fraser. Marks and Spencer's employees who have been with the

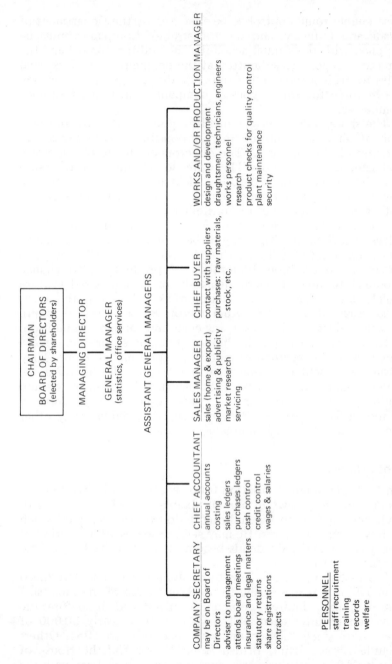

Organisation chart of a public manufacturing company.

CHAIRMAN
BOARD OF DIRECTORS
(elected by shareholders)

MANAGING DIRECTOR

GENERAL MANAGER
(statistics, office services)

ASSISTANT GENERAL MANAGERS

COMPANY SECRETARY
may be on Board of
Directors
adviser to management
attends board meetings
insurance and legal matters
statutory returns
share registrations
contracts

PERSONNEL
staff recruitment
training
records
welfare

CHIEF ACCOUNTANT
annual accounts
costing
sales ledgers
purchases ledgers
cash control
credit control
wages & salaries

SALES MANAGER
sales (home & export)
advertising & publicity
market research
servicing

CHIEF BUYER
contact with suppliers
purchases: raw materials,
stock, etc.

WORKS AND/OR PRODUCTION MANAGER
design and development
draughtsmen, technicians, engineers
works personnel
research
product checks for quality control
plant maintenance
security

16

firm for more than five years receive 4p for each £1 of gross salary for the year.

The CBI (Confederation of British Industry) conducted a survey which showed that 85 per cent of workers believed that profit-sharing leads to higher efficiency and prosperity, but some companies, with outsiders as stockholders, are afraid that employees may cash their shares and lower the standing of the company on the stock exchange. Some trade unions are opposed to profit-sharing.

Limited liability

It must be emphasised that every shareholder is liable for the company's debts *only* up to the amount he has invested, and not beyond it. If he has bought £100 worth of shares, that is the total amount for which he is personally liable, even if the company owes thousands of pounds.

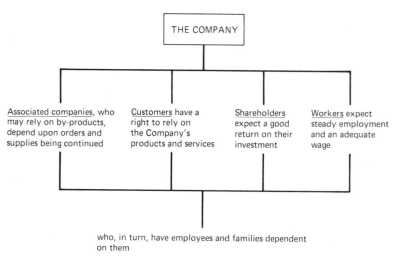

THE COMPANY

Associated companies, who may rely on by-products, depend upon orders and supplies being continued

Customers have a right to rely on the Company's products and services

Shareholders expect a good return on their investment

Workers expect steady employment and an adequate wage

who, in turn, have employees and families dependent on them

A Company's productivity, activity and efficiency also affects the business livelihood of the local community

The obligations of a company.

17

Non-profit making organisations

There are a number of organisations which have never been owned by profit-seeking owners (or shareholders) and these, though they must of course make a profit in order to continue in business, are owned and controlled by the members and are organised for the benefit of its members/customers.

Co-operative societies

These developed from the original retail co-operative set up in Toad Lane, Rochdale in 1844 by twenty-eight weavers to meet the needs of working people suffering from the profiteering of wealthy shopkeepers. The intention was, and is, that profits should be distributed to the customers in proportion to the amount they spent, and this principle was adopted by similar societies which were set up throughout Britain and in many other countries.

Each society was, and is, an independent body, governed by a committee elected by customers who had become shareholders on buying at least £1 of share capital.

As national chains of highly efficient shops and supermarkets have developed in recent years, using modern selling techniques, the co-operative societies have faced ever-increasing competition and difficulties. This has led to mergers forming regional organisations, such as the Co-operative Retail Society (CRS) and the London Society. There are now a number of very large regional societies, using modern marketing methods. These large societies provide commodities for nearly every domestic need as well as

Manchester and Salford's Co-operative Society's store in a shopping precinct at Stretford.

banking, insurance, wedding and funeral undertakings. The Co-operative Bank became a member of the London Bankers' Clearing House in 1975.

The co-operative societies have about eleven million members, and an annual turnover of nearly £3000 million.

The **Co-operative Wholesale Society** (CWS) was formed in 1863 to provide the needs of the retail societies, and it has developed into a highly-professional and well-organised body. Shares in the profits of CWS are distributed to retail societies in the same way as dividends are distributed to 'co-op' customers, ie, in proportion to the amount they buy.

As stated, a customer is established as a shareholder, with a vote, by purchasing £1 of share capital. Co-op shares, unlike shares in a public company, cannot be sold but are repayable on demand. Any member can attend meetings and use a vote to elect members of the Board of Directors (committee) which organises the society. Only one vote is allowed to each member, regardless of how many shares he or she may have.

Traditionally, the co-op 'divi' paid to members, based on the amount spent and not on shares held, was calculated every half-year, and each member could withdraw it or leave it in the society as share capital earning interest. The amount of dividend on each £ of purchases was fixed by the governing body after considering the previous year's trading surplus.

Today, the majority of societies use the National Dividend Stamp Scheme to return dividend to customers. Books of stamps are redeemable for cash, or other goods, or can be deposited in a share account.

The principles of the co-operative system, established by the 'Rochdale Pioneers' in 1844 and since, are:

- open membership to buyers of shares
- democratic control with one vote per member
- election of a committee to run the society
- payment of limited interest on capital
- dividend distribution (now usually in stamps) in proportion to purchases
- promotion of education for members, officers, employees and the general public
- co-operation among co-operatives nationally and inter-nationally
- shares can be redeemed, but not transferred or sold
- share capital supplemented by the CWS

One change in principle is that, while the Rochdale Pioneers refused to allow credit, today's co-operative societies operate a variety of credit-trading schemes, as well as radio and television rentals.

It should be noted that, unlike profit-making organisations, the co-operative societies are responsible to the Registrar of Friendly Societies, and not to the Registrar of Companies.

Building societies

These were established originally as local bodies providing funds for home ownership, and although many building societies today are large concerns with branches in nearly every town and city, their function remains the same. The building society obtains its funds from thousands of savers who receive interest on their deposits.

They are non-profit making organisations because their capital is available to their customers and not to private owners, and their annual accounts, auditors' reports and directors' reports go to the Registrar of Friendly Societies. They are subject to the

	Ownership	Control	Share of profits or losses	Liability	Legal Responsibility
Sole proprietor	One person	The one owner	The one owner	No limit	Full
Partnership	2-20 persons (with exceptions)	The active partners	Equally or otherwise by agreement	No limit	Fully on the partners
Public limited liability company	Shareholders, minimum 2, no maximum	Directors elected by shareholders	Divided amongst the shareholders according to the type and number of shares held	Limited to amount which each share-holder has agreed to contribute	On the Company
Private limited company	minimum 2, (excluding employees)	Directors elected by shareholders	Divided amongst the shareholders according to the type and number of shares held	Limited to amount which each share-holder has agreed to contribute	On the Company
Co-operative society	Shareholders, any number	Committees elected by shareholders (members)	Divided amongst the members according to their purchases	Limited	On the Society

Forms of ownership in the private sector.

Building Societies Act of 1962, and control is in the hands of groups of directors elected by voting members. These are usually members who have lent money to the society.

Other institutions

Friendly Societies, which originated in the same way as building societies, but with the object of providing insurance for their members, are also non-profit making bodies. Others include the Trustee Savings Bank, the National Trust and a wide range of clubs and societies formed by people with common interests, ranging from photography to caravanning, and from choral singing to pot-holing, and including almost every sport. They elect their officers and make their rules, and in many cases there is a national federation to help them, such as the Rambler's Association and the National Federation of Music Societies.

Questions

It may be necessary to study Chapters 9 and 10, Finance for Industry and Capital, before answering some of the questions

1. (a) State *two* advantages of trading as a sole trader.
   (b) When and where is it necessary for a business to display the name(s) of its owner(s)?
   (c) State one way in which a private limited company differs from a public limited company.
   (d) With regard to the formation of a public limited company, explain briefly *two* of the following:
   (i) a prospectus
   (ii) articles of association
   (iii) a certificate of trading

(EA)

2. Jack has just formed a small private limited company with one of his friends as the other shareholder and co-director to open a shop selling freezers and frozen foods. His brother Jim, a chartered accountant, has just entered into partnership with another accountant. Compare these two forms of business organisation, bringing out the reasons which led the two brothers each to choose the particular form he did.

(YR)

3. **Shareholders : partners : board of directors : one man**
   Using the above words in your answer, explain the differences in ownership, control and profit sharing in the following business units:
   (a) sole proprietor
   (b) partnership
   (c) limited company

   (NR)

4. Cadbury–Schweppes, National Westminster Bank, Imperial Tobacco, and ICI have all begun to offer their employees an opportunity to become shareholders in their companies:
   (i) By what name is the scheme known?
   (ii) Who was responsible for the introduction of the scheme?
   (iii) Explain in detail how the scheme works and what options are available to the investor at the end of the term.

   (SW)

5. Two partners, both of whom are skilled motor mechanics, own a garage/filling station/repair shop for motorists. They have no written agreement, and ask you to advise them on this matter. Write a short report to them giving reasons for recommendations.

   (RSA)

6. (a) Describe four features of the structure and organisation of a retail co-operative society.
   (b) A co-operative society is regarded as 'non-profit making' although the managers would argue that their function is to make profits (or surpluses). Explain *briefly* what 'non-profit making' means in respect of a co-operative society.

   (RSA)

7. Write a paragraph about the principle of limited liability.

   (RSA)

8. (a) You have bought £200 of Preference Shares in MacAndrew Ltd. Complete the Share Certificate opposite adding all the necessary details.
   (b) The company has a very successful year and declares a dividend of 20%. How much will you receive?
   (c) As a result of the successful year's trading the shares are now quoted on the Stock Exchange at £1.25 each. What are your shares now worth?
   (d) You have been given the opportunity of changing your Preference Shares for Ordinary Shares in the same company. What factors would you take into consideration before you came to a decision?

   (WY)

6% PREFERENCE SHARES

A/c No. _____   Amount of Shares

Certificate No. _____   £

                                        Represented by ____Units of
                                        £1 each.

MACANDREW LTD.
Incorporated under the Companies Act, 1862.

This is to certify that _____

_____ is/are the Registered Holder(s) of

_____ pounds six per cent Preference Shares of

MacAndrew Limited subject to the Memorandum and Articles of

Association of the Company.

The Common Seal of MacAndrew Limited was hereunto affixed

this _____day of _____ 19_____ in the presence of

Director   *Secretary*

3

Ownership—the public sector

The public sector of Britain's mixed economy consists of various Government Departments concerned with providing services to the public, Public Corporations set up to run nationalised industries, and undertakings run by local authorities. (See page 9). In many fields Government and private enterprise are involved together. For instance, the Government has shareholdings in various companies: it has major holdings in BP Ltd (British Petroleum) and, through the National Enterprise Board, in BL Ltd (British Leyland) and Rolls-Royce Ltd.

Since the beginning of the nineteenth century it has been generally considered that some services should be made available to all citizens, regardless of the ability of those citizens to pay for them as individuals, and that these must be provided via central or local government. Since the Second World War, Government participation has increased enormously with the nationalisation of various industries and services, as it has seemed wise to have central control over the essential services, such as transport, communications and fuel, both for economic reasons and with the aim of increasing efficiency. At the end of the war there was an urgent need for overhaul and re-organisation in these areas, and a shortage of private capital to carry them out. Public control would obviously be required if public money were to be used to modernise and reorganise essential services.

Public corporations

The majority of these have been set up by Act of Parliament (though some, such as the BBC were established by Royal Charter) to deal with a particular activity. They are not a government department, or even part of a department, but, being under public control, each is responsible to Parliament in various ways for day-to-day management of the industry or service.

The Board of Directors, including the Chairman, is appointed by the Minister, and may be dismissed by him; and although the

Minister does not concern himself with day-to-day management he has power to lay down overall policy, and expects to be kept fully informed and consulted.

Some of the nationalised industries are expected to be self-supporting over a period, but others, particularly those supplying a social need, are subsidised by Government grants. However, even those whose finances are expected to be self-supporting have needed help from the Treasury to cover losses.

As regards finance for capital expenditure, money which cannot be found from internal sources may be obtained either by Government loans, on which interest is payable, or by borrowing from abroad.

Parliamentary control over the Corporations is maintained partly by:

- regular examinations of accounts and reports by a House of Commons Select Committee on Nationalised Industries,
- an annual debate, and
- answers to parliamentary questions from the Minister, though these should not be concerned with administration.

Consumer Councils have been set up for most nationalised industries, in order that they may deal with complaints and suggestions from the public, and they may also advise the Minister or the board on changes considered desirable.

Public Corporations include those for:

fuel—British Gas Corporation; the Electricity Council; National Coal Board; UK Atomic Energy Authority; British National Oil Corporation.

transport—British Rail; National Freight Corporation; National Bus Company; British Airways.

communications—the Post Office; the British Broadcasting Corporation; the Independent Broadcasting Authority.

finance—the Bank of England.

industry—British Steel Corporation; British Aerospace; British Shipbuilders.

Goverment ownership of industry outside the public corporations has been transferred largely to the National Enterprise Board (NEB) which is itself a public corporation established under the Industry Act of 1975. It has become a holding company for Government shareholdings in industry and a channel for government funds to selected sectors of private industry. It is intended to develop the economy, promote industrial efficiency

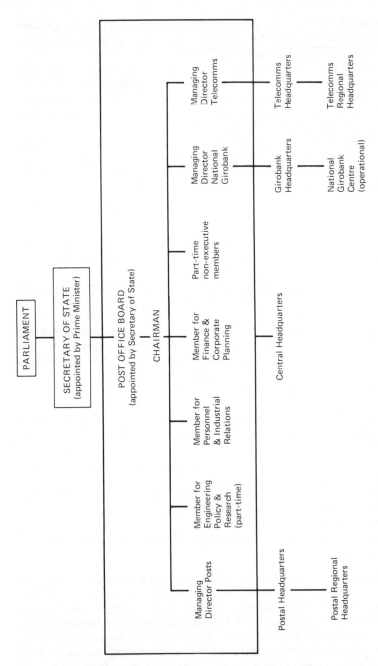

PARLIAMENT

SECRETARY OF STATE
(appointed by Prime Minister)

POST OFFICE BOARD
(appointed by Secretary of State)

CHAIRMAN

Managing Director Posts

Member for Engineering Policy & Research (part-time)

Member for Personnel & Industrial Relations

Member for Finance & Corporate Planning

Part-time non-executive members

Managing Director National Girobank

Managing Director Telecomms

Postal Headquarters

Central Headquarters

Girobank Headquarters

Telecomms Headquarters

Postal Regional Headquarters

National Girobank Centre (operational)

Telecomms Regional Headquarters

Organisation chart of the Post Office headquarters.

26

and provide productive employment (while obtaining an adequate return on its outlay). (See also Chapter 9, Finance for industry.) The Board acquires shares in industry in return for funds, as in the case of BL (British Leyland), where it has a majority holding, and can influence operations, just as a shareholder can influence operations in a public limited liability company by acquiring 51 per cent of voting stock. In the case of BL, the intentions, in addition to those above, were also to protect jobs and to protect the economy by providing a British product to compete with imported foreign cars.

One of the latest investments of NEB is £50 million in the micro-electronics industry.

Government departments

These own or have control of a large amount of property outside the public corporations, ranging from HMSO (Her Majesty's Stationery Office), which has eight printing works and six binding works, to motorways which have an essential part to play in industry; from Ministry of Defence Ordnance factories and Royal Dockyards to the Royal Mint; and from the Forestry Commission which has 4.93 million acres of woodland to the Inland Waterways Board controlling 2000 miles of canals.

Local authorities

Local authorities consist of two main groups: **county councils** (the top tier) which are responsible for major services, and **district councils** (the second tier) which are responsible generally for more local services. In connection with the provision of these services, the councils require a considerable amount of property and maintain a large work-force, employing about 2.8 million workers, including administration, professional and technical staffs, manual workers and teachers.

The county councils require facilities to provide the protective services (police, fire, civil emergency); education, including schools, further education colleges, libraries and youth centres; and health services which include refuse and sewage disposal, pollution control and abattoirs. However, housing for rental is provided by district councils, which own about 6.6 million houses and flats. For example, 47 per cent of the 314 600 dwellings built in 1976 were built by district councils. Some were built by the district councils' own labour, others by private firms. Housing accounts for one-third of the total capital expenditure of local authorities.

Local authorities are also responsible for the building of non-trunk roads, and for the maintenance of all roads within their boundaries. Provision also has to be made for the elderly, mentally ill and handicapped, and for children. This includes 2500 homes for the elderly, training centres and day centres for the handicapped, day nurseries, and homes for children in the care of the local authorities.

Other local authority property, which is in use by the general public every day, includes museums, art galleries, parks and sports-grounds, and commercially run car parks, bus services, swimming pools and restaurants and libraries.

Management of these services and the property necessary for their upkeep is in the hands of unpaid members of the council, who are elected by the voters at local government elections. Most councils use the committee system, where policies decided by the full council are administered for each service by the appropriate committee. For some functions it is necessary for neighbouring councils to appoint joint committees.

It is obvious that the unpaid 'amateur' councillor is in need of expert advice, and also help in the carrying out of council policy. For this purpose officials are employed, and they range from highly qualified heads of departments, such as the County Treasurer, to clerical and manual workers.

Finance for local authority undertakings is obtained from the rates, from Government grants, from rents, licence fees and profits from trading. A popular way of increasing revenue is local authority lotteries. Money is also raised by loans from the Government's Public Works Loan Board and from the general public and also from bonds issued on the Stock Exchange.

The National Health Service

The National Health Service was set up in 1948 and is based upon the principle that medical care and advice should be readily available to everyone, at little or no cost. The service is financed largely from general taxation revenue (over four-fifths) while the rest is met from a small part of the national insurance contributions paid by employers and employees and from charges paid by people using certain services.

Area health authorities are responsible, through Regional Health Authorities, for area planning and operational control of all health services in their area and are statutory agencies of central government. They co-operate closely with local authorities responsible for social work, environmental health, education and other services. Area authorities and health boards have a certain amount of discretion in determining the best patterns of services for their area but they must also take account of national priorities. In most areas the day-to-day running of services is carried out by management teams in districts which usually contain a general hospital.

The health authorities and boards consist of unpaid part-time members. Those in English regional authorities are appointed by the health minister concerned. They consist not only of representatives from the medical profession and health service but from professional, local authority, university and other interests.

The ultimate responsibility for all aspects of the NHS lies with the health ministers—the Secretary of State for Social Services in England, and the Secretaries of State for Scotland, Wales and Northern Ireland; and the health departments for each country (the Department of Health and Social Security in England) are responsible for strategic planning.

Logos of some public corporations.

In January 1982 the NFC became the National Freight Company (rather than Corporation) on being transferred to the private sector. Shares were bought by staff and management with outside financial backing. Similar 'privatisation' (public participation in capital) may take place with the BNOC, British Aerospace and British Airways.

Nationalisation: arguments for and against

For
1. *Natural monopolies*. It would be inefficient and expensive to have some services provided by a number of private companies.
2. *Expense*. Industries in need of extensive modernisation after the 1939–45 War could not obtain sufficient funds from private sources.
3. *Socially desirable*. Some services should be available to all members of the public, either free or at reasonable cost, and so should be subsidised from taxes.
4. *Basic economic importance*. Industries which are essential to the economic life of the nation should not be in private hands.
5. *Unemployment*. Industries which employ large labour forces should not be allowed to decline.
6. *Labour relations*. Industries with poor labour relations would benefit from public ownership.
7. *Government control*. In times of war or national emergency the Government should have certain basic needs under their control.

Against
1. *Politics*. It is argued that nationalisation is on political grounds.
2. *Inefficiency*. Very large organisations tend to become inefficient. This is especially true where there is no contact between management and work force.
3. *Motivation*. Waste, inefficiency and under-production result from knowledge that public money is available to cover losses.
4. *Over-manning*. Public corporations tend to overman administrative departments.

Public corporations

Year of Original Act	Name of Corporation
1927	The British Broadcasting Corporation (BBC)
1940	BOAC, joined in 1946 by BEA, became British Airways in 1971
1946	The Bank of England
1946	The National Coal Board (NCB)
1947	The Electricity Council
1947	British Rail (BR)
1947	British Transport Docks
1947	British Road Services (BRS)
1948	British Gas Corporation
1954	UK Atomic Energy Authority (UKAEA)
1954	Independent Television Authority (ITA), became Independent Broadcasting Authority (IBA) in 1973
1965	British Airports Authority (BAA)
1967	British Steel Corporation (BSC)
1968	National Freight Corporation (NFC)
1968	National Bus Company
1969	Post Office Corporation (previously a Government Department)
1975	British National Oil Corporation (BNOC)
1975	The National Enterprise Board (NEB)
1976	British Aerospace (BAe)
1977	British Shipbuilders

Which of the reasons for nationalisation given in this chapter is most appropriate to each of the above corporations?

Questions

1. What do you understand by a mixed economy?
2. Which of the following people are employed by public corporations?
   A stewardess on a British Airways aircraft;
   a railway porter; a BBC announcer; a taxi driver;
   a coal miner; a teacher.

3. (a) Name the nationalised industries responsible for each of the following:
   (i) transport (ii) power (iii) communication
   (b) How is any *one* of these industries controlled, and how does it obtain its income?
   (c) State *one* argument *for* and *one* argument *against* nationalisation of industry.

(Metro)

4. (a) State *three* ways in which the central government and *three* ways in which local authorities obtain their funds from citizens.
   (b) Describe *three* ways in which each spends its money for the benefit of citizens.

(Metro)

5. (a) Give *two* examples of industries owned by central government and *two* owned by the local authority.
   (b) How does a nationalised industry differ from a public company in the way it raises capital?

(WY)

4

Buying and selling

Goods produced or manufactured for sale must be put on the market, and the four principal methods of distributing manufactured goods, as shown in the diagram below, are:

- manufacturer to retailer via wholesaler
- manufacturer direct to retailer
- manufacturer direct to consumer
- manufacturer to mail order warehouse

The choice of route depends often on circumstances and on the type of goods. For example, for a very large item such as a ship or an aeroplane, a customer will go direct to the maker to place an order. A grocer on the other hand, will stock a choice of biscuits by ordering from a wholesaler who specialises in grocery items and who has biscuits from a number of manufacturers. Some manufacturers and producers now have their own shops or may offer a mail order service 'direct to the public at factory/farm prices'.

Wholesaling

Traditionally the wholesaler (sometimes called the dealer, merchant, agent, or factor) is the link between producer or manufacturer and the retail selling outlet and is often referred to as the 'middleman'. Wholesalers, for example, dominate the distribution of groceries and provisions and cash and carry wholesale warehouses have increased in number in recent years. These are used by small local shopkeepers, hoteliers, catering establishments etc, who collect their requirements. By buying in bulk and by cutting out credit and delivery facilities, the cash and carry wholesalers can offer substantial price discounts to their customers. In fact, cash and carry wholesalers account for about 40 per cent of turnover of all grocery warehousing.

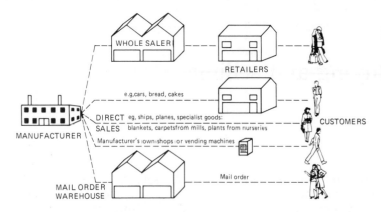

The chain of distribution.

Multiple traders (those with ten or more branches) generally by-pass the wholesaler and have their own buying and distribution organisations. Branches then order stock through their Head Office to the central store.

To try to compete with this, many wholesalers have joined with independent retailers to form voluntary organisations (eg, Spar, Bob, Vivo, Mace) in order to give smaller retailers the advantages of bulk-buying and co-ordinated distribution and, in

A cash and carry warehouse.

34

fact, over one-third of all independent grocers are members of voluntary groups.

The co-operative movement in Britain has established its own wholesale organisation, the Co-operative Wholesale Society (CWS), to serve the needs of retail co-operative societies, and is a manufacturer, trader, importer and provider of many services.

Methods of wholesale distribution vary according to the type of merchandise handled. Fish, for example, is auctioned at the ports to port wholesalers who in turn may sell to inland wholesalers or direct to retailers. Increasingly, however, it is sold by contract to fryers and processors.

Wholesale markets play a leading part in the distribution of foodstuffs, including the famous ones in London;

New Covent Garden for fruit and vegetables,
Smithfield for meat and poultry,
Billingsgate for fish.

The wholesaler makes his profit by buying in bulk at a discount from the manufacturer and selling to the retailer at a higher price. Although there is the feeling that if the number of people between the manufacturer and the consumer were smaller, then the price of goods would be lower, the wholesaler still performs a useful service.

Services to the manufacturer

- purchases in large quantities for selling in smaller lots;
- relieves manufacturer of warehousing costs;
- saves manufacturer packaging and paper work;
- cuts down employment of salesmen by manufacturers by selling to wholesalers rather than to hundreds of retailers;
- advises manufacturer on current demands.

Services to the retailer

- provides a place where buyers can choose products of more than one manufacturer;
- provision of small quantities at frequent intervals means that retailer needs less storage space, his capital is not tied up in stock, and there is less likelihood of obsolete goods left on his hands;
- storage and supply of seasonal goods;
- offers credit facilities to regular customers, which enables retailer to sell goods before he has to pay for them unless cash and carry facilities are used.

Farmers, agricultural and horticultural producers market their goods either through private trade channels, through co-operatives formed by producers, or through **marketing boards** set up by Parliament to help with the production and marketing of particular products.

There are two types of marketing boards. One is either the sole buyer of the commodity from all producers, or the controller of contracts between buyers and sellers (eg, hops, milk and wool); the other is the type of board which, whilst having a wide control over the market, actually leaves the producers free to deal with their own buyers (eg, the Potato Marketing Board). In Northern Ireland pig and seed potato boards fall into the first category.

The marketing boards are producers' organisations having statutory powers to regulate the supply and marketing of particular products. A minority of board members are appointed by the ministers concerned. The schemes which they operate must be approved by Parliament. The boards also provide market intelligence, promote research and development, safeguard the interests of both producer and consumer and, in some cases, arrange for promotional advertising (eg, by the Egg and Milk Marketing Boards).

The diagram below shows the various ways that most fruit and vegetables reach the housewife. A good example of a producers' co-operative marketing association is the egg-packing station.

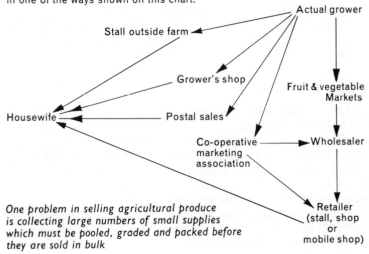

Fruit and Vegetables and other raw produce may reach the consuming public in one of the ways shown on this chart.

One problem in selling agricultural produce is collecting large numbers of small supplies which must be pooled, graded and packed before they are sold in bulk

Shopping habits and places

People's shopping habits vary according to their personal circumstances, where they live and the transport available. The high proportion of 'working wives' has led to 'late-night openings', and the availability of family cars has meant the expansion of superstores, with large car parks, away from town centres. This is often at the expense of markets and high street shops. For the same reasons, and the growing use of deep freezers, Cash and Carry and bulk buy supermarkets have flourished, enabling housewives to shop periodically, say once a month, and also enabling them to take advantage of the price reductions which result from buying in bulk.

On the other hand, the cut-back in local bus services could make users of public transport rely more on the shopping facilities in their locality, whether they are shops in a village, on a housing estate, or mobile shops. The prices might be slightly higher but this could be offset against the cost of transport.

Today there is a trend in town planning to provide pedestrian shopping precincts where vehicular traffic is excluded. In some cities this means car parking on the perimeter with free bus services to the city centre.

In all shopping areas where customers serve themselves from open displays and then take the goods to a cash desk or 'paypoint', the owners have found it necessary to budget for annual losses of thousands of pounds as a result of shop-lifting.

A pedestrian shopping precinct.

There is a tendency nowadays for most shopping centres to look alike, with shops having the same names and similar decor in each town. There are fewer individual 'sole traders' in town centres, largely because of the high rents charged and the inability to compete with the low prices of the multiples. These individual shops are more likely to be found in the side streets and on estates where rents and property are cheaper.

Retail businesses in Britain may be classified under four main headings:

- independent retailers,
- multiple traders,
- department stores, and
- retail co-operative societies,

although there are other outlets to consider. In addition, there are gas and electricity showrooms which, although forming part of a nationalised industry, are retail selling points for a variety of gas and electric appliances by different manufacturers.

Sole traders

Although in decline owing to the competition from larger undertakings, the single unit shops still play an important role in terms of convenience, service and range of goods stocked. They are often situated near homes (the 'corner shop'), provide personal service and interest, stay open late, give credit to regular customers (purchases are put 'on the slate'), and may have a delivery service. A newsagent for instance may stock items ranging from confectionery, hardware and patent medicines to haberdashery. The butcher may also sell vegetables and grocery items. In the side streets of town centres the fashion boutique and hairdresser are often sole traders; the owner's only shop.

The proprietor of a smaller shop may have another means of livelihood, the business being looked after by his wife. Alternatively, the shop may be owned by the wife. The development of self-service trading and pre-packaged goods over the last two decades has enabled the single unit shop-keeper to save on the employment of shop assistants and, as mentioned under wholesaling, the sole trader can belong to a voluntary group to finance central buying in bulk at lower prices.

Multiple traders

The multiple or chain store may have grown from the expansion of one single shop, or it may have been set up as a chain by its owners. This series of retail shops may sell one type of goods, eg, footwear (Saxone), clothing (Richard Shops), or electrical goods (Curry's), or may be 'variety chain stores' selling different types of goods, eg, Woolworth, Marks & Spencer, Boots.

Most multiple chains have their own warehouses and so buy direct from manufacturers. The head office is responsible for ordering stock and for the payment of rent, rates, wages, etc.

The design and naming of the multiple shop front is the same at each branch and this has the advantage of being easily recognisable by the shopper as well as saving on architects' fees when a new store is planned. Multiple traders are to be found in almost every town, and their large turnover enables them to employ advertising agencies, market research experts, and pay for the best sites in town. There are training schemes for staff which result in efficient service and the customer knows that the quality of goods and service is consistent throughout branches.

Department stores

Department stores are those with a number of departments under one roof. These departments may sell furniture, fancy goods, clothing, footwear, household and electrical goods and appliances, china, books and stationery, and also provide services such as a restaurant, hairdresser and travel agency. Some large establishments may even provide a crèche while mothers do their shopping.

Department stores usually sell quality goods, have pleasing décor, lifts and escalators, and are situated centrally in well-populated areas. They also offer budget accounts, monthly charge accounts, and credit facilities to enable their regular customers to pay for their goods over a period or at a later date.

Department stores may be owned by multiples, by independents or by co-operative societies. Many old-established independent department stores have been taken over by other groups and some still retain their original name. Some, notably Harrods of London, are world-renowned and attract many thousands of overseas visitors. Because of their high overheads (expensive premises and fittings, well-paid and trained staff, good working conditions), department stores need to be situated in busy areas in order to get sufficient custom to provide a good turnover. However, the quality and variety of their goods tend to attract customers from smaller towns from a considerable distance.

The layout of most department stores follows the same pattern: small items, stationery, beauty counters, haberdashery, etc readily accessible to shoppers on the ground floor; fashion on an upper floor, with furniture, restaurants and hairdressing on the top floors. China, electrical items and the food department may be in the basement.

Retail co-operative societies

About 13 000 shops in Britain are co-operative shops. They are situated both in town centres and suburbs. There are large department stores, self-service supermarkets, small shops, bakeries and dairies, and a recent development is the superstore providing car parking facilities. The societies provide commodities for nearly every domestic need as well as banking, insurance, wedding and funeral undertakings.

The ownership of co-operative shops and the dividend paid to members is discussed in Chapter 2. However, the basic difference between co-operative shops and others is that they are owned and controlled by the people who shop there. Anyone can join a co-operative society on payment of a few pence towards his first share. Once a member, he can attend meetings and exercise his vote in electing members on to the Board of Directors which governs each society.

Mail order

Mail order trading, either through a mail order business or direct from retailer, wholesaler or manufacturer (direct selling), accounts for about 4 per cent of total retail sales, the main products being clothing, textiles and soft furnishings. There are opportunities for 'direct from factory' or special offer prices, although the cost of post and packing often has to be added to the offer price.

There are various ways of reaching the buying public—by catalogue, sales representatives, agents or newspaper and magazine advertisements. Some well-known département stores (eg, Selfridges, Gamages) do a considerable amount of mail order business through newspaper advertisements.

The mail order service is useful for isolated, busy or infirm people who can select their purchases in their own home in their own time. Customers cannot usually see goods before purchase but reputable firms give money-back guarantees for dissatisfied customers.

Payment can be by various methods: advertisements in the press require either cheque or cash with order (CWO), allow payment by instalments, or use the Post Office Cash on Delivery (COD) service (see Chapter 7). Care should be taken before sending money to an unknown firm as there have been instances when goods have not been received, and it is all too easy for letters of complaint to be ignored or 'lost'. It should be remembered, too, that there is unlikely to be any after-sales service for appliances and equipment.

Thriving mail order businesses are the book and record societies which send monthly information sheets to members from which a selection can be made. There is usually a minimum number to be ordered annually but initially free or very cheap books or records are an inducement to join.

Other mail order companies recruit agents by offering a percentage of sales; these agents are often housewives who build up a friendly circle of customers. Goods are chosen from large, glossy catalogues and ordered and paid for through the agent. Payment is allowed by instalments at no extra charge and the local agent pays the weekly collections usually over the Post Office or bank counter into the National Giro or bank account of the mail order company.

The mail order business has the advantage that it does not require expensive shop fronts in town centres but a warehouse, packing bay and office in a less expensive area. Although the overheads may be comparatively low the mail order business has other costs to take into account: packaging, carriage costs, correspondence, advertising, security, returned goods and bad debts. Goods may be delivered by parcel post, by road transport, or by rail.

Mobile shops and hawkers

The simplest way of selling is to take the item for sale to a possible buyer. In the past the hawker was a man with a basket walking from house to house offering for sale rather cheap and sometimes inferior quality goods. This type of hawker does still exist but the modern extension of the hawker is the mobile shop, offering for sale perfectly sound goods. Mobile shops are mainly concerned with food sales: bakers, grocers, greengrocers, butchers, fishmongers and ice-cream vendors, with only a small proportion specialising in paraffin supplies and hardware. Milk delivery vans now also sell foodstuffs in some areas.

The mobile shops are generally independently owned, often by sole traders as an extension of their business. However, a thriving part of the co-operative societies is their sales through mobile food shops.

The advantages to the housewife are obvious: convenience, choice of fresh foods and friendly service. The owner has few overhead expenses so his prices are likely to be competitive. His potential market may be reduced, however, by the modern tendency of wives to be out at work during the day.

Street traders and market stalls

The 'barrow boy', as he is called, may have one single barrow, be the owner of a fleet of barrows, or even have no barrow as such. These street traders usually carry small stocks, aiming to clear their goods quickly and, when perishables are concerned, to be left with no stock at the end of the day. The barrow is a moveable selling point and there are laws stipulating where barrows may be placed.

The next step up the ladder is the market stall. These stalls are very much sought after and traders often wait many years to get the stall they want, perhaps in a favoured position. The landlords are very often the local councils and there are strict hygiene regulations.

A market stall may be an extension of a single unit shop, or it may be the holder's only selling outlet. He may travel from one market to another with his wares. Egg producers and market gardeners often have stalls in order to sell direct to the public. The market is also a place where sub-standard goods and 'seconds' (factory rejects) are sold, notably in china, fabrics, household linen and clothing.

Because there are few overheads, goods from the market may be cheaper than in the shops, and from farm stalls the food is likely to be fresher. However, there are a few unscrupulous traders who are continually on the move and so the buyer should beware. There are few facilities for trying on clothes and we all know that the beautiful display of fruit does not guarantee the same quality in our shopping basket.

Nevertheless, the market place is a very popular shopping attraction. Most large towns have indoor market halls but there are still many towns that hold the traditional market day in the market place which was originally linked to the cattle market.

Automatic vending machines

Many of the vending machines in use are installed in offices and factories, supplying drinks and meals. These installations have increased in recent years to save labour costs in the provision of refreshments. Other items sold from vending machines include cigarettes, confectionery and, of course, postage stamps. As mentioned in Chapter 14 it is possible to get immediate and instant travel insurance from a machine at some airports and railway stations.

The buyer knows in advance what he is going to get from the machine, or he is able to select his purchase from items on view through a glass front by manipulating the appropriate buttons and inserting the correct change. This form of selling has the great advantage that it operates for twenty-four hours each day for seven days a week. As with most machinery there are, of course, occasional breakdowns and the customer must have the correct change.

There are firms which specialise in the supply of vending machines and their products. Their terms for the installation of machines vary according to individual conditions.

Supermarkets

Supermarkets are not in any particular category since they can be owned by sole traders, multiple concerns, co-operative socie-ties or department stores. There is, however, a difference in the meaning of the various terms used.

Supermarkets are defined as self-service shops with a mini-mum selling area of 2000 square feet (186 square metres).

Superstores, also known as **hypermarkets**, are increasing in number. They generally operate a selling area of between 20 000 and 100 000 square feet (1860 and 9290 square metres respec-tively); hypermarkets have a minimum selling area of 50 000 square feet (4645 square metres). These stores operate on super-market lines but with a much wider range of goods. They are generally associated with exclusive car-parking facilities and situated away from established central shopping areas.

Supermarkets rely on attracting custom and they do this in various ways:

- late-night shopping times,
- reduced prices and special offers,
- trading stamps (with 'bonus' days),
- shoppers' bus
- car parking facilities

Some items, known as **loss leaders**, are sold at a loss in order to attract custom; they rely on shoppers then being tempted by other merchandise. Displays are strategically placed to catch the eye of the shopper, especially by the pay-out till where that bar of chocolate can be placed in the basket at the last minute. If shoppers become too used to the layout of a store they will go straight to the items required so that some stores have a policy of periodically changing the layout so that customers pass, and are tempted by, other items.

Stores also benefit by manufacturers organising competitions, offering special purchases at reduced prices and including coupons for a price reduction on the next purchase in order to boost sales. Free-tasting and free sample stands are also a feature to be found in stores.

The giving of **trading stamps** is on the decline in favour of greater price reductions. Shoppers prefer an immediate saving rather than to save stamps which have themselves fallen in value over the years. However, the cycle may turn again (as it has in America) and the trading stamp companies are looking at ways to bring trading stamps back into favour. It is possible now, for instance, to add cash to a stamp collection in order to get the item required.

There is another type of supermarket, called a **cash and carry discount store**, which dispenses with much of the trimmings to be found in other stores. The displays are likely to be samples only and the customer takes his purchases from crates or from

A hypermarket (or superstore). Note the car parking facilities.

large boxes on shelves, and rather than buy a single tin of fruit he will be expected to buy a box of tins. Some items, like dried fruit, cooking oil, coffee, etc will be in large cartons or containers. The prices are generally lower than in normal supermarkets but the initial outlay for the housewife will be higher because she is buying in greater quantity than for her immediate needs. Such an establishment is useful, however, for the working housewife who likes to keep her shopping expeditions to the minimum. Groups of housewives may decide to join together to buy in bulk, sharing out the purchases later.

There are also discount stores which specialise in consumer durables such as cut price electrical goods and, again, display is often kept to a minimum, the shopper being expected to know and ask for exactly what he wants. The store may even display catalogues or leaflets from which goods may be chosen. Such a place is unlikely to offer credit or instalment facilities or after-sales service.

Methods of buying

By description or grade

Some articles can be so carefully graded that the buyer knows exactly what he is getting without seeing the articles beforehand. Items which can be acquired with absolute certainty in this manner are securities bought on the Stock Exchanges. In industry and commerce a great deal of buying is done in this way, merely on paper, of goods capable of grading and description, eg, cotton and wool.

Among items bought by the general public are drugs, screws, bolts, car parts or roses, which can be accurately ordered from a catalogue.

By sample

This means that there is an opportunity of examining a small part of something which is much larger; it can be part of something supplied in bulk or a single example of articles which are mass-produced. By law (The Sale of Goods Act 1893) it is laid down that the buyer may expect the bulk to correspond with the sample and, if it does not, the buyer is not obliged to accept the goods.

In commerce, goods such as tea and the lesser grades of wool are bought by sample. Also, samples of wool and material are often sent out with catalogues and descriptive leaflets so that the buyer can judge quality and colour before ordering. A customer can also choose wallpaper, carpeting and curtaining from sample books.

45

By auction

There are three main kinds of auction:

Auction sale: The auction sale is well known both in business and private experience and is used to dispose quickly of a large or miscellaneous collection of items. The auctioneer acts as agent for the seller and normally goods are sold to the highest bidder although there may be a reserve price stated by the seller. The sales may be by sample, the items may themselves actually be in the sale-room for inspection, or property may have been viewed beforehand.

Dutch auction: At a Dutch auction the auctioneer names a price and then reduces the price until he receives a bid. This unusual form is used for some perishable goods when the price named by the auctioneer is usually the average for the day preceding. It is often used when auctions are held for charities when the auctioneer starts the bidding at a very high price. Some market stall holders or travelling salesmen may use this method for selling such things as cheap china or cutlery.

Tender: Tendering is the term used when the buyer states what he wants and the sellers are each allowed to make one bid which cannot be changed. Although not necessarily so, the lowest bid will usually get the order from the prospective buyer.

Futures contracts

These are a form of buying by traders, often in the produce or commodity market, who need to secure a fixed price for goods which they will require for future delivery, say in three or six months' time. The buyer and seller will be trying to cover themselves against opposite risks; the buyer that the prices may rise after he has fixed his own selling price, or submitted a tender, thus destroying his profit; the seller that the price of his stock may fall before he can dispose of it. The advantages to the buyer are that he can plan his costs in advance, and be sure that his profit margin is secure; that his capital is not tied up in materials for which he has no immediate use; and that he does not need to find storage space for the goods. On the other hand, he takes the risk that prices may fall after agreeing a price, and that he could have bought more cheaply in the open market.

The advantage to the seller is that he is guaranteed a market in advance for his goods, but he takes the risk of prices rising in the interim period, and being forced to sell below market price.

Futures contracts can only be made in goods which can be accurately graded and sold by description. Metals, corn, wool, and produce such as cocoa, coffee, wheat, sugar and potatoes all come into this category.

By inspection

Most people make nearly all their purchases by inspection of the goods, by direct dealing between the buyer and the seller. The customer relies on the seller to present him with a variety of goods and relies on his own judgment in deciding whether the goods are suitable for his purposes and whether the price is such that he is willing to pay it.

Commercial documents

When buying goods over the shop counter the transaction between the buyer and the sales assistant is often quite informal and spontaneous with very little paper work between the two parties other than a till receipt being given to the customer for cash received.

The procedure follows a pattern: first of all there is an **enquiry** ('Have you any black shoes, size six?'). Details are given in reply with the **price** and, if this is acceptable, the customer **orders** the shoes; they are wrapped and **delivered** and **payment** is made. If the shoes are in any way faulty they may be returned to the shop and a **credit note** given against future purchases, or the goods exchanged or the money refunded.

Several shops may be approached in the first instance to see what each has to offer before a decision is made. The decision may be based upon the quality, style, suitability or price of the goods or even whether the shop (or make of shoe) has a good reputation and gives good service.

The procedure is much the same for a formal transaction between business firms wishing to buy and sell, the difference being that some paper work and documentary evidence is involved at most stages as written records and proof are needed. Buyers in business have also to decide which supplier to choose and in addition to those points outlined above the decision will also be based on the delivery date and terms offered (ie, discounts, length of time for payment, carriage costs, etc).

The chart below sets out what is done, and the documents involved, at each stage of a sale in business. It should be remembered that not all steps are essential in every transaction.

Buyer	**Seller**
1. Enquiry: by letter, form or telephone to suppliers selected from trade directories, Yellow Pages, publicity literature or by recommendations or previous association. ──────────▶	
◀──────────	*2. Quotation:* by letter, form, catalogue and price list, pro forma invoice or in the form of a tender or estimate. Gives price, terms, delivery date.
3. Purchase order: official written order to selected supplier. States goods required, quantity, price, catalogue or reference number, delivery date (ie, repeats terms given on quotation). ──────────▶	
	Invoice set: set of documents, the top copy of which is the invoice, prepared by supplier on receipt of order. (Other copies, with prices obliterated often in different colours for easy recognition.)
◀──────────	*4. Advice note:* acknowledgement of order sometimes sent.
	5. Despatch note: to despatch department for assembling and packing of goods.
◀──────────	*6. Delivery note (or packing note):* enclosed with goods.
7. Goods received note (GRN): issued to purchases department and accounts to notify receipt of goods. Quantities and quality of goods checked against purchase order, and supplier notified of discrepancies in writing within the maximum time allowed as shown on the advice or delivery note. ──────────▶	

← *8. Invoice:* bill setting out—full description of goods, price, discounts, terms of payment, VAT, names of buyer and supplier, invoice number, date and buyer's order number.

9. Invoice checked against purchase order and GRN.

← *10. Credit note:* corrects shortages or losses in delivery if these are not replaced. Returnable crates are invoiced and credited when returned empty. (Credit notes often printed in red to distinguish from invoice.)

← *11. Debit note:* corrects undercharges on an invoice (eg, delivery charges not known when invoice made out).

← *12. Statement of account:* statement, usually monthly, showing debit and credit transactions and balance due at the end of the month.

13. Remittance: payment made (after statement of account checked against invoices and credit notes received), usually by cheque, bank giro or National Giro bank. *Remittance advice note*, which may accompany cheque, is sometimes a tear-off portion of invoice. →

← *14. Receipt:* only if requested, since cleared cheques act as receipts.

49

There are various abbreviations and terms associated with commercial documents and some of these can be seen in the illustrations of an invoice and statement on pages 51 and 52.

Carriage forward (Cge fwd) means that the buyer pays for the carriage of the goods purchased. The sender may pay the charges and include the cost on the invoice.

Carriage paid (Cge pd) means that the supplier (seller) of the goods pays for the carriage of the goods purchased.

Cash discount is an allowance to encourage the prompt payment of accounts. '$2\frac{1}{2}$ per cent monthly' means that $2\frac{1}{2}$ per cent may be deducted from the invoice total if it is paid within one month of the date of the invoice. Cash discount is usually a small percentage (say $1\frac{1}{2}$-5 per cent) and is not shown on the invoice as a deduction.

Strictly net, or **net monthly** printed on the invoice indicates that no cash discount is deductable and that full payment is expected within one month of the invoice date.

Trade discount is a discount between trades usually when the buyer is buying with the intention of re-selling; for example a retailer buying from a wholesaler or manufacturer. The allowance represents the retailer's gross profit when the goods are resold. For instance, if the wholesaler's catalogue price for an item is £100 and trade discount of 25 per cent is allowed, the buyer actually pays £75; his profit margin when he resells the goods at £100 is £25. Trade discount is generally a high percentage (say 10-$33\frac{1}{3}$ per cent) and is shown on the invoice and deducted from the gross price of the goods. VAT is charged on the net price of the goods *after* the deduction of any discounts, ie, on the price actually paid.

Quantity discounts are sometimes offered by traders for items bought from them in quantity or bulk. The percentage may vary according to the amount ordered: the larger the order the higher the discount.

E & OE (errors and omissions excepted) is printed by many firms at the foot of their invoices, estimates and quotations. These letters mean that if an error or omission has been made in the prices on the document the firm selling the goods may put it right subsequently. The error could be arithmetical or typographical. If the error occurs on an invoice, undercharges will be adjusted by a debit note and a credit note will be issued for any overcharge. Therefore, buyers must not accept the figures on these documents, but check them carefully, since they will have to pay the adjusted price.

50

INVOICE

Sutton and Drewery Limited

Office Equipment and Supplies

Head Office, 51 Castle Street, Lincoln, LN1 3HU, (registered office)

Telephone 0522 78987
Telegrams OFFQUIP LINCOLN
Telex 56913

VAT Reg No 912 3456 78
Registered number 000111 England

NEWBOLT ENGINEERS LTD
Greenwall Estate
BLACKBURN
BB2 8ER

Customer Order No 706		Despatched by JR	Invoice No 1253	Invoice Date/Tax Point 4/11/82		
Cat No	Quantity	Description		Price	£	
1045	5000	Paper clips, assorted		50p per 1000 net	2	50
1026	500	Double pocket files, manilla		75p per 10 less 33½%	37	50
			Gross Value of Goods		40	00
			Less Trade Discount		12	50
			Net Value of Goods		27	50
			Plus V A T @ 15%		4	12
	E & O E		Invoice Total		31	62

Terms: Cge Pd, Net monthly account

An invoice

A pro forma invoice is a preliminary invoice stating the value of goods and notifying the recipient that they have been despatched. It is not a demand for money, and might for instance accompany goods sent off on approval or be sent as a form of quotation since it gives details of prices.

51

Sutton and Drewery Limited

Office Equipment and Supplies

Head Office, 51 Castle Street, Lincoln, LN1 3HU,

Telephone 0522 78987

VAT Reg No 912 3456 78

NEWBOLT ENGINEERS LTD
Greenwall Industrial Estate
BLACKBURN
BB2 8ER

Date ___30 November 1978___

Account No ___G 142___

Date	Reference and Number	Debit	Credit	Balance
1978				
October	brought forward	32.60		32.60
4 Nov	Csh		32.60	------
4 "	Gds - Invoice 1253	29.70		29.70
8 "	Cr - C/N 56		2.16	27.54 DB

GDS Goods
CR Credit
CSH Cash
DIS Discount
DB Debit Balance
CB Credit Balance

The last amount in
this column is the
amount due

Terms: Net monthly
E and O E

A statement of account.

Value Added Tax (VAT) is a form of indirect taxation on goods and services. It is collected at each stage in the production and distribution process when value has been added to the goods or services, the final tax being borne by the consumer.

VAT was introduced in April 1973 to replace two other forms of taxation, purchase tax and selective employment tax, and is designed partly to bring the UK taxation system more in line with Common Market systems.

Any business with an annual turnover in *taxable* goods and services of £10 000 and over is liable to register with HM

How value is added at each stage of the manufacturing and distribution process. VAT is shown at a rate of ten per cent.

	Cost price excluding tax*	Value added	VAT payable (at 10%)	Price to customer including VAT (at 10%)
Manufacturer sells dress for	£10.00	£10.00	£1.00	£10 + £1 = £11.00
Wholesaler buys dress for	£10.00*			
Wholesaler sells dress for	£15.00	£5.00	50p	£15 + £1.50 = £16.50
Retailer buys dress for	£15.00*			
Retailer sells dress for	£20.00	£5.00	50p	£20 + £2 = £22.00

Final cost of dress, excluding VAT £20.00
VAT (at 10%) £2.00
Final purchase price of dress £22.00

*The cost price at each stage excludes tax because registered traders, although they pay tax on their purchases, can recoup this.

Customs and Excise and will therefore be required to keep VAT records, which include tax returns to Customs and Excise.

Whenever a trader buys a product or service, he will get from his supplier a tax invoice showing the price of his purchase and the amount of tax charged on it. When, in turn, he supplies taxable goods and services to his own customers he will charge them tax.

At regular intervals, usually quarterly, he will make a tax return to Customs and Excise. He will add up all the tax charged to him by his suppliers in the tax period (his *input tax*) and then all the tax he has charged his customers on his sales in the same period (his *output tax*) and will pay the difference to Customs and Excise.

If in any period his input tax is greater than his output tax— perhaps because he is stocking up or has purchased expensive equipment—he will be entitled to claim a refund of the difference.

The example on page 54 illustrates the basis on which VAT is calculated by registered traders. For ease of reckoning and recognition the VAT rate is assumed to be ten per cent.

An example of how a retailer might calculate VAT due to HM Customs and Excise. Again, VAT is calculated at 10% for simplicity.

Purchases	Quarter ending 30 June	Quarter ending 30 Sept	Quarter ending 31 Dec
	£	£	£
Opening stock	nil	500	1500
Purchases for stock (exclusive of tax)	2500	3000	1500
Tax charged by suppliers	250	300	150
Other purchases (stationery, etc)	300	200	200
Tax charged by suppliers of stationery, etc	30	20	20
Total tax charged	280	320	170
Sales			
Closing stock	500	1500	500
Sales (exclusive of tax)	3000	3000	3750
Total tax on sales	300	300	375
Tax payable to or to be repaid by, customs (ie the difference between the sums in boxes)	20	−20	205

VAT is chargeable at a **standard rate** (currently 15 per cent).

Some goods and services may get relief from VAT and are **zero-rated**. This means that no tax is chargeable on these goods, but a trader supplying zero-rated goods can reclaim from Customs and Excise the tax on his inputs, for example the tax on services and equipment needed for his business. The most important supplies to which zero-rating applies are most types of food (except in the course of catering); books, newspapers and periodicals; fuel including gas and electricity but not petrol and other fuels for road use; construction of buildings; exports; public transport fares; young children's clothing and footwear; and drugs and medicines supplied on prescription.

Zero-rating should not be confused with **exemption**. A trader in the exempt fields does not charge any tax on his supplies, but unlike the trader in zero-rated goods and services, he cannot reclaim any tax which has been charged to him by his suppliers. Exemption, in the main, relates to land (including rents), insurance, postal services, betting, finance, education, health, burial and cremation.

The keeping of VAT records is essential for the registered business and their invoices clearly show the amount of VAT involved (see invoice on page 51). As far as the shopper is concerned, most prices on display include VAT but some catering establishments for instance show the price of meals excluding VAT, and 'plus VAT' may be printed at the foot of the menu.

Questions

1. Describe important changes which have taken place in recent years in the retailing of food and household goods. Your answer may include the following ideas:

    (a) Branding and improved packaging
    (b) Increased proportion of married women going to work
    (c) An increase in car ownership
    (d) Shopping precincts and city development
    (e) Deep freezers

    (EM)

2. (a) What is a wholesaler?
    (b) Describe *two* services which the wholesaler provides for (i) the manufacturer (ii) the retailer.
    (c) How does a cash-and-carry wholesaler operate?
    (d) Give one reason why the wholesaler has become less important in recent years.

    (EA)

3. How have the following altered the links that existed for many years between wholesaler and retailer?

    (a) supermarkets and hypermarkets
    (b) voluntary chains
    (c) cash-and-carry wholesalers
    (d) catalogue discount stores

    (RSA)

4. (a) Describe *two* ways in which retail co-operative societies differ from other retail outlets.
    (b) Give *two* advantages which multiple stores may have over smaller retailers.
    (c) Describe *two* distinguishing features of a department store.
    (d) (i) Why are department stores usually found in city centres?
    (ii) Why are smaller retailers usually found on housing estates?

    (EA)

5. Write a short essay on Value Added Tax.

    (RSA)

6. Each of the following terms may be met in a business transaction: invoice, cash discount, trade discount, credit note, debit note and statement. Explain in detail *each* of the terms, and state how they could all arise in a single transaction.

(SW)

7. (a) Define what you believe to be the role of the small retailer, and
   (b) indicate how the development of hypermarkets might affect his business.

(RSA)

8. Two ways by which the housewife may stay at home and yet still do her shopping are by mail order and mobile shops. Describe the *advantages* to the housewife of these methods of retailing.

(EM)

9. (a) What is a mail order business?
   (b) Write a paragraph on each of the following aspects of a mail order business:
      (i)   How it obtains its customers
      (ii) How the goods are delivered
      (iii) How payment is made
   (c) What do you consider to be the advantages to the customer and to the company of this type of trading?

(MR)

5

Trading overseas

Britain is a small, highly-populated and heavily industrialised island, and although it has less than 2 per cent of the world's population, it is the fifth largest trading nation in the world. Overseas trade is therefore vital, not just to our economy, but to our existence. Even with a mechanised and very efficient agricultural industry we have to buy overseas (import) almost half of our food, and most of the raw materials we need for our major industries are also imported, including timber, metal ores and oil. In return, in order to pay for these, we sell to overseas markets (export) a whole range of manufactured goods, including machinery, electrical goods, aircraft, metal manufactures, chemicals and vehicles. Similarly, all countries today are dependent to some extent on international trade.

Britain tries to keep a favourable **Balance of Trade**. This is the difference between the total value of all goods sold out of this country and the total value of all goods imported. When we sell more than we buy, the Balance of Trade is favourable. If we have to buy more than we sell, the Balance is unfavourable, and we have a **trade gap**.

For some years Britain has had a trade gap, the figures for 1976 indicating a deficit of £3600 million, but it must be remembered that the Balance of Trade refers only to visible, tangible goods. Fortunately Britain has 'invisible exports', and without them we could hardly pay our way. They are mainly services we sell to foreign countries and foreign businessmen, and they include financial services such as insurance and banking, together with shipping and civil aviation services, travel and tourism, and overseas constructions and technical advice. Other 'invisibles' include returns on investments overseas in the form of interest or dividends.

It must be remembered that there are also 'invisible imports', including Government aid to developing countries, British holidays abroad, and the cost of maintaining British forces abroad. However, largely because businesses throughout the

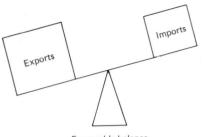

Favourable balance

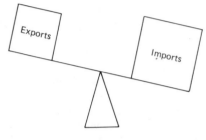

Unfavourable balance

Favourable and unfavourable balances of trade.

world use Britain's financial services, Britain has maintained an 'invisible credit balance' for many years, the credit balance in 1976 being £2166 million.

When we add together the costs of visible and invisible exports, and the visible and invisible imports, we have the **Balance of Payments;**

Britain's Balance of Payments 1976

visible exports	£25 416 000	invisible exports	£13 838 000
visible imports	£28 987 000	invisible imports	£11 672 000
visible balance −	£3 571 000	invisible balance +	£2 166 000

visible balance	− £3 571 000
invisible balance	+ £2 166 000
Balance of payments	**− £1 405 000**

Over the period 1966–1976 the Balance has ranged from a surplus of £1084 million (1971) to a deficit of £3380 million

(1974). It should be remembered that there was a marked increase in oil prices at the end of 1973.

We have to consider how these goods find their way abroad, or into this country. Most export and import trade is in the hands of private enterprise, but the Government has the power to stop both import and export of goods, and to impose restrictions on the movement of capital in the national interest. There has been, until recently, a total ban on trade with Rhodesia. The Government can also influence trade in the following ways.

To reduce imports:

- impose **tariffs**: making goods more expensive on the home market, therefore reducing demand which in turn would reduce imports
- impose **import quotas**: import licences would state the maximum each country was permitted to supply
- **devaluation of the pound**: making goods relatively dearer.

Obviously the Government cannot impose too many restrictions on imports for fear of reciprocal measures being taken by other countries.

To increase exports:

- give 'bounties' to exporters, eg, tax concessions
- **devaluation of the pound**: reducing the value of currency makes exports cheaper and more attractive to the overseas buyer and makes imports relatively dearer. However, this is a drastic step and cannot be used repeatedly or currency will become completely worthless.

In trading overseas, at one end of the chain is the manufacturer who makes the goods and at the other the overseas customer who eventually buys them.

The exporter faces many problems, he must:

- know something of the customs and needs of the country to which he hopes to export
- make contact with consumers overseas
- arrange for goods to be marketed abroad
- see to the transport of the goods: safely and promptly
- make shipping and insurance arrangements, with all the necessary documentation
- collect payment (exchange problems to be overcome).

Banks help the exporter in areas other than that of finance.

The clearing banks maintain in London large Overseas or Foreign branches dealing with international operations, but there are also specialised branches in most other large cities handling the day-to-day business of overseas trading. Every branch bank, too, has its own experts to deal with the foreign trade problems of its customers. They will arrange for:

- business visits abroad for exporters wishing to meet prospective agents or buyers
- introductions to banks abroad who will provide on-the-spot help and technical advice
- information on economic conditions abroad
- information on foreign import and export regulations
- the supply of suitable trade contacts abroad
- status reports on the credit-worthiness of foreign companies and individuals
- help and advice on exchange control regulations
- supply of traveller's cheques and foreign currency and attend to passport and visa queries.

The British manufacturer who is making goods for the export market may sell his goods to someone else (an **export merchant**) who will then do all the exporting work—financing, storing, packing, shipping and selling. But many manufacturers employ an agent to do these jobs for them, though they themselves continue to own the goods until they are sold to the overseas customer. These agents have several different names and do different work (for example, **export agent** or **shipping and forwarding agent**) and more than one agent or broker may be concerned in any transaction. **Export houses** play a very important part in overseas trade, the larger ones buying and selling on their own behalf, the smaller ones acting as agents. In some cases trade is carried on by the firm's own branch office overseas or by a subsidiary company.

Every transaction in overseas trade is both an export transaction (from the point of view of the exporting country) and an import transaction (from the point of view of the importing country). So there are agents and merchants in both the countries concerned, linking the manufacturer in one country to the buyer in the other.

Payment overseas

In trading overseas, the distances and the times taken to cover them, sometimes mean that a trader is anxious to obtain money in the early stages, perhaps even to finance the movement of the goods to the buyer. The exporter obviously wants to be paid at once, and the importer wants to delay payment for as long as possible. The bank and other institutions have developed methods to deal with this situation. The simplest method is for the exporter to get a loan or overdraft from his own bank.

Another method, is for the foreign buyer to tell his bank, through its international connections, to 'open a credit in favour of' the exporter at the exporter's British bank. The banker, in a Letter of Credit, in effect undertakes to pay the price for the goods as soon as the exporter proves by producing documents (the Bill of Lading, Insurance Certificate and Invoice), that he has sent off the goods. This method of opening a bank credit in a foreign country is part of a process known as '**documentary credit**'.

But the overseas buyer may not want to pay at once for the goods: he may not have enough money to pay for them until he has sold them to someone else. In this case he may want to use a delayed action means; either an Acceptance Credit—an irrevocable undertaking by a bank to pay the exporter—which is saleable by the exporter, or by payment with a **Bill of Exchange**. This is an order to pay, at a fixed future date, a certain sum of money. If the exporter wants his money at once he can take the Bill of Exchange (ie, the buyer's promise to pay in, say, three months' time) to a financial institution that specialises in Bills of Exchange (a merchant bank or a discount house or bank). If the institution is satisfied that the overseas buyer is reliable it will 'discount' the Bill of Exchange, that is, buy the Bill from the exporter at its face value (ie the amount the overseas buyer is eventually going to pay), less a deduction for the time the institution will have to wait before the overseas buyer pays up. If a bank 'guarantees' or 'confirms' a Bill of Exchange this means that the exporter is sure of all of his money at once and that the bank has taken the risk that the overseas buyer will fail to pay up. There are now specialist financial firms, called Confirming Houses, which will also take this risk.

In recent years there has been a marked growth in the number of factoring organisations. The factor buys from his clients their invoiced debts. The factor pays the client up to 90% of their value and then himself takes over, invoicing, collecting and bookkeeping, and the bad debt risk. He has nothing further to do with the seller of the goods unless there is difficulty in delivery. Many financial institutions, including the banks and Merchant banks, and export houses, have bought interests in such factoring organisations.

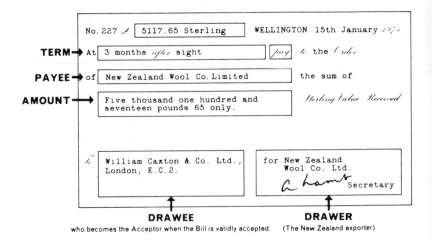

No. 227 ◢ | 5117.65 Sterling | WELLINGTON 15th January *19..*

TERM → At | 3 months *after* sight | *pay* *to* the *Order*

PAYEE → of | New Zealand Wool Co. Limited | the sum of

AMOUNT → | Five thousand one hundred and seventeen pounds 65 only. | *Sterling Value Received*

To | William Caxton & Co. Ltd., London, E.C.2. | for New Zealand Wool Co. Ltd. *a Lamb* Secretary

DRAWEE | **DRAWER**
who becomes the Acceptor when the Bill is validly accepted. | (The New Zealand exporter)

A bill of exchange.

Government help

It would be dangerous for businessmen to trade overseas if there was any doubt of payment being received, and received promptly. So they make use of the banks and specialised finance houses. Help is also given by the Department of Trade, which sponsors the work of the British Overseas Trade Board (BOTB) in providing export services. These include the provision of up-to-date information and statistics, help in finding customers and agents abroad, the provision of trade fairs, and aid for firms taking part in overseas missions. Much of the information comes from the British Diplomatic Service, whose commercial attaches not only send back up-to-date information on markets, but are always ready to help exporters, particularly where difficulties arise over government regulation.

The Board of Trade is also responsible for the Export Credits Guarantee Department (ECGD), which offers to exporters insurance against the risk of non-payment by the buyer. This covers not only refusal to pay or inability through bankruptcy, but prevention of payments by government action or even by war. The ECGD will also guarantee repayments to banks which have financed exporters.

Export documentation

You remember that the exporter had to prove he had sent off

62

the goods before he could get any money out of a documentary credit opened for him at his bank. He gives the bank this proof by showing them three documents. These are: a **Bill of Lading** or an **Air Waybill**, an Insurance Certificate and an Invoice. The Invoice and Insurance Certificate are self-explanatory. A Bill of Lading is used when goods are sent by ship, and an Air Waybill when they are sent by air. They are both receipts signed by the ship's or aircraft captain certifying that the goods have been received by him on board his vessel or plane. They are also 'documents of title' which means that possession of the document acts as proof of ownership of the goods. Therefore if an exporter wishes to sell the goods while they are on the seas, he does so by selling the Bill of Lading and the person to whom it is sold can claim the goods on their arrival. The Bill of Lading shows:

the name of the shipper,
the name of the ship,
the place to which the goods are going,
a description of the goods,
the weight,
the name of the person to whom they are to be delivered and the date.

If the captain of the ship (or the 'master' as he is more correctly called) finds that the goods delivered to him are in any way damaged he will call them 'dirty' goods and sign a 'dirty' Bill of Lading. If they are in good order he will sign a 'clean' Bill of Lading (in the same way that we say a 'clean bill of health').

Two other documents are often required when goods are being sent overseas. These are Certificates of Origin and Consular Invoices and they are needed so that customs duty can be correctly assessed. A Certificate of Origin (as its name implies) states where the goods were manufactured and it is often used in the *entrepôt* trade, in which goods are bought abroad and pass through this country on their way to be sold in another.

A Consular Invoice is an invoice stamped by the Consulate of the importing country certifying that the price shown on the invoice is a true reflection of their value, according to current market prices.

Bonded warehousing

Import trade is very concerned with customs regulations. Customs duty is one of the sources of Government revenue for the country. Not all goods are subject to customs duty when they enter this country. If they are free from duty they can either be taken straight away from the docks by the importer or stored in one of the warehouses for that type of goods, and looked after by a dock company or wharfinger until the importer (or his agent) claims them.

With dutiable goods (e.g., tobacco, wines and spirits) the procedure is different. To allow the landing of cargo on which duty has not been paid there is a system of **bonded warehouses.** The goods are weighed or measured and checked in the presence of the customs officials and carefully guarded at all times. Importers may own their own warehouses, or space may be rented. Owners enter into a 'bond' with HM Customs which is an undertaking that no goods shall be removed from warehouses until the duty has been paid. If the bond is broken, the owner forfeits his deposit with HM Customs and puts his livelihood in jeopardy.

As each part of the consignment is sold the dock warrant for the consignment is altered to show how much remains unsold in the bonded warehouse. A dock warrant, like a Bill of Lading, is a document of title and gives a right to claim the goods as their owner.

Duty on goods can be substantial, and the system of bonded warehousing means that capital is not tied up in duty until the goods are required. The system of bonded warehouses applies also to dutiable goods produced for sale on the home market.

Markets

Many of the raw materials imported into this country are sold at the great **Commodity Markets** or **Commodity Exchanges.** Most of these are in London (in the City around Mincing Lane, St. Mary Axe and Coleman Street) but some are in the other great British ports like Liverpool, traditionally the market for raw cotton. They are some of the oldest and most interesting of British trading institutions. They hold daily sales or auctions and deal not only with raw materials that physically enter the country but also in those that never actually come into Britain, but of which the ownership is sold here. Sometimes samples of the materials to be sold are shown but often they are sold by description only. Sometimes they are open to the public, and anybody can buy, but often they have a membership governed by very strict rules to ensure fair dealing.

The London Commodity Exchange Group, in Plantation House, Mincing Lane, is a group of separate commodity markets for products such as cocoa, coffee, copra, fishmeal, jute, rubber, sugar, vegetable oils, and general produce (spices, aromatic oils, ivory, etc.).

Other commodity markets include: The Fur Market, The London Wool Exchange, The English Grains Market in the Corn Exchange, The Gold and Silver Bullion Markets, The Manchester Royal Exchange (for cotton, rayon yarn and cloth), the Bradford Wool Exchange, and The Liverpool Cotton and Wheat Exchanges.

At the Baltic Exchange in St. Mary Axe, shipping and air freight space can be hired or chartered.

There are also special **wholesale produce markets** which deal in both imported and home produce, including the famous Billingsgate Fish Market, New Covent Garden (for fruit and vegetables), and Smithfield Meat Market.

Britain and the European Economic Community

Britain's highly developed industry until recently has been able to provide work for a large population. As already stated, this population is too large to be fed from our own agricultural land, and Britain must export manufactured articles to pay for imported food. This has become particularly true since the Second World War, during which Britain lost or sold many over-seas investments to pay for the war effort. These had previously provided income to pay for imports. At the same time many other countries have become highly industrialised and offer strong competition in world markets, including those where Britain virtually held a monopoly. Because of this competition, many countries have found it necessary to use tariffs to restrict the free entry of goods. **Tariffs** are taxes imposed by importing countries on certain goods, not to raise money, but to raise the prices of the goods in the home market, and so make them more expensive and so less desirable than home-produced goods. In this way the home manufacturers are protected against foreign goods which have been produced more cheaply.

In this situation, one factor which was of extreme import-ance to Britain was her relationship with the rest of the Com-monwealth, in particular with the three great food-producing countries Canada, Australia and New Zealand. Their products were allowed to enter free of duty into the British market, which meant that they were cheap compared with similar products from European countries against which tariffs were raised. In return we enjoyed preferential tariffs when exporting goods to Commonwealth countries. About 25 per cent of our imports came from the Commonwealth and the same percentage of our exports went there.

In 1957 six West European countries (West Germany, France,

Italy, Belgium, Holland and Luxemburg) agreed eventually to abolish all tariffs between themselves and to establish a common external tariff wall against the rest of the world. Internal tariffs and all other obstacles to free trade were to be removed by stages over a period of twelve to fifteen years. The **Treaty of Rome** also contained clauses dealing with investment and the freedom of movement of capital and labour (so that it was possible for a citizen of any of the six countries to operate a business or take a job anywhere within the group); with agriculture; with banking, insurance and transport; with social services and conditions of work. The general effect of all this was to transfer some responsibility for these matters from the individual governments of the Six to the Executives of the Community.

These Executives of the European Community administer the customs union, or **European Economic Community (EEC)**, popularly known as the **Common Market**, and two other organisations. The first of these is the **European Coal and Steel Community (ECAS)** (formed as long ago as 1951), which provides central control for these industries throughout the Six, and the other is the **European Atomic Energy Commission (Euratom)**, whose task is to create within the Community a powerful industry for the peaceful use of atomic energy. The objective of the Common Market was stated to be: 'To promote throughout the community a harmonious development of economic activity, continuous balanced expansion, increased stability, a more rapid development in the standard of living, and closer relationships between its member states'.

Britain did not take part in the Treaty of Rome when it was ratified because we did not wish to surrender any sovereignty or abandon our policy of subsidising our own agriculture, and because we wanted to maintain our preferential tariffs with the Commonwealth, which would have been impossible from inside the common tariff wall. This attitude appeared to be justified by the fact that at that time our exports to the Common Market were less than our exports to the Commonwealth.

Subsequently Britain made two applications for membership of the Community which were rejected in 1963 and in 1967. Britain re-opened negotiations to join the Common Market at the end of June 1970. At the same time, Denmark, Ireland and Norway also began negotiating for membership of the Community. The talks continued for almost a year and on 23rd June, 1971, agreement was reached on most issues for Britain's entry. In October 1971 Parliament by a narrow majority took a decision in principle that Britain should enter the EEC and on 22nd January, 1972, the Prime Minister signed a Treaty of

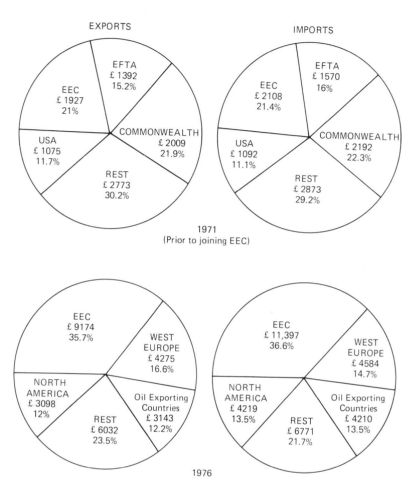

EXPORTS

EFTA
£ 1392
15.2%

EEC
£ 1927
21%

COMMONWEALTH
£ 2009
21.9%

USA
£ 1075
11.7%

REST
£ 2773
30.2%

IMPORTS

EFTA
£ 1570
16%

EEC
£ 2108
21.4%

COMMONWEALTH
£ 2192
22.3%

USA
£ 1092
11.1%

REST
£ 2873
29.2%

1971
(Prior to joining EEC)

EEC
£ 9174
35.7%

WEST
EUROPE
£ 4275
16.6%

NORTH
AMERICA
£ 3098
12%

Oil Exporting
Countries
£ 3143
12.2%

REST
£ 6032
23.5%

EEC
£ 11,397
36.6%

WEST
EUROPE
£ 4584
14.7%

NORTH
AMERICA
£ 4219
13.5%

Oil Exporting
Countries
£ 4210
13.5%

REST
£ 6771
21.7%

1976

Changes in Britain's trade pattern.

Accession which, after ratification by Parliament, made Britain
a full Community member from 1st January, 1973. Ireland and
Denmark also joined on that date, but Norway rejected membership in a referendum held in 1972. Britain held a referendum
(the first ever held) in June 1975 which endorsed membership
by a 2-1 majority: 67.2 per cent in favour and 32.8 per cent
against.

Although the Community aims for complete political and
economic union eventually, the effects on Britain so far and in
the near future are mainly related to agriculture, finance, indus-

67

try and trade.

Before entry Britain and eight other European countries, Austria, Denmark, Finland, Iceland, Norway, Portugal, Sweden and Switzerland, belonged to the **European Free Trade Association**. Britain carried on a great deal of trade with the members of EFTA. Like the EEC, EFTA aimed to promote trade among member countries by the removal of restrictions, such as import quotas and customs duties. Virtually all tariffs between the EEC and EFTA had been removed by July 1977, when EEC tariffs had been eliminated. Now that Britain is in the EEC, she must abolish duty on goods from the other countries of the Community and apply the Common External Tariff to imports from all non-member countries. However, the provisions of the Community allow for special trade agreements to be made with non-member states and Britain has negotiated the continuation of favourable treatment for New Zealand dairy products and for sugar from developing nations.

The original six members of the EEC had given their former colonies a close economic association with the Community, and a similar arrangement was made with twenty-two developing Commonwealth countries in Africa, the Caribbean and the Pacific (ACP) in 1975. A total of forty-six ACP countries whose economies are dependent on their exporting particular agricultural products, including sugar, have their interests safeguarded.

As already stated, New Zealand dairy products are still accepted into the Market, and commercial agreements have been made with India (1974), Sri Lanka (1975) and Pakistan (1976).

The principle of a transition period for Britain as a new member applied in the area of finance. At the end of the five-year transition period, the controls on the movement of capital to Community countries were abolished. Therefore, at the beginning of 1978 there were no restrictions on anyone who wished to invest money in other countries of the EEC.

The Department of Trade has issued reprints of a number of articles dealing in detail with the Treaty of Rome, legal and industrial policy, technology, labour and commercial policy, and these may be referred to in order to cover more fully all aspects of the relationship between Britain and the EEC. To indicate how the relationship has grown one aspect, agriculture, can be studied in some detail.

Agriculture and the EEC

The Community's agricultural prices and financing arrangement has been applied gradually over five years. Under the Community's Common Agricultural Policy (CAP) each member pays into a fund which finances the complex system of managing market prices and contributes to the cost of the modernisation of agriculture. Market prices are managed by the Community to ensure farmers a steady income while keeping prices in the shops stable. Farmers get special treatment in most developed countries of the world because natural conditions, like the weather, can mean scarcity one year and an abundance the next. Scarcity pushes prices up. An abundance of produce pushes down prices but this could force some farmers out of business, making produce more scarce and thus much more expensive the following year. Besides being difficult for the home consumer, these price fluctuations could have a harmful effect on the export of farm produce. Therefore, it is important for a trading nation like Britain to keep farm prices stable.

For many years before her entry into the EEC Britain had a system of farm subsidies or grants paid to the farmers by the government. These subsidies assured farmers of their income while keeping retail prices stable. Farmers sometimes had to sell produce at a lower price than was profitable to them and their losses were made up by government subsidies. Because these subsidies kept down food prices in the shops, people on low incomes were helped. The subsidies were paid out of general taxation, so that in effect the ordinary taxpayer was helping those below this level to buy food cheaply. In the year immediately before entry, Britain had been finding this system increasingly expensive and was ready to change to the EEC's system.

In the EEC farming is treated like a commercial operation and it is expected to make its profit from the commodities it produces. EEC farmers get all their income from selling their produce. British farmers adopted the EEC's system immediately after entry. Over the transition period the prices paid to farmers for their produce have gradually increased to EEC levels and at the same time the farmers have gradually lost their government subsidies. This has meant an inevitable rise in the cost of food, although the increase was spread over the five-year period from the date of Britain's entry.

The Community's Common Agricultural Policy (CAP) includes a system to keep market prices stable. For certain farm produce, such as cereals, beef, sugar and milk, the EEC sets a target or guide price which they feel the farmer should receive when he sells these commodities. If the price of a commodity falls because of a surplus, the EEC organisations, the national intervention boards, step in at a certain point, called the intervention price, and buy all the produce at that price. This guarantees the farmers a minimum price for the commodities they produce. In this way Community farmers are protected from a collapse in market prices, although they are expected to look after their own profits in normal circumstances. It also results in the creation of stock-piles of produce, including the 'beef-mountain', the 'butter-mountain' and so-called 'wine-lake'. In the case of beef, in December 1977 a new system of support for the beef sector was introduced following the UK system of support buying mixed with premiums to the producers. This was intended to make a more flexible system, enabling consumers to enjoy lower retail prices when there were plentiful supplies, and to reduce over-large 'beef-mountains' by encouraging consumption. The so-called Green Pound refers to the special exchange rate used to calculate Community prices into each national currency.

The Community also helps its farmers deal with the importing and exporting of food. As with other goods, there is no tariff on farm produce exported from one member to another. Trading in farm produce outside the Community is, however, more difficult. Many commodities sold on the world market are surplus to the requirements of each country and these are sold at a lower price than the domestic production costs. If a farmer wants to export his produce outside the EEC, the Community helps him by giving the farmer a grant or 'restitution', that will allow him to sell his goods at the lower world trading price. On the other hand, if world prices rise above the EEC level, the Community may exact a levy on exports to prevent internal prices rising to world levels.

Imported food presents a different problem. Where world food prices are lower, cheap imported food could flood into the Community and put the Community farmers out of business. To prevent this, the EEC only allows farm produce to be imported if it is a certain price. Then the importer must pay a levy, which is like a tariff, that brings the price of imported produce up to the price of Community produce. The levy is variable so that it can be adjusted when there is a scarcity or abundance in the Community. For example, if the Community production of beef declines, then the governments must take action to keep the butcher shops supplied. By lowering the import levy on beef, the Community can attract greater beef imports. In times of a

The European Community.

1 Belgium
2 Denmark
3 Fed. Rep. of Germany
4 France
5 Ireland
6 Italy
7 Luxembourg
8 Netherlands
9 United Kingdom

The Common Market has four main institutions-

The Commission makes proposals for action and carriers them out when decisions to act have been taken.

The Council of Ministers makes the decisions; it is made up of Ministers representing the 9 national governments.

The Court of Justice is the final court of appeal. It ensures that Community law is observed.

The European Parliament-
helps to shape decisions taken by the Community;
has a say in the Community Budget : how much is spent and on what;
is consulted by those who take decisions (the Council of Ministers) and by those who carry them out (the Commission).
It can not extend its powers without the permission of the national Parliaments.

On June 7th-10th 1979 were held the first elections for Members of the European Parliament (or European Assembly) which enabled voters in each of the Community countries to elect their own European MP's. Prior to this, members had been nominated by the national Parliament of the European Community countries. The

European elections in June 1979 saw the world's first international elections.

the nine Heads of Government European Council meetings (Summits) three times a year by the nine Heads of Government

Greece became the tenth full member of the EC in January 1981. Portugal and Spain have applied to join too.

Community surplus of beef, the levy can be raised to protect Community farmers from foreign competition.

The Community has also established rules for marketing farm produce and these must be observed by farmers in all Community countries. For example, most fruit, vegetables and plants are graded very carefully and eggs are put into seven different grades. These rules should give the consumer a better guide to the farm produce that is sold in the shops.

The EEC also gives aid to member countries, and in 1977 aid to the United Kingdom amounted to over £4$\frac{1}{2}$ million for projects ranging from drainage pumping stations to constructing carrot packhouses.

Now that Britain has joined the EEC, her economy should in theory be stimulated and expanded by increased competition and a much larger 'home' market. In addition, Britain's trade in world markets ought to be helped in the long term as she is now part of a major trading bloc that can compete on equal terms with countries the size of the United States. It is only fair to add that there is still much disagreement on this subject in this country and among EEC countries.

The European Monetary System (EMS)

The intention of an EMS is to keep the value of the currencies of the member-states of the EEC in a fixed relationship against each other, within a range of 2$\frac{1}{4}$ per cent either way.

With this, exporting and importing firms would not have to consider the effects of changes in the value of their currency and would be able to reckon accurately and more surely the price of goods bought and sold, thus encouraging trade within the Community, and thus investment. At present 'internal' trade between EEC members is the most important element of each country's international trade (see page 67). Greater certainty over exchange rates would in fact make the community like a home market; and inflation should fall when countries can no longer devalue their currency to boost exports.

In order to maintain currencies within tight limits, especially during periods of intense speculation, a pool of reserve currency would be needed. Into this any member would dip when its currency was under pressure, borrowing whichever currency was required. Conditions would be attached to long-term borrowing, but it is anticipated that short-term credits could be arranged between the central banks of the members. It has been suggested that the currency pool should be about £17 000 million, big enough to tackle most EEC currency problems. The money from the participating countries would be deposited in the **European Monetary Fund (EMF)**.

No one currency denomination, such as the mark or franc, would be used for accounting the fund. An artificial weighted average called the **European Currency Unit (ECU)** would be used. It would not be a currency in its own right, though perhaps it might eventually provide a basis for a common European currency.

One of the necessities for a system of this kind is a co-ordinated economic policy, so that rates of growth and rates of inflation, and therefore trade balances would remain compatible, with the currency remaining in the same relationship. (Indeed, some economists believe that the co-ordinated economic policy should be achieved first, and that the co-ordinated currency, or even common currency would then follow as a matter of course.) However, compatible rates do not mean that they would have to be the same. Britain's North Sea oil would give it an advantage on balance of payments, while other countries might have higher growth through higher productivity, or by foreign capital investment.

Britain, France and Italy are at present following similar monetary policies, and the discipline of a fixed rate might cause greater co-operation. Some countries might require a greater lee-way than $2\frac{1}{4}$ per cent, and it has been suggested that Italy might be asked to keep the lira only within 6 per cent of its agreed rate.

British Chancellors of the Exchequer have become accustomed to using the weapon of devaluation to combat inflation, and this weapon would no longer be available to them. A more serious hazard is that the strong German Deutschmark (D-mark) will continue to rise against non-European currencies (the dollar and the yen) and, dragging European currency with it, make European goods less and less competitive in price in the world markets.

At the time of writing no firm decision has been made by Britain, beyond an agreement to ally itself with the EMF. This does not include locking the pound within the narrow exchange limits. This could be a future commitment. Two facts may be relevant to this decision to have 'associate-membership' only. It has been made clear that there will be no massive transfer of resources to help the poor members; and it appears that Britain, seventh richest of the nine countries in terms of per capita income, might well be the main contributor to the Community budget by 1980.

Questions

1. (a) Why is it important for the United Kingdom to trade with foreign countries?
   (b) Distinguish between visible and invisible trade and give *two* examples of each for the United Kingdom.

(MR)

2. (a) An adverse balance of payments means that we are not paying our way. Discuss this statement.
   (b) Distinguish between the balance of trade and the balance of payments.
   (c) How can tariffs protect the home manufacturer?

(NW)

3. (a) Describe briefly the part played by each of the following in the exporting of goods:
       (i) an export agent   (ii) a bill of exchange
   (b) Describe briefly one of the functions of the British Overseas Trade Board.
   (c) Describe *two* ways in which a commercial bank can help exporters.
   (d) State the function of the Export Credits Guarantee Department.

(EA)

4. An importer of goods has to deal with four main interested parties: the exporter, the shipowner, the port authorities and HM Customs. Explain in detail the part each would play in the import of raw materials.

(SW)

5. What effect has entry into the European Economic Community (EEC) had upon the commercial life of this country?

(EA)

6. If a country's imports of goods in any one year are in total worth more than its exports of goods, the country is said to have for that year.
   (a) an adverse balance of payments
   (b) too much money chasing too few goods
   (c) a balance of trade deficit
   (d) a currency devaluation crisis.

(RSA)

6

Transport

Transport is vital to the chain of production. Raw materials or component parts have to get to the manufacturer and very often several factories are involved before there is a finished product. The goods have to be delivered to the selling point, the buyer has to travel to see the goods he wishes to buy and the products have to be transported to his home.

In January 1978, a local strike of long-distance lorry drivers in a town away from the main line railways, paralysed the fishing port of Grimsby: factories closed or lay idle because there were no supplies of raw materials. The finished products that were made had no market and had to stay in store, with great loss to the frozen food companies concerned as they depend on a quick turn round of products. There were no deliveries of fresh milk and housewives stripped the local shops of powdered and long-life varieties. Deliveries of fuel ceased—soon there were no buses because there was no diesel fuel, and no oil for heating factories. Fortunately the strike did not last long, but in that short time it could be seen what chaos resulted from the withdrawal of road transport facilities. In fact, the strike was over the introduction of tachographs into lorry drivers' cabs. These are discussed under the section on road transport.

Besides the transport of goods, there is the transport of people: people have to get to and from work and to places where they can buy the goods they have helped to produce, either directly or indirectly. Businessmen, salesmen and buyers need to travel the country and the world to carry on and to expand their businesses. Not only that, children need to be educated to help them to live a full life for the prosperity of themselves and the country; all ages need relaxation and entertainment, and the services that help and protect us need the mobility that transport provides.

Of course, we can walk from place to place, we can carry goods in our arms, on our backs, push them in front or drag them behind us. We also have animals to help transport us or

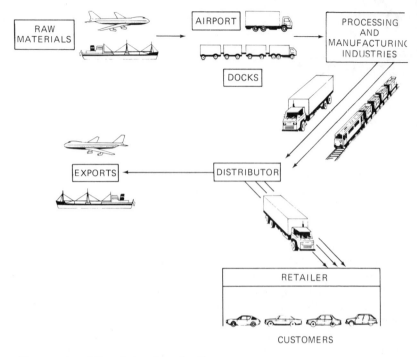

RAW MATERIALS

AIRPORT

PROCESSING AND MANUFACTURING INDUSTRIES

DOCKS

EXPORTS

DISTRIBUTOR

RETAILER

CUSTOMERS

Transport and the chain of production.

our goods, but civilisation and world-wide inter-dependence demand more than these primitive means.

We in Britain have several means of transport available: we have railways, smooth-surfaced roads and a great variety of vehicles to use them; we have the sea with port facilities; navigable canals and rivers; aircraft and airports; and pipelines for special purposes. Behind these physical assets, which are constantly being modernised, we need the supporting network of administration and the law of the land to control their use. Because of the growth of the private car, traffic congestion, pollution from traffic, the closure of railways and noise from aircraft, transport has become a very much discussed subject. It is one of the responsibilities of the Department of the Environment under the immediate jurisdiction of the Minister for Transport.

The method of transport we choose depends on individual circumstances, and we take into account convenience, cost, destination, speed and availability. The choice of transport for

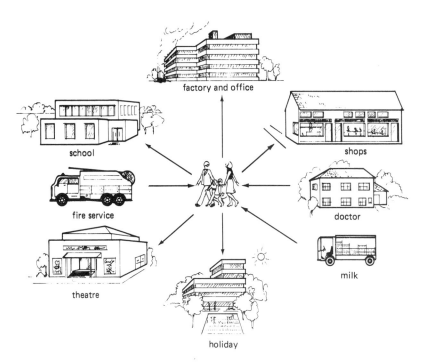

Transport and People.

goods depends largely on their nature: whether they are small or bulky, perishable or durable, valuable or cheap, whether they are urgently required or not and the distance they are to be carried. Remember that 'goods' will include anything from safety pins to steel towers for oil refineries, to diamond rings, or petrol, or potatoes.

The cost of a journey may be linked with convenience and speed. For example, it will be worthwhile for a firm to send their Managing Director by an expensive but quick and convenient means of transport (say air or chauffeur-driven car) in order that he arrives at his destination fit and ready for work at once, rather than waste his expensive time on a slower, though cheaper, form of transport. Similarly, a whole production process may be held up because a machine has broken down and is awaiting the arrival of a spare part: it would be best to send that spare part by the quickest means available, even if it is not the cheapest. Therefore the actual cost of a journey or of transport is not necessarily the deciding factor, as the cheapest means may be inconvenient and time costs money. Convenience may also be a great money-saver, for some big firms choose to use public goods transport systems rather than have the expense and work of running their own delivery department.

Safety and comfort also have to be taken into account. If goods are valuable or fragile, the safest form of available transport is chosen, bearing in mind the risks of theft, loss or breakage.

Obviously the geographical situations of the sender and receiver and what forms of transport are available are often deciding factors, and for long-distance travel several kinds of transport may be involved. Most towns do not have an airport, there are more towns inland than on the coast, and canal and river transport is not available in most cases. Industry and transport systems, though, have developed simultaneously over the years to their mutual benefit. For example, there are railway sidings beside mines and steelworks, there are canals throughout the potteries, and light industries by major roadways.

Container traffic on road, rail and water, is the most recent, influential and revolutionary development in the transport of freight. Although initially expensive, the use of containers (often specially designed for the type of goods carried—refrigerated, lined, in compartments) means that the goods themselves are not handled from the day they are locked in, to the time they reach their destination. There is, therefore, less risk of loss or damage to goods in transit. Container traffic has also meant major changes in port procedure and handling, with fewer people involved and special cranes and gantries being designed. There are now special container lorries, trains, ships and barges to carry the increased load of container traffic. Containers are easier and quicker to handle than individually packed items and containerisation has meant fewer checks at boundaries between countries. The containers and equipment for handling are standardised so that the containers can travel by ship, barge, rail and road right across the world without difficulty.

Rail transport

The first railway was opened in 1825 and the railways that developed belonged to private companies until they were nationalised and came under public ownership in 1947. The British Railways Board has overall responsibility but, for ease of administration, 'British Rail' is divided into five geographical regions: London Midland, Western, Southern, Eastern, and Scottish.

A container ship being loaded by high capacity cranes especially designed
to move containers from road vehicles.

British Rail operates about 11 000 miles (18 000 kilometres)
of track with nearly 3000 stations, and carries almost 800 million passengers annually. The main freight commodities are coal,
coke, iron and steel, but carriage of petroleum products, cars
and motor components and construction materials is on the
increase. Approximately 200 million tonnes of freight per
annum is carried. However, this represents only about 16 per
cent in terms of tonne-kilometres of freight carried; their chief
competitor being road transport.

The most important recent developments have been the replacement of steam by diesel and electric traction, the improvement of inter-city passenger services and greater mechanisation
in the carrying of freight. High speed trains (HST's) have been
introduced, and the quality of tracks and of signalling methods
are being improved to ensure that safety standards are maintained at these high speeds. The HST's (the world's fastest diesel
rail service) run at a sustained speed of 125 mph (210 km/h)

and higher speeds will follow the introduction of the Advanced Passenger Train (APT) capable of speeds up to 155 mph (250 km/h).

British Rail's Inter-City 125. The high speed train.

The carriage of freight is being improved by the introduction of larger wagons and a network of regular high-speed freight services. Freight traffic is being concentrated at fewer, better sited and equipped marshalling yards and terminals and the whole process is computer-controlled. Express container services are growing in importance and the 'merry-go-round' system, whereby trains are loaded and discharged automatically while in motion, is being used more widely.

The freightliner services are operated by Freightliners Ltd a company owned jointly by the National Freight Corporation (NFC) (see also Road Transport) and the British Railways Board. Freightliners Ltd operates a network of purpose-built terminals linked by fast, scheduled services of container-carrying trains. These terminals transfer the freight containers from road or ship to rail or vice versa, using massive cranes which straddle the road and rail tracks. By this means the road collection and delivery of containers is linked to fast rail haulage; or (increasingly) deep-sea container ships. The company also operates container services to Ireland and the Continent, the latter developing fast because of European railway links Freightliners Ltd has its own vehicle and container fleet, but customers' or hauliers' vehicles and containers also have access to the system.

By the streamlining of freight operations and with overall control by the NFC over rail and road traffic, British Rail hopes to tempt custom back to the railways and they are negotiating long-term contracts with various companies.

Subsidiaries of British Rail

British Rail Hovercraft Ltd run hovercraft services across the Channel and the Solent to the Isle of Wight for passengers and accompanied cars. There are also privately-owned hovercraft

Rail transport

Advantages	Disadvantages
Good organisation	High charges result from high capital outlay, maintenance costs and overheads
Large quantities can be moved at a time (bulk trainloads)	Other transport needed to get goods to and from terminals or goods yards
Suitable for long distances	Limited for awkward sizes by tunnels, bridges and opposite track
Fast service between main centres	Some areas of country not accessible
Highspeed freightliner gives door-to-door collection and delivery for containers	Subject to delay through breakdown, track repair or industrial action
NFC provides co-ordination between road and rail services	Diffusion of responsibility makes it difficult to locate or remedy pilfering, delay or negligence
Provides parcel service for items too big or heavy for parcel post	Under 200 miles, road transport is more economic

Examples of freight: coal, coke, iron ore, steel, china clay, oil, grain, refuse, sand and gravel, chemicals, cars, milk, newspapers, mail, livestock firms but British Rail is the world's largest operator.

The ferry fleets which carry lorries, cars and passengers between Europe and Great Britain, and Ireland and Great Britain, are among the biggest earners for British Rail.

British Transport Hotels Ltd own about thirty hotels and control Travellers Fare, the catering facilities provided on trains and platforms.

British Rail also have engineering works and a technical centre for research and development.

British Rail's Shipping and International Services division carries more sea-going passengers than any other fleet in the world and provides passenger and freight services on domestic and European routes.

Road Transport

Roads

To give some idea of the amount of traffic on the roads, in 1974 there were eighty-four vehicles for every mile of road, or one for every twenty-three yards. In 1977, at the height of the holiday season, on the M6 near Birmingham 100 000 vehicles daily were recorded. Because of the popularity of and increase in road transport, the Government has a road programme designed to complete a network of routes of high quality, but such heavy use makes road repairs a very expensive item indeed.

There are three main categories of road in Great Britain: trunk roads (including motorways), classified roads and unclassified roads. Trunk roads link industrial areas, towns and ports, and motorways are designed for long-distance, high-speed traffic and are based on six main routes. The Secretaries of State for the Environment and for Wales are responsible in England and Wales for the construction, improvement and maintenance of trunk roads; county councils look after classified roads; and district councils the unclassified roads.

A large programme of bridge and tunnel building has been undertaken in recent years and modern bridges include the suspension bridge across the Firth of Forth and the Severn incorporating major advances in suspension bridge design. A bridge being constructed across the River Humber will have a span longer than any bridge in the world. Recent tunnel schemes have been across the Mersey and the Thames at Dartford, Kent.

Road haulage

Most of the passenger and freight traffic of Great Britain is

The Severn Bridge.

carried by road (about 67 per cent, compared with 16 per cent by rail).

Most of the road haulage industry is privately-owned (there are some 145 000 operators), mainly small firms with an average fleet of four vehicles, but the biggest freight operator in Great Britain and in Europe is the National Freight Corporation (NFC) which is a public corporation. Nevertheless, it does not have a monopoly as it handles only about 10 per cent of road freight. The NFC was formed under the 1968 Transport Act to run all publicly owned freight services and to streamline and integrate road and rail freight services. It has a number of subsidiaries, including British Road Services Ltd (BRS), National Carriers Ltd (NCL), Roadline UK, Freightliners Ltd, and Pickfords. Between them they will carry anything from a small parcel to a giant turbine. See page 29 re ownership of NFC.

Besides the vehicles owned privately and publicly which are solely for hire, for the distribution of other people's goods, there are many general trading firms and manufacturers who have vehicles for the carriage of their own goods only.

The outstanding development in road transport has been the provision of very large containers capable of easy transfer from

The Roadline symbol.

The NCL symbol.

road/rail and water (see Container traffic, page 78). Long container vehicles bearing continental registrations and the letters TIR (Transports Internationaux Routiers, or International Road Transport) are familiar sights on our roads, having crossed the sea by ferry. Likewise British lorries are familiar sights on the Continent.

Road haulage operators are subject to licensing and other controls. There is legal control over speeds, gross weights carried, size and type of vehicle and regulations control the emission of smoke and noise by lorries and the carriage of dangerous goods. There are rules on drivers' hours and types of records kept; vehicles are subject to annual tests and drivers are subjected to driving and medical tests. European Community legislation requires commercial vehicles to be fitted with a **tachograph,** an instrument which automatically records driving hours, the vehicle's speed and distance covered. A tachograph is soon expected to become a required fitting and drivers will be limited to 281 miles (450 kilometres) a day.

Passenger traffic

This ranges, of course, from pedal cycles, scooters and motor cycles to motor cars and public transport vehicles. Cars on the road exceed all the others and amount to over three-quarters of licensed vehicles. Household car ownership is an important factor, affecting shopping habits as well as travel, although household cars are used primarily for getting to and from work. It is estimated that by 1980 there were 13 million households with one car and $2\frac{1}{2}$ million with more than one, compared with $4\frac{1}{2}$ million with no car.

Public road passenger transport in Britain is provided mainly by publicly-owned operators. In England and Wales this is the National Bus Company which operates through locally based and named subsidiaries, such as the Western National Omnibus Company and Ribble Motor Services Ltd. County Councils, as Passenger Transport Authorities (PTA's), are also responsible for local bus services and the London Transport Executive, appointed by the Greater London Council (GLC) is responsible for the central bus and underground rail services.

There are some 5000 privately-owned fleets but only a small proportion of these are concerned with scheduled bus services. Long-distance luxury coaches for home and overseas travel are now quite common on our roads.

In Great Britain there are about 34 000 taxicabs, mainly in urban areas. In London there are almost 12 000 taxicabs that ply for hire in the streets and these are privately operated by companies or by owner-drivers and are licensed annually by the Metropolitan Police. Elsewhere taxis are licensed by local authorities. There are also numerous car-hire and rent-a-van firms in operation.

Road transport

Advantages	Disadvantages
Good service	Limited amount per load
Door-to-door, therefore less handling and less risk of damage	Bad weather (fog and ice) can hold up deliveries
Quicker and cheaper than rail (fewer overheads), particularly for short journeys	British roads often inadequate—traffic jams, road accidents
All country accessible	Not very safe from pilfering especially when parked overnight
Container vehicles for inland and overseas deliveries	Drivers' hours limited which slows down long-distance distribution
Awkward sizes and shapes can be carried more easily than by rail	Contributes to pollution, accident hazards and road congestion
	Dangerous substances carried through built-up areas

Examples of freight: Deliveries of all types of goods for manufacturers, wholesalers and retailers, eg, furniture, food, clothing, building materials, milk, household goods, chemicals, oil products, tobacco, drinks

Water transport

Water transport must be considered under three separate headings: Inland Waterways, Coastal Shipping, Ocean Shipping.

Inland Waterways

There are over 2000 miles (3000 kilometres) of navigable rivers and canals controlled by the publicly-owned British Waterways Board, and about 340 miles (550 kilometres) are maintained for freight-carrying vessels. A further 1200 kilometres of canals are available mainly for recreational purposes, and since the development of canal traffic as a holiday facility many well-known canals carry large numbers of passengers, and every year more formerly disused canals are being re-claimed for holiday use. A holiday on the canals will show you some of the most beautiful countryside in Britain, and some unknown parts of towns.

Canals were the traditional method of transporting coal, clay to potteries, and china products when completed, because there was less breakage than when carried by horse-wagon. Today canals play only a minor part in freight carriage (under 3 per cent) compared with roads and rail. Freight traffic of about five million tonnes per annum is mostly on the rivers and broad canals of Yorkshire and Humberside, though the Manchester Ship Canal, which enables sea-going vessels to penetrate into the heart of Manchester, carries a substantial volume of export traffic from Merseyside.

New canal facilities are being provided with the introduction of container barges, and a specially designed interlocking

Canal transport

Advantages	Disadvantages
Low maintenance costs, therefore low charges	Very slow—therefore lot of capital tied up in goods in transit
Smooth for fragile goods	Limited area covered by canals
Loading and unloading cheap and easy	
Goods transferred straight from ships to barges—saves docking time and charges	Sometimes difficult transferring from one canal system to another
Can handle container traffic	

Examples of freight: Coal (represents one-third of total goods), bulk liquids, sand and cement, pottery, timber, flour modular barge system. The British Waterways Board operates docks, warehouses and inland freight terminals, and has a fleet of barges, but much of the freight is handled by independent carriers or by traders in their own craft. Much of the material carried is coal or liquids in bulk, but the use of containers is widening the scope of carriers.

Sea transport

The British merchant fleet is one of the largest merchant fleets in the world and nearly all of the fleet is privately-owned, about two-thirds of the tanker fleet belonging to oil companies. Some ships are owned and/or operated by nationalised industries—by British Rail in particular (see Rail Transport). British liners are operated by a small number of large groups.

The Department of Trade is the Government department responsible for most matters connected with merchant shipping and administers regulations for safety and welfare, for example certifying the load-line (or Plimsoll line) that shows that a ship is not overloaded. A complete record of all British ships is kept.

There are other organisations concerned with shipping activities. **Lloyds Register of Shipping** is an organisation which surveys and classifies ships; it gives technical advice on vessels of all nations during the building stage, during service and after accidents. By referring to Lloyds Register, would-be users can find out a ship's age, size, type, owner, etc, which is of particular interest to a company wishing to charter or insure a ship. Ships are classified and it is from this that the expression 'A1' (at Lloyds) comes.

The Baltic Exchange originated in one of London's seventeenth century coffee houses and is the world's largest market for the chartering of ships of all nationalities. In addition, the sale and purchase of ships, and the chartering of aircraft are carried on there.

The monies earned by Lloyds Register and the Baltic Exchange are among the 'invisible exports' which help to keep this country's Balance of Payments favourable (see Chapter 5, Trading overseas).

Large-scale modernisation of ports has been taking place in recent years as a result of the increase in Britain's trade and of technological advances in shipping. The growing size of tankers and bulk carriers has necessitated more deep-water berths, and mechanical handling methods, containers and 'roll on/roll off' services have created a demand for new types of port facilities. There are special tanker terminals, for use by oil tankers, which are owned and operated by the oil companies.

Port authorities are of four main types: nationalised bodies, public trusts, local authorities and statutory companies. Ports run by nationalised undertakings (The British Transport Docks Board and the British Railways Board) represent over a quarter of the total capacity. The British Railways Board controls certain ports which are largely used for cross-Channel services of the railways. Examples of public trust port authorities are the Port of London Authority (PLA), the Tees and Hartlepool Authority and the Belfast Harbour Commissioners. The members of the Trust traditionally consist of representatives of importers, exporters, shipping companies, local authorities and trade unions with non-executive members appointed by the Government. Local authorities own about one-third of Britain's ports, including Bristol and Sunderland and there are also statutory companies owning, for example, Manchester and Liverpool. There are some private ports which deal with the movement of commodities such as china clay, petroleum or paper pulp by individual industrial firms.

Coastal shipping. Because Britain is an island, it is possible for products to be carried around the coast, from port to port and, indeed, about 15 per cent of the country's goods are carried in this way. Almost one-third of cargo passing through the ports of Great Britain is coastal traffic. The type of commodity is generally goods in bulk (petroleum and coal). Many companies owning 'coasting tramps' and 'coasting liners' also trade between British and foreign ports.

Ocean shipping. Almost all Britain's overseas trade is carried by sea and British ships carry over a third of foreign seaborne trade. Apart from 'special' ships such as oil-tankers, ocean-going ships are 'tramps' or 'liners' too. Those described as **'liners'** sail regularly between fixed ports, like a bus or a train (and like a bus or train or anything else that runs to a regular timetable on set routes, whether full or empty, they are 'common carriers'). The **'tramps'** are wanderers, like taxicabs. The 'tramp' can be chartered, by using a document called a **'charter party'**, to carry practically anything anywhere (though there are many specially equipped tramps for carrying oil or other cargoes requiring special kinds of carriage).

Modern tramp shipping has developed rapidly, and the ocean-going tramps now carry their cargoes, crew and their small number of passengers in considerable comfort. Tramps compete with liners for goods traffic, but liners are the main passenger carriers. The new container ships have automatic controls and instead of being issued with a Bill of Lading (B/L) at the quay-side (a document giving details of cargo on board), details of cargo put on board are computerised and telexed to the ship the day after it has left port. Thus there is no delay over document-ation. The containers and container handling equipment is standardised worldwide and so a container can be carried across land and sea by any means of transport.

Sea transport

Advantages	Disadvantages
Cheaper than air for overseas trade	Port-to-port only—other forms of transport needed
Large quantities can be handled	Slow: unsuitable if speed is important
Heavy, bulky and awkward goods can be handled	Delays at ports
Little damage to goods	Pilfering of cargo not uncommon if loose
Modern port facilities	
Container ships for safety and ease of handling and delivery	Packaging can be expensive to protect goods from salt air
Computerised documentation	
Access to most parts of the world	

Examples: Imports — raw materials, petroleum and petroleum products, eg, oil, rubber, raw cotton, ores, grain, phosphates, molasses, ground nuts
Exports — iron and steel, tinplate, machinery, chemicals, manufactured goods, eg, vehicles, clothing

Air transport

The story of British aviation is a rapid and exciting one. In 1911 British airmen carried the first mail by air. In 1919 a daily passenger service was put into operation between London and Paris and in that year, two British airmen, Alcock and Brown, made the first non-stop crossing of the Atlantic. The first over-seas service was to India in 1929; in 1931 there was a service to Africa and, in 1935, to Australia. In 1939 an experimental service to the USA began for mails. In 1924 four small air companies were given a Government grant on their merger to form Imperial Airways Ltd. This company carried many thou-sands of passengers in conditions that would both shock and frighten air passengers today. Compare the photographs of 1937 aircraft and modern aircraft, and remember that pre-war aircraft did not have the benefit of radio and radar services and that air-ports were ill-equipped to land aircraft in bad weather conditions. In 1940 (a year after the beginning of the Second World War), the two largest operating companies, Imperial Airways and British Overseas Airways, were taken over by the Government and the public corporation, British Overseas Airways Corporation (BOAC), directed the airways during the war. After the war (in 1946) British European Airways (BEA) was formed separately and in January 1973 the two merged to form British Airways.

The chief competitors of the ocean liner for passenger transport, the civil air services, are run both by the State and by independent airline companies.

British Airways is a government owned commercial enterprise and has the power to operate air transport services, either scheduled or charter, without restriction as to the nature of these services. In practice, the airline's main activity lies in providing scheduled passenger and cargo services between Britain and a wide area of the world, and also domestic flights within Britain. British Airways has more miles of unduplicated routes than any other airline in the world and if they were all unravelled and put in a straight line, they would stretch to the moon and back! In terms of passengers carried and kilometres flown, it is the largest airline in the world. For administration purposes it is divided into three departments: Commercial Operations (structure of routes, development of passenger, cargo and mail markets), Flight Operations, and Engineering and Planning.

British Airways also operates and markets a wide range of inclusive holidays, under various trade names, including Sovereign, Enterprise and Speedbird, and many of these passengers are carried by British Airtours Ltd, a Gatwick-based subsidiary. These inclusive tour operations and British Airtours are profitable and self-supporting.

The helicopter division—British Airways Helicopters Ltd— operates a scheduled service between Cornwall and the Isles of Scilly, undertakes charter work, provides links between oil rigs in the North Sea and the mainland, and operates some air-sea rescue services.

Cargo, including freight and air mail, earns British Airways about one-eighth of its total revenue and a high proportion is carried in the holds of passenger aircraft. There has been considerable growth in cargo charter and as success in the cargo field depends on first-class service on the ground, major reconstruction and reorganisation is in hand.

Only about 15 per cent of the value of imports and exports are carried by air but this is partly due to the value of oil (carried by sea) having increased so much in recent years. The main commodities carried by air are machinery, medicinal and pharmaceutical products, and diamonds. It is obviously quicker and safer than by sea for small items but it is more expensive. Besides carrying air mail items, all mail to Europe goes by air.

The independent companies (for example British Caledonian Airways and Laker Airways) compete with British Airways over several domestic and international routes, and are used on chartered and scheduled passenger and freight services. In addition, many companies are engaged in miscellaneous aviation activities such as supplying North Sea oil rigs, crop-spraying, aerial survey and photography, and flying instruction. There are over forty companies engaged in air-taxi operations who carry over 400 000 passengers a year.

Special aircraft can be chartered to fly cargoes or passengers and the dealing between brokers is done at the Baltic Exchange, London.

A helicopter delivering cargo.

The latest development in the design of civil aircraft is the supersonic jet, Concorde, which has a cruising speed of twice the speed of sound. It was developed in co-operation with Air France and the world's first supersonic scheduled passenger service was the highly publicised one to Bahrain in January 1976. This was followed in May by a service to Washington DC and in 1977 to New York. Routes were also approved to Singapore and to Melbourne, Australia. Its main advantage over other aircraft is its speed, cutting the length of a journey by almost half the flying time. Its disadvantages are the cost and the fact that airport authorities and local residents object to its noise level. However, great attention is being paid to noise abatement and the flights are now attracting regular commuters, apart from passengers travelling for interest and experience. Time is money to businessmen and London to Melbourne, for instance, takes thirteen and a half hours in Concorde, compared with twenty-two and a half hours by subsonic aircraft.

Airports must be able to accommodate the increased traffic flow and size of aeroplanes and most of the main airports in Britain are undergoing programmes of redevelopment and improvement. There are approximately one hundred and fifty civil airports in Britain, with fifty Service aerodromes available for civil use. The British Airports Authority (BAA), a statutory body set up by Act of Parliament, owns and manages London's airports (Heathrow, Gatwick and Stansted) together with four other major airports: Glasgow, Prestwick, Edinburgh and Aberdeen. Most of the other public airports are controlled by local authorities. London Heathrow is the world's largest international airport and as overseas airways account for half the traffic this is good for Britain's national economy and balance of payments.

The Civil Aviation Authority is an independent statutory body, with members appointed by the Secretary of State for Trade. It is responsible for licensing scheduled and charter flights by British operators, and air travel organisers. It is also responsible for safety requirements in airline operations, in-service training of air crews, and in fire and rescue services, and for the airworthiness certificates of civil aircraft. The CAA also is responsible for National Air Traffic Services, which controls the flights of high-level aircraft.

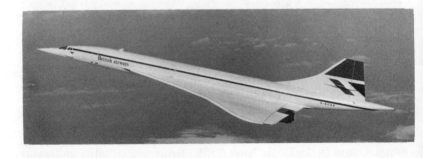

Concorde.

Air transport

Advantages	Disadvantages
Very quick—for perishables and urgent items	Expensive
Safe—for valuables	Limited quantities per load
Efficient—at airports and customs	Limited size and bulk
Suitable for domestic and overseas routes	Away from centre of population, therefore other forms of transport needed
Insurance costs low (risks are smaller than by surface vehicle)	
Protective packaging costs low and often unncessary	
Little risk of pilfering	

Examples of freight: mail, newspapers, gold, valuable stones, jewellery, films, flowers, table delicacies, animals, machinery, medicinal and pharmaceutical products, very fragile goods

Pipeline

The only commodities suitable for transport by pipeline are liquids and gas and The Pipelines Act 1962 was designed to secure the orderly development of privately owned industrial pipelines. Crude oil pipelines are in operation in Britain between harbours and refineries, and tankers can discharge their contents into pipelines at tanker terminals for direct transmission to refineries. Pipelines also carry refined products from the refineries to the major marketing areas (Manchester, London and the Midlands, for example). Submarine pipelines carry oil from off-shore oil fields to the mainland.

A pipeline system was commissioned in 1964 for the delivery of liquified natural gas from Algeria and since then a national pipeline system has been formed for the transmission of natural gas from British fields in the North Sea. The switch over to natural gas is now virtually complete—the gas being delivered by pipeline. Canvey Island is the terminal for Algerian gas and a central system is supplied by feeder mains from the North Sea short terminals. As with oil, there are submarine pipelines in connection with the exploration for, and production of, off-shore gas.

Britain's water resources are, with progressive development, sufficient for domestic and industrial requirements and water supplies are piped to users, the local authorities levying a charge through the rating system.

A full glossary of transport and delivery terms can be found on page 283.

Questions

1. Explain the abbreviations:

fob	carr pd	for
TIR	cif	PLA
BAA	B/L	NFC

2. There are a number of factors to be considered when business-men decide which method of transport to use for their goods. Say how *four* of these factors apply, using an appropriate example in each case.

(Metro)

3. Some commodities, among them water, gas and oil, are trans-ported in pipe lines. Compare the advantages and disadvantages of the pipe line with other methods of transporting such commodities.

(YR)

4. In the 1960's and 1970's a study of the index of ton-miles for inland goods transported shows that road transport has been gaining freight, the railways losing it. What advantages does road transport possess that might account for this? What transport policies have been adopted to reverse this trend?

(AL)

5. Under what circumstances is it more advantageous for a trader to export his goods by air in preference to exporting them by sea? Give *five* examples of goods that would clearly be sent by air freight and state the main differences in the documents involved in this form of transport as compared with transport by sea.

(SW)

6. Describe the changes which have taken place in the methods of transporting goods in both home and overseas trade as a result of the increasing use of containers.

(YR)

7. To travel or send goods by air is not usually the cheapest method of transport. In view of this, explain why air transport has become so important today.

(EA)

7

Communications and the Post Office

During the twentieth century there has been tremendous progress in methods of transport, and we can understand how isolated and comparatively primitive our lives would be without, for example, petrol-driven engines, electric and diesel trains, and jet aircraft. The modern inter-dependence between people, countries and nations has led to an equal need for rapid communication. We need to be able to send and receive letters, orders and parcels rapidly and reliably; and to be able to have discussions with people without actually travelling to meet them. Television, radio and newspapers also keep us in touch with events and are means of giving and receiving information.

The Post Office

The Post Office is a public corporation and provides the means for the transport and delivery of letters and parcels and various communication and remittance services, including the National Giro banking service (see chapter 11, Means of payment). In this chapter we consider the Post Office as a means of communication. Because the Post Office has a monopoly of postal and communication systems, there is an organisation independent of the Post Office which acts as a watchdog on the consumers' behalf. This is the Post Office Users' National Council (POUNC).

Much of the activity of the Post Office does, of course, take place behind the scenes, out of the public eye. However, there are high street and district Post Offices and sub-Post Offices which provide a counter service for the general public. It should be remembered that Post Offices not only sell postage stamps and accept telegrams, but provide over-the-counter services unconnected with communication, including:

- sale of licences (motor vehicle, drivers', dog, radio and TV, gamekeepers', etc);
- issue of British Visitors' Passports, and application forms for regular passports;

- issue of pensions (widows', retirement, etc);
- allowances (maternity, child benefit, industrial injury, etc);
- benefits (sickness, invalid, child interim, etc);
- acceptance of money for various Government savings schemes;
- acceptance of money for the payment of telephone bills, for the National Giro system and for remittance services.

Letters and parcels, postcards, printed papers, samples and newspapers may be sent at varying rates both by inland and overseas post. There are certain prohibitions as to the type of articles which can be sent through the post, and details of these restrictions are given in the **Post Office Guide** published annually by the Post Office. This guide also gives current prices of postage, and details of all postal and telecommunication services. Buyers are kept up-to-date by the issue of supplements. In addition, local Head Postmasters and Telephone Managers are more than willing to advise business firms if they have any special communication problems: for example, bulk postings, urgent deliveries, the training of switchboard operators, an internal telephones system, etc.

Subject to the permission of the Post Office, companies may buy or lease a **franking machine** to frank their mail with the cost of the postage, rather than have the laborious task of buying and sticking on postage stamps. The use of a franking machine has other advantages besides the obvious one of time-saving:

- cost of postage is metered and recorded, thus eliminating separate records and calculations
- a dial can be adjusted for any denomination of stamp
- it is safer—there is less risk of loss of stamps or cash (the machine can be locked when not in use)
- the machine can be set up to print a slogan, or the company's name, in addition to franking the postage
- labels can be fed through the machine for the franking of parcels and other bulky items
- quicker procedure through the mail as franked mail bypasses the system where postage stamps are cancelled

There are different types and sizes of franking machine available according to the requirements of the customer. Only four firms are authorised to produce and supply the machines, and these are given in the Post Office Guide, together with the regulations for their use.

Another way of speeding the mail through the post is to use

the **postal code**. Postal towns, districts and streets are incorporated in the code and this aids mechanised sorting. Each envelope passes on a conveyor belt and pauses in front of an operator at a keyboard. The operator taps out the code seen on the envelope and this action places phosphorescent dots on the envelope which are then 'read' by the sorting machinery.

Principal postal services

In addition to the following services there are express delivery services and variations for mail sent overseas and for full details the Post Office Guide should be consulted. Royal Mail leaflets should be consulted for up-to-date prices, fees and compensation limits.

Letter service

Students will be aware of the two-tier system of postage for inland letters, cards and postcards. The sender has a choice of sticking on a stamp to the value of first-class postage, or a lesser amount for the second-class service if the letter is not urgent, or has been posted in plenty of time. Business firms usually have a policy regarding which service they choose. For example, everything may go second-class, unless specifically marked otherwise. On the other hand, some firms may, for prestige purposes, or because the nature of their work requires that clients, customers or patients get mail quickly, like everything to go first-class. But cost is often a deciding factor and busy companies can spend several hundreds of pounds on postage costs each week.

It is not perhaps always realised that quite bulky items can be sent by letter post, which is quicker than parcel post. The maximum size allowed is 610 mm × 460 mm × 460 mm (about 2 ft × $1\frac{1}{2}$ ft × $1\frac{1}{2}$ ft), which is quite a considerable size for a letter! There is no limit on weight if sent first-class, but the maximum weight by second-class is 750 grams.

There are special facilities for business firms who post circulars and literature in bulk: they can be franked by the Post Office, and there are rebates if more than 4250 identical items are sent. Newspapers or other publications posted by the publishers, printers or their agents, can travel by first-class mail at second-class postage rate.

The Post Office has the power to make an extra charge for letters weighing less than the basic weight of 60 grams if the envelope does not conform to the **Post Office Preferred (POP)** range of envelopes. The Post Office has not yet made use of this power, but may do so if too many envelopes outside the POP range of sizes continue to be used. Most envelopes are now sold with the POP symbol on them, particularly envelopes bought with greetings cards. The large greetings cards that are so popular may, if weighing under 60 grams, at some future date, be outside the POP range and therefore be liable for a surcharge.

Letter post for Europe is sent by air as the normal means of transmission, and is referred to as the **All-up Service**. To other countries, senders have a choice of sending mail by **Air Mail** or surface mail. Air Mail is more expensive and, as with all mail, the charges vary according to weight. Special lightweight Air Mail forms and stationery are available.

Poste restante   Postal packets and letters may be addressed to a Post Office to await collection by the addressee. The words Poste restante, or 'To be Called For', must be clearly shown in the address:

```
Mr G K N Holsworthy
POSTE RESTANTE
The Post Office
ILMINSTER
Somerset
TA19 OAJ
```

The addressee must show evidence of identity when he collects his post. This service is useful for travellers, anyone on a touring holiday and for someone with a temporary address (except that it must not be used in the same town for more than three months).

Business Reply Service (BRS)   This is a very popular service used by business firms wishing to encourage replies from clients, customers and potential customers. It encourages a response because the client is not put to any postage expense, as a prepaid card or envelope is provided. Sometimes a newspaper or magazine advertisement incorporates a fold-up and tuck-in form with the BRS design. Before using this service the company must apply for a licence and will pay an additional $\frac{1}{2}$p, in addition to the normal postage rate, for each BRS card or envelope returned by post to the licensee. The licensee may choose first- or second-class service.

Freepost   This, like the BRS, is designed to encourage replies from customers without their having to pay postage costs, but

A Business Reply Service Card.

under this service, reply-paid stationery is not supplied. The customer merely includes the word *Freepost* in the address. As with the Business Reply Service, a firm wishing to use a Free-post address must obtain a licence from the Post Office and also pays an additional $\frac{1}{2}$ p postage every time the Freepost address is used. Freepost packets are treated as second-class mail—the firm has no choice as it has with the BRS. Besides a saving in stationery and printing costs, firms can also save on advertising space as a response is encouraged without their having to pay for space large enough for a BRS form.

Printed Postage Impressions (PPI)   This facility may be used by customers making single postings of not less than 5000 letters, 1000 packets or 100 parcels. They may print or stamp a *postage paid* impression on their own envelopes, labels or wrappers and then pay the postage when the items are handed over to the Post Office, either at the time of posting or through an account. The local Head Postmaster will advise on the permitted design and arrangements must be agreed prior to posting.

Registration   All items sent by the inland first-class letter post may be registered and all letters containing coins, notes, and jewellery must be registered. The registration fee (which is on a scale according to the value of the package) provides for com-pensation (maximum £800) in the event of loss or damage. Packets for registration must be dealt with over the Post Office counter- -a certificate of posting is given to the sender, and a special blue and white label is affixed to the packet. The packet then receives special security treatment in the mail and a signature is obtained upon delivery. The sender must pay special attention to packing and registered letter envelopes, available at the Post Office, must be used for currency and tokens of monetary value. These envelopes are linen-backed and have blue lines across them. Overseas packets cannot be registered but may be insured.

Recorded Delivery Service Any item sent by the inland letter postal service, first- or second-class, can be sent by this service which provides proof of posting and of delivery. There is a small fee to pay in addition to the cost of posting but there is no special treatment in the mail apart from a signature being obtained upon delivery. There is only limited compensation (not exceeding £18) in the event of loss or damage. Recorded Delivery packets must not contain items of monetary value and its use is for documents of importance: for example, examination papers and scripts, legal documents, etc or when proof of posting and delivery is required. RD packets must be handed over the Post Office counter as the sender gets a receipt and an orange label is affixed to the package.

For both the registration and the Recorded Delivery services, the sender can be advised of the delivery of the packet if he pays an extra fee and completes an *Advice of Delivery* form. Proof of delivery can be requested afterwards, but the fee would be higher.

Datapost This provides a highly reliable, door-to-door, overnight delivery service. Packages are collected at a place and time agreed between the Post Office and the customer, and are delivered on the next working morning, again at an agreed place. They may include documents, medical samples or spare parts. In this way for example, a bank in Carlisle using this service can have mail for Datapost collected daily at, say 4 pm, and be sure that it will be delivered direct to its head office in London the next morning. The service is available anywhere in the country, and the regulations regarding size, weight and contents are similar to those for letter post. It must be realised that each organisation using Datapost enters into an individual contract with the Post Office for collection from and delivery to specified addresses, and this may be on a daily, weekly or monthly basis, or for specified dates. Charges for the service are negotiated separately for each contract.

Datapost 'D' (On Demand) is available for organisations which require occasional and not regular delivery. For this, the customer takes his mail to his nearest Head Post Office.

The package may travel by any of the normal methods: air, rail or road. An international service is also available to ten countries. Conoco Oil Refineries, for instance, have a regular collection and delivery service from their Humberside refinery to their parent company in the United States.

Selectapost Many firms have a post room for sorting incoming mail, but the Post Office is prepared to subdivide a firm's mail into departments prior to delivery. The charge for this service is negotiated separately for each customer.

Callers Services The Post Office provides Callers Services through which mail may be received earlier or at a more convenient time than normal delivery by the postman. Each service involves the addressee (or his authorised representative) calling at the Post Office to collect the mail. All mail must bear the full address including the box number if a private box is used, for example:

```
A D Jones & Co Ltd
P O Box 100
30 Main Street
SCUNTHORPE
DN17 1AJ
```

Reply Coupons If a reply is required from a friend or client abroad, a British stamp cannot of course be enclosed. It is possible, however, to buy an International Reply Coupon from a Post Office and enclose this with the communication. These coupons may then be exchanged abroad for stamps representing the minimum postage payable for a letter from that country to this country.

Inland Parcel Service

There are limits of weight and size imposed on parcels acceptable by the Post Office. The weight is 10 kg and the size (laid down precisely) is roughly that of a guitar. Over and above that it would be necessary to send a parcel by an alternative method, for example by rail or road transport. There is a reduced charge made by the Post Office for **area parcels** (ie those which are to be delivered in the same delivery area as the area of posting. The Post Office make special arrangements with businesses who have regular large postings; they will collect from the premises and offer contracts to their mutual advantage.

Compensation Fee (CF) Parcels   This service provides compensation (maximum £225) for loss or damage. A fee is paid at the time of posting. A form is completed by the sender and the relevant box is ticked according to the value of the parcel. Postage stamps for the fee payable are affixed to the form which is then date-stamped by the counter clerk. This portion is then returned to the sender as a receipt. The parcel is not marked in any way, receives no security treatment and there is no signature obtained upon delivery. Packages of great value should, therefore, if possible, be sent by the registered letter service, even though it is much more expensive.

Postage Forward Parcel Service   This service for parcels is similar to the Business Reply service for letters in that customers or clients can send parcels to firms or advertisers without having to pay postage. Reply-paid labels are supplied instead of envelopes or cards. The licensee pays the postage costs plus an additional six pence for each parcel sent to them. This service is useful for companies who run a 'free approval' service.

Cash on Delivery (COD) Service   The addressee (receiver) of a COD parcel or package pays a **'trade charge'** to the postman or Post Office before the parcel is handed over. This trade charge (not over £100) is usually in payment of the contents of the parcel and is specified by the sender at the time of posting. This amount is then forwarded by the Post Office to the sender. The COD service is very useful to both parties; the sender is sure of getting his money for the goods, and the receiver does not run the risk of sending a cheque or cash with his order (CWO), not knowing whether he will receive the goods or not. The COD service must not be used to send unsolicited (unrequested) goods. The sender fills in a form and pays a fee at the time of posting.

Telecommunications

British Telecom (separated from the Post Office in 1981) has the

102

most up-to-date systems of world-wide communications. **Sub-scriber Trunk Dialling (STD)** is now available throughout the country and most large European cities and many others throughout the world can be dialled directly without going through the operator. STD calls are charged at a fixed rate for a unit of time; the length of time varying according to the distance and time of day. There are also services for telephoning ships, and mobile radio telephones can be installed in personal cars.

British Telecom advices business firms on the type and size of switchboard most suited to their needs. There is, for example, the PMBX (Private Manual Branch Exchange), where the company's switchboard operator obtains and receives all calls, whether internal or external. With a PABX (Private Automatic Branch Exchange) however, the operator receives and routes incoming calls only because extension users can dial each other and also dial their own outside calls.

Businesses can also rent private telegraph and telephone circuits from British Telecom. In this way the subscriber has his own line between points quite separate from the public system. This means instant, confidential communication between the transmitters, for example from a Head Office to its branches. The BBC has this facility between London and the regions. The British Steel Corporation has an internal telephone system called COTEN (COrporation TElecommunications Network) which enables 20 000 telephones, located on ninety BSC sites throughout Britain, to have desk-to-desk dialling facilities without going through any switchboard.

There are **telephone answering machines** available which answer the telephone and may record a message for the sub-scriber. The subscriber can connect the answering machine either when he is not going to be there himself, or when it is not neces-sary for telephone calls to be personally acknowledged. Some firms, for example, have a special telephone line to receive orders and enquiries. Television and newspaper advertisements which say 'ring now' generally indicate that there is a telephone answer-ing machine on the other end of the line. The answering machine can also be useful for old, blind, disabled or infirm people.

There are special telephone call services available to tele-phone users and subscribers and, as with the postal services, full details and costs are given in the Telecom Guide. Information can also be obtained from telephone directories and dialling code booklets which are issued free to all subscribers. One directory contains a list in alphabetical order of the names of all subscribers in the area; the classified directory ('Yellow Pages') lists firms and traders according to classification of industry or trade, plus government and professional entries. The telephone dialling code booklet gives information on STD codes, cost of calls, and of the various special services available.

Advice of Duration and Charge (ADC)   The cost and timing of a call through the operator will be notified on its completion provided the caller asks at the time of booking the call. This service is useful to subscribers wishing to keep a record of their long-distance or overseas calls, or to anyone using someone else's telephone and wishing to pay for the call. There is an additional fee payable.

Transferred Charge Calls   The charge for a call from any telephone may be debited to the called subscriber provided he agrees in advance to accept the call. The receiver pays the cost of the call plus a transfer fee.

Freefone   This is a service similar to the postal Freepost service, in that it enables customers, clients, agents or employees to call a firm without having to go to the trouble and expense of paying for the call. A Freefone number is allocated to the business subscriber and calls are obtained through the operator giving the Freefone number. In addition to the cost of the calls the subscriber pays a quarterly charge plus a transfer fee for each call. Freefone numbers are often connected to an answering/recording machine.

Telephone Credit Cards   These may be supplied to subscribers to enable them, or their employees to make telephone calls and send telegrams from any telephone without payment at the time. Calls are made through the operator quoting the credit card number and are charged to the telephone account on which the credit card was issued. They are useful for journalists or representatives who travel on behalf of their companies and who need to make regular or frequent telephone calls on their journeys. There is a quarterly charge and calls are charged for at the appropriate operator rate plus a transfer fee.

Personal Calls   For a fee the telephone operator will put through a call to a particular person, or a named substitute. If that person is not available the personal call fee only is payable. The charge for the call does not begin until the person required speaks on the telephone. If the person called is not available, the operator will leave a message to contact the caller. This service is useful for long-distance and overseas calls through the operator when it is essential to speak to one particular person. However, it may well be cheaper and quicker to dial direct by STD if that is possible, rather than involve the operator.

Fixed Time Calls   A call may be booked in advance for connection at a specified time. There is an extra charge for this service which is not made if the call is not effected within 10 minutes of the time stated.

Alarm Calls   These may be booked by subscribers if they wish to be rung early in the morning, or as a reminder at any other time of the day or night. There is a charge for each alarm call.

Telephone Information Services   Recorded information services are available in many towns and full details can be found in local telephone directories. The charge is that for a call to the number concerned. Examples of services are: Time (the Speaking Clock), Teletourist (events and places of interest in London and Edinburgh), Cricket (scores and prospects of play during Test and other matches), Dial-a-Disc (a different hit record each night), Recipe, Financial Times Index and Business News Summary, Motoring Information (road conditions), Bedtime Stories, Gardening Information, Weather Information and Forecasts (local forecasts).

The '999' Emergency Dialling Service   This enables callers to be connected as quickly as possible, free of charge, to the service required: police, ambulance, fire brigade, coastguard, lifeboat or rescue.

Services for the speedy transmission of written messages are also expanding.

Inland and overseas telegrams   These can be sent either by hand from a Post Office, by telephone, by Telex or via a Post Office messenger. It is possible to hand in a telegram in advance for delivery on a specified day. **Telemessage**, a recent Telecom service, is a telegraphed message at a fixed rate. There is a basic charge for a telegram plus a charge for each word. Delivery can be made by hand, by Telex or by telephone, when a confirmatory copy will be delivered by post if requested.

Phototelegrams Pictures, photographs, drawings, plans and documents can be transmitted from London to many places in the world. When the phototelegram is received by the overseas telegraph office, it is posted to the addressee by express or registered post.

Facsimile transceivers The use of facsimile transceivers by business companies is growing. This is a copying machine attached to the telephone system which will transmit and receive facsimile copies of any kind of original document over telephone lines. An A4 size document can be transmitted in about thirty seconds As there are several makes of transceiver on the market it is necessary for the caller and receiver to have compatible machines.

Telex is a fast means of transmitting a message which is printed out on teleprinters on both the sending and receiving installations. The telex network in the United Kingdom is fully automatic and subscribers can have immediate connection by direct dialling. This direct dialling is also available to many subscribers in Europe and elsewhere but otherwise telex subscribers are connected by the London operator. Telex has the speed of telephoned verbal messages, but, being in typescript, is unlikely to be subject to human errors of mishearing or recording, and is more likely to be acceptable as written instructions or confirmation or an order. Since no operator is needed for receiving messages when Telex and answering machines are used, these machines have overcome the difference in time between continents.

Complicated, detailed or lengthy communications can first be punched onto tape by the means of a special attachment to the Telex teleprinter. The preparation of punched tape means that intricate messages can be checked before transmission and, as tape is transmitted at a higher speed than typed messages, there is a saving on call time.

Datel is a Telecom service which enables a large amount of digital data to be transmitted through telegraph or telephone systems at very high speeds. For transmissions over telegraph system, a computer prepares a five unit code on punched paper which is decoded by the receiver's computer. For transmission over the telephone network signals from the computer are fed into a piece of Telecom equipment called a modulator/demodulor (Modem for short). This turns the signals into pulses, which can be transmitted at much higher speeds than other signals. The

106

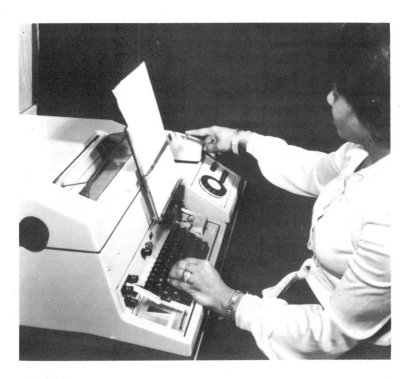
Telex machine.

pulses enter a modem at the receiving end for reconversion to signals for the recipient's computer.

Several types of datel services are available, offering different speeds; and also facilities for simultaneous two-way transmission between two points. Automatic error detection equipment is also available.

Datel is thus a method of transmitting information between computers at very high speed via telex, private telegraph or telephone circuits. Datel services are used by many businesses whose operations demand the constant feeding in and retrieval of information. For example, banks and building societies have now computerised their records and data about each day's transactions is transmitted to the computer centre where it is stored until required. Similarly, manufacturers and wholesalers keep track of their sales and stock position by having a central computer linked to each of their sales offices.

The Datel service is nationwide and there are international services to the USA and seventeen European countries have been established by using satellite telephone circuits.

Viewdata is a service linking private telephones to specially modified television sets, and enables subscribers to obtain a wide range of information for display on their television screens. Information, stored in a computer, includes consumer guidance from the Consumers' Association, stock market prices and tourist information, including road and rail travel information. Subscribers pay for the call to their nearest Viewdata centre at ordinary rates, plus a charge for the information obtained.

Confravision is another development in the field of communication introduced in 1971 and operated by British Telecom. It is an audio-visual conference facility operating, at the present time, between five cities in Great Britain (London, Birmingham, Bristol, Glasgow and Manchester). Studios are booked in advance and two or three studios can be interconnected for the video conference. The facilities offered are customer-controlled and designed to allow meetings to be conducted over the system as though the participants were face-to-face. The minimum hire is for a half-hour and the hire charge varies according to distance. However, it could well be cheaper than executives travelling across country to meetings.

The Telecommunications Tower in central London provides a new centre for a network of microwave radio links for telephone services and transmission of broadcast radio and television programmes. Possibly the most interesting development of all is the radio communication between distant parts of the globe using space satellites as reflectors. Such a system provides cheap, efficient international telephone services, and international television transmission, without the need for expensive underwater cables.

Questions

1. Explain why the Post Office is often one of the busiest 'shops' in a town centre.

(NR)

2. Explain what is meant by:
   (a) Recorded Delivery; (b) Cash on Delivery;
   (c) Poste Restante; (d) Selectapost;
   (e) Freepost.

(RSA)

108

3. The Letter Post, the Telephone system and the Telex system are all means of communication.

Explain how *each* of them is useful to the business community.

(YR)

4. (a) Apart from postal and telegraph services name *five* distinct facilities available over a Post Office counter.

(b) Name (i) *one* specialised service available by telephone that is free of charge,

and (ii) *two* specialised services for which the normal telephone charges are payable.

(c) In 1971 the Post Office introduced 'Confravision'. Briefly explain what the service is, and where you would have to be in order to use it.

(SW)

5. (a) Write short paragraphs on any *four* of the following:

(i) Yellow Pages (ii) STD (iii) Telex (iv) Datel (v) Freefone

(b) Describe any other two telecommunication services of special interest to people in business and finance circles.

(RSA)

6. 'All business firms are assisted by services provided by the Post Office'. Describe these services with particular reference to the mail order firm.

(EM)

7. (a) Describe a set of circumstances when a businessman might prefer to use a telephone rather than a letter.

(b) Describe a situation when a business would use Recorded Delivery.

(NR)

Special note

The British Telecommunications Bill 1981 set up British Telecom to run the telecommunications and data processing services of the PO and to break the telecommunications monopoly, thus giving greater scope for competition both in the supply of parts for attachment to the public network and in the provision of services.

Cable and Wireless, BP and Barclays Merchant Bank are to set up a new telecommunications network, known as 'Mercury', initially covering major cities in England and offering national and international services to large governmental and commercial users.

8

Banking

The business of a bank is money. Its customers include men and women of all kinds, some wealthy and some of limited means; and businesses large and small, at home and abroad. Britain has one of the most highly developed banking and financial systems in the world, and every day millions of pounds worth of money change hands without a note or coin being handled by the parties concerned. At present about 50 per cent of the adult population have current accounts with banks, and this number is increasing because more and more employers are paying wages directly into the bank accounts of their employees. This means that many young people starting work need to open a bank account.

The development of banks

Lombard Street in the City of London is the centre of British banking and the high street banks have their head offices and clearing houses there. The street is named after the Lombards, from the Plains of Lombardy in northern Italy, who came to do business in London in the seventeenth century and set up their benches (bancos) in what became known as 'The Street of the Lombards'. They worked and sold gold at these benches. If they were unable to pay their debts, angry creditors smashed up their benches, hence the term 'bankrupt' (bench broken).

Eventually banking came to be developed by London goldsmiths who, in addition to their normal business, stored and guarded gold in their vaults for people who wanted a safe place for their wealth. These 'depositors' were given a receipt, and if they wanted to withdraw some of their deposits would produce their receipt. Naturally, the depositor paid the goldsmith 'bank charges' for the privilege of having his wealth safely guarded.

It became apparent that unnecessary risks were being run by depositors in withdrawing large sums of money in order to pay another person. It would be simpler and safer merely to ask the banker to transfer funds from their account to the account of the person to whom they owed money (their *creditor*). These written letters of instruction to the goldsmith (banker) asking for the transfer of wealth to a creditor were the forerunners of the cheque system today.

The goldsmiths soon realised that large amounts of money were lying around unused in their vaults and that it was profitable to lend some of it to people anxious to borrow money.

This, then, was the basis of the modern banking system: keeping an account of customers' receipts and withdrawals; safeguarding money for them; paying others on their behalf; and lending money to those who required it.

The banking system

The three main categories of institution in the British banking system are:

- The **Bank of England.** The central bank of the United Kingdom.
- Specialist banking institutions, such as **Merchant Banks**, which specialise among other things in the financing of trade both at home and abroad. These are discussed in Chapter 9, Finance for industry.
- **Commercial, joint stock, or deposit banks**, whose traditional role has been to undertake all types of banking business for the general public.

The trustee savings banks are governed by special statutes and are discussed separately in Chapter 13, Saving and investing.

The Bank of England

The Bank of England (the 'old lady of Threadneedle Street') was founded in 1694 to provide money for the war against France, when stockholders subscribed money required for the war. The bank developed into a national institution and was regulated and strengthened by the Bank Charter Act of 1844. This laid down restrictions on existing note-issuing banks with the result that the Bank of England eventually became the only bank which issued notes in England and Wales. (Certain banks in Scotland and Northern Ireland have a limited right to issue bank notes.) The 1844 Act allowed the Bank to issue any amount of notes backed by gold coin or bullion and up to a specified value beyond this backing. (Bullion is uncoined gold.) The amount of notes issued over and above gold backing is called '*fiduciary issue*'. Today the backing is in the form of

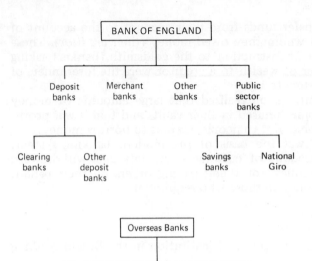

The structure of the banking system in Britain.

Government and other securities and the amount of gold held is very small. The Gold Standard was suspended in 1931 so that most of today's currency is fiduciary issue.

As a result of the Bank of England Act 1946 it became a public corporation (nationalised), the ownership passing to the Treasury. Its affairs are managed by a board of directors (known as the 'Court'), all appointed by the Crown on the advice of the Government. The Chief Cashier's signature appears on bank notes 'For the Governor and Company of the Bank of England'.

The Bank of England is the central bank of the United Kingdom.

- It acts as banker to the Government and to other banks, including overseas banks.
- It is responsible for the issue of our currency and notes; new notes are issued and withdrawn in large numbers each day. Only the Bank of England and the Royal Mint can replace notes and coin, and decide when they are unfit for further use.
- It acts as Registrar for Government stock, which involves

112

making four million dividend payments annually.
- It acts as agent for the Government in important financial operations and is adviser on many aspects of financial policy.
- The Bank also undertakes the management of the National Debt and administers a fund called the Exchange Equalisation Account (EEA) which ensures that the value of British currency in the foreign money market remains as steady as possible.

The Bank of England is, therefore, an agent of the Government and it is through the Bank that monetary policy is implemented. By deciding on and announcing the Minimum Lending Rate, the Bank of England influences the amount of interest charged to borrowers by banks, building societies and finance houses, and also the amount of interest paid to savers on their deposits. The rate fluctuates according to how much control the Treasury wishes to exercise over spending. At its simplest level, cheap loans encourage borrowing and spending whereas high interest rates deter borrowers and are likely to increase investment. (See note on page 127.)

The Bank of England is the centre of what is known as the money market and all the City financial institutions, the insurance companies and the Stock Exchange are closely linked to it. (See Chapter 9, Finance for industry.)

Pressure is growing for new legislation to clarify and strengthen control of the banking system, since weaknesses were shown up by the banking collapse of 1973-74 which involved a number of secondary banks. The Bank of England averted a financial disaster by calling upon the main clearing banks to assist the twenty-six ailing secondary banks.

Commercial, or joint stock banks

The primary business of the commercial or joint stock banks is the receipt, transfer and cashing of deposits (money) and they are the banks with which everyone is familiar because they deal with the general public, both as business and private customers. All the cash used by the public passes through the branches of these banks and by looking at the 'cash-in' and 'cash-out', bank managers can estimate how much, if any, they need from their central source. It is the duty of the bullion department of a bank to supply branches with currency and to relieve them of any surplus. The banks are the only agency throughout the country for distributing cash; even the Post Office calls upon local banks for its own local needs.

As a result of a number of mergers between banking groups the principal banks in this group are the six London *clearing banks:*

| Barclays | Coutts | Lloyds | Midland | National Westminster | Williams & Glyn's |

Symbols of the six London clearing banks.

In addition there are three Scottish clearing banks and two Northern Ireland banks. In 1975 membership of the London Bankers' Clearing House was extended to the *Co-operative Bank* and the *Central Trustee Savings Bank.* These banks provide full banking services throughout Britain and operate through some 14 000 branches. The clearing bank groups have been extending their foreign operations by setting up branches abroad and by going into partnership with foreign banks in order to compete in international markets.

The commercial banks are public companies and, as such, they exist to make a profit for their shareholders. They do this mainly by lending money at interest to their customers and investing deposits in safe securities. Like all public companies, bank shares are bought and sold on the Stock Exchange.

Accounts and services offered to customers by the banks include:

Deposit account Money kept in a deposit account earns interest for the account holder. This is usually 2 per cent below the minimum lending or bank rate. Interest received has to be declared to the Inland Revenue because income tax is payable on it. Credit slips are used to pay in to the account and withdrawals are requested and signed for over the bank counter. Since the banks invest money left on deposit, in theory account holders are required to give seven days' notice of withdrawal. In practice, except for large sums, amounts can be withdrawn on demand. Account holders may, however, lose seven days'

114

interest on the amount involved.

Savings account These are designed for small personal savings and below a certain amount may earn less interest than a deposit account. The account is useful for the saver of small amounts as money boxes are provided, the key being held by the bank. When the box is full the account holder takes it to the bank to be unlocked and the money is credited to his or her account. Parents often open savings accounts on behalf of their children.

Current account A current account is the account used for the transfer of money and with it the holder gets a cheque book. Money kept in a current account does not usually earn interest because it is continually 'on the move'. Bills can be settled and cash withdrawn by the use of cheques. Money can be transferred between account holders by using the *credit transfer* (or *bank giro*) system, the *direct debit* system, or by *standing order*. Goods and services can also be obtained by the use of *credit cards* (e.g., Access or Barclaycard) and payment made at a later date. Full details of these services are given in Chapter 11, Means of payment.

Amounts are paid into a current account by the use of a *paying-in slip* or *Bank Giro Credit slip* (see illustration). The credit slip, when completed, is handed over the counter of the customer's own bank, or at another branch, and need not be paid in personally by the account holder. The cashier checks that the money agrees with the slip and then stamps and initials it and accepts both slip and remittances. Paying-in books are available to bank customers and these have a counterfoil or duplicate copy which the cashier stamps as a record for the account holder. Alternatively, individual credit slips are available at bank counters.

A current account credit slip.

The use of paying-in slips is not, however, the only way an account can be credited because many employees now have their wages or salaries paid directly into their bank accounts by their employer, and creditors can receive settlement of bills by their debtors through the various transfer systems mentioned above and in Chapter 11.

At regular intervals, current account holders receive a bank statement of account which records all the transactions in and out of the account and shows the balance in the account at the date of the statement. The customer should not accept the balance shown on the statement without checking whether any transactions have taken place since. He can do this by referring

Lloyds Bank

COLCHESTER   D   5 *

22FEB78

S FOREST ESQ
31 ANY STREET
COLCHESTER
ESSEX

FOREST S   0187342

Date	Particulars		Payments			
1978	Opening Balance				49 67 *	
15JAN	CREDIT BY POST			11 03		
		149703	30 00		30 70 *	
19JAN	SUNDRY CREDIT			19 28		
		149706	13 65			
		149707	5 42			
		149708	55 05		24 14 OD	
22JAN		149711	12 17			
	CASHPOINT CARD 1		20 00			
	CASHPOINT CARD 1		18 00			
		149710	1 50		75 81 OD	
25JAN	BANK GIRO CREDIT			266 27	190 46 *	
29JAN	DAVIES & NEWMAN	DIV		25 75	216 21 *	
30JAN	LEGAL & GENERAL	D/D	9 50			
	LOAN A/C	S/O	15 00		191 71 *	
31JAN	KALAMAZOO	DIV		8 51	200 22 *	
1FEB	BUCKS CC	DIV		7 14		
	SHELL T & T	DIV		13 21	220 57 *	
6FEB		149701	60 00			
	CASHPOINT CARD 1		14 00		146 57 *	
13FEB	INVESTMENTS SOLD			209 15	355 72 *	
14FEB	LEEDS P B S	S/O	20 50		335 22 *	
20FEB		149712	192 36		142 86 *	
22FEB	CASHPOINT CARD 1		20 00		122 86 *	

The items and balance shown on this statement should be verified and any enquiries directed to the above Branch

A bank statement.

116

to paying-in book counterfoils and cheque book stubs. When businesses do this, they prepare what is called a *bank reconciliation statement*. They 'reconcile' the bank statement with the true, up-to-date state of affairs as shown by the Cash Book. Cheques, when they have not been cleared through the banking system (not yet returned to the drawer's bank for his account to be debited) are known as *unpresented cheques*.

Banks may levy what are known as *bank charges*, which is a service fee. The amount levied is largely at the Bank Manager's discretion and depends on the average balance in the account and the number of entries involved. Therefore, if the account is used frequently, with a small balance held, the bank charges will be higher than for an account used infrequently and with a large balance in hand. The bank statement will show the customer how much the account has been debited. Some banks do not levy changes if the balance of the account does not fall below a minimum amount.

Overdrafts Customers may, with the Bank Manager's consent, and at his discretion, overdraw their current account within a set limit. Interest is charged on the amount overdrawn and is calculated daily on any debit balance. The rates of interest range from one to five per cent above the declared minimum lending or bank rate. The amount overdrawn will, of course, fluctuate as amounts are credited to the account. When the account is overdrawn this is shown on the bank statement by the abbreviation OD or DR beside the balance figure. Interest charges are also shown on the statement. This can be one of the cheapest methods of borrowing because interest is charged only on the amount overdrawn.

Bank loans Banks advance money to customers for a wide variety of reasons: for household goods, motor cars, home improvements or extensions, professional equipment (eg, for dentists), and for advances required by industry, commerce or trade.

Personal loans are for fixed periods and for a specified amount. A fixed rate of interest is charged based on the current bank rate. They are normally short-term loans ranging from six months to three years and are repayable by equal monthly instalments. Some security (collateral) may be required by the bank in case of default and this can be in the form of property deeds, life assurance policies, Stock Exchange securities, or some other form of security.

The normal procedure is for a special Loan Account to be opened. The amount of the loan is transferred from this to the borrower's current account as required so that cheques can be drawn without overdrawing the current account. The Loan Account is then debited and is credited as repayments (including interest charges) are made to it (by standing order payments from the current account).

The bank manager, before agreeing to overdrafts or loans, has several factors to consider:

- Government policy concerning public borrowing (a credit squeeze is sometimes in force)
- the bank's own policy and resources
- the personal position of the borrower: his credit worthiness and prospects
- the type of security offered by the borrower
- the purpose of the loan; for instance, the enlarging of business premises for greater profitability would be viewed more favourably than a holiday
- the length and amount of repayment

Bridging loans These are short term loans agreed for a limited period over and above any loans or mortgages outstanding. An example of their use is when a family are moving house and have to pay towards their new home before the old one is sold. They, therefore, need a loan to 'bridge the gap'.

Night safe facilities In one of the outside walls of the bank is an opening with a shutter (rather like a letterbox). This is used by people such as shop-keepers who may have large sums of money to deposit after 3.30 pm or at week-ends when the banks are shut. Money for the night safe must be put in special bags provided by the bank. When the bag is 'posted' into the opening of the night safe it drops into the vault of the bank. The following morning either the bank, by arrangement with the customer, opens the bag and banks the money, or the customer himself opens the bag, and pays the money into his account.

Cash dispensers A *cashcard* may be issued to approved customers. With this, the customer can obtain £10 in notes from a dispenser outside his own or any other branch of the bank at any time of the day or night. Each customer has a personal code number which is indicated on the card only by a series of holes, and these can be 'read' by the machine in the dispenser. To obtain the money, the customer places his card in the dispenser and taps out his number on a set of buttons. If the number tapped corresponds to the code on the card, a plastic wallet containing £10 is issued. The card is retained by the machine, and returned to the customer after his account has been debited.

The use of a code on the card for the customer's number prevents its being used if it is lost or stolen. If the wrong number is tapped out on the buttons the dispenser rejects the card. The customer has three chances to tap out the correct number, and after a third 'wrong number' the machine retains the card.

Cashpoints These are cash dispensers situated inside the banking hall and are available only during bank hours (9.30 am to 3.30 pm, Monday to Friday with generally one 'late night' opening one evening a week). Their purpose is to relieve pressure on counter staff and to provide a quick cash service for customers. The operation is similar to that of the cash dispenser mentioned above, but since the sum is not limited to £10, the amount as well as the customer's number, is tapped out on a keyboard. The maximum amount obtainable is £100 or five transactions in a day. The machine is linked to a computer which checks that the customer has sufficient funds in his account before the notes are released. The machine also releases the cashpoint card once the coded information has been 'read'. The complete transaction takes only a few moments.

Holders of cashcards should beware that there is no cheque stub to check on withdrawals but the use of the card is recorded on the bank statement (see illustration).

Cheque card or banker's card The cheque card, which has a number and is signed by the holder, acts as a form of identification for the customer. When a customer writes a cheque, the person receiving it writes the number of the cheque card on the back of the cheque and compares the signature with that on the cheque card. The bank guarantees to honour that cheque and pay the payee. This guarantee is for sums up to £50. With

A cheque card.

a cheque card the customer can use his cheque book to buy goods and services or can use it to cash cheques at any bank in the British Isles and at banks abroad showing the Eurocard symbol. In the case of Barclays Bank the Barclay card which is a credit card (see Chapter 11) is also accepted as a cheque card.

The cheque card, therefore, is a card of authority for drawing cheques and of guaranteeing payment to the payee for any amount up to £50.

Other bank services Banks give advice and help on all financial matters. They will arrange with leading insurance companies for all types of insurance, such as life, property, marine, fire, theft and travel. Customers with funds to spare can be advised on investment prospects and the bank will act as broker for the purchase and sale of shares on the Stock Exchange. They also arrange for payments overseas and discount Bills of Exchange (see Chapter 5, Trading overseas).

At quite short notice a bank will obtain and supply foreign currency and travellers cheques. Special foreign departments also help with the wide range of problems arising from foreign trade and travel. Banks have extended their export facilities, particularly in providing information on overseas markets and securities.

Banks also have departments for executor and trustee work, which deal with the money that people leave when they die or that they place on trust for other people during their lifetime.

Customers can arrange for the storage of valuables and important documents in the bank's vaults for either a short or a long term. In some branches there are safe deposits where the customer holds the key to a private safe in the bank's strongroom.

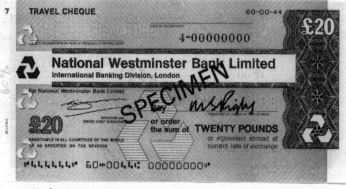

A traveller's cheque.

To summarise, a business can, by using current account services, arrange for the receipt and transfer of money, safely and accurately; it can have wage and salary payments transferred into its employees' bank accounts; it can use the night safe to deposit sums of money after bank hours; if its prospects are promising, a bank overdraft will be allowed for temporary finance such as an increase in stock, and a loan can be arranged for the purchase of new machinery or the modernisation of plant. The bank will also give the business advice on expansion; sort out taxation, investment and insurance problems; help with overseas affairs: exporting, documentation, payment, passports, visas, travel insurance and currency; and when new transactions with other business firms arise, the bank will give a reference as to the company's standing and ability to pay debts.

A private customer can make use of many of the same services for the payment and receipt of money and, if his income is regular and particularly if his pay is paid direct into his bank account, he may be able to arrange for an overdraft to cover a sudden influx of heavy bills, or a loan for a home extension, double glazing, or a new car. The bank will obtain his holiday money and store the family silver while he is away. If he is left some money in a will they will advise him how best to invest it and help him with any income tax or insurance problems. Some banks even have 'budget account' facilities to help customers spread their expenditure over the year instead of having some heavy and some light months (see Chapter 17, Budgeting and money management), and he can apply for a credit card to buy larger items than a cheque card will allow and to defer payment on expenditure (see Chapter 11, Means of payment). And when he wants to rent a flat or buy something on hire-purchase, a bank manager will supply the bank reference that may be needed. Since 1981 banks have also offered mortgage facilities.

Opening a current account

First of all, the prospective customer must decide which bank to approach. He may choose the one nearest to his home, or place of work, or one that his family uses. He should then go to the enquiry counter where he will be attended to. Unless he is recommended by his employer, the bank will require the name and address of a referee—someone who will testify as to the prospective customer's reliability. A specimen signature will also be required so as to identify future instructions. Once he has decided which form his signature should take (using initials and/or Christian name) he must keep to this style and notify the bank of any change. He will be required to open his account with a sum of money, and will be issued immediately with a paying-in book or Giro credit slips, but he will not be given a cheque book until the reference is taken up. Cheques are now 'personalised' with the printing of the customer's name above the signature space, so, once approved, he may be given a temporary cheque book until the printed ones are ready.

It is possible to have a *joint bank account* (eg a husband and wife) with either or both having withdrawal facilities. Anyone of a 'responsible' age can open a current account and banks now offer attractive terms to students to encourage their custom. Although a bank manager will act as referee, he will only do so with the permission of the customer and details of a customer's account are regarded as strictly confidential.

The clearing system

The diagram illustrates the clearing system for cheques. In the past decade rapid strides have been made by the clearing banks in the use of computers which carry out the work of the clerks in the various branches, head offices and clearing departments. This use of mechanisation, automation and computer techniques has made it possible for almost all cheques to be cleared through London, the only other clearing house being in Liverpool. All branches are linked to a computer centre, so that it can do the book-keeping for outlying branches, the necessary information being transmitted as electrical impulses by land line. It is necessary, however, in order to understand what is involved and what has been taken over by the computer centres, to follow the story of a cheque.

You will see from the diagram that the drawer gave a Barclays Bank cheque to her grocer. The grocer paid it into his account at a branch of the National Westminster Bank and his account was credited. His branch sent it, with all the other cheques paid in that day, to the Head Office of the National Westminster Bank. The Head Office listed and microfilmed all the cheques it received. These cheques represented the sums of money owed to the customers of Nat West by customers of other banks. The National Westminster Bank then distributed these cheques to the Head Offices of the banks on which they were drawn and the Head Offices sent them on to the branches named on them. The drawer's cheque would thus be sent to her own branch of Barclays Bank and her account debited.

At Head Office, the cheques were listed and checked. The lists were taken to the London Bankers' Clearing House, so that

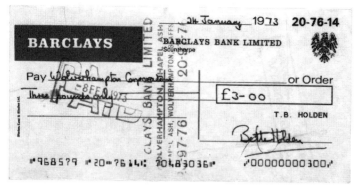

A cleared cheque. It was paid into the bank account of the payee—, Wolverhampton Corporation—Barclays Bank, Wolverhampton. The amount of the cheque (£3) has been added in magnetic ink characters for automatic reading. It was received at the drawers bank—Barclays Bank, Scunthorpe—on 8 February where the drawer's signature was verified and the account debited.

the amounts owing to each other by the various banks could be settled. All the clearing banks have accounts at the Bank of England and money is transferred from their accounts as necessary. Thus if, after a day's transactions, customers of Nat West drew cheques amounting to £26 million in favour of customers of Barclays Bank, and Barclays Bank customers owed a total of £23 million to Nat West customers, then £3 million would be paid to Barclays Bank by the National Westminster Bank and the banks' accounts with the Bank of England adjusted accordingly. In this way, relatively small amounts are transferred between accounts rather than the total value cleared daily—which averages about £4000 million.

The members of the London Bankers' Clearing House are the six London Clearing Banks, the Trustee Savings Banks, the Cooperative Bank and the Bank of England. As outlined above the clearing house provides a simple but effective way of dealing with the clearing of cheques and arranging for the debiting and crediting of accounts held by the clearing banks with the Bank of England. It also processes and clears other payment documents such as credit transfers, direct debits, bills and drafts. The Scottish and Northern Ireland banks have their own clearing arrangements for cheques drawn on banks in their own countries, but for cheques drawn on banks in England and Wales they make arrangements for a London clearing bank to act as agent, as do other banks who are not members of the London Bankers' Clearing House.

In England and Wales the time taken to clear a cheque is

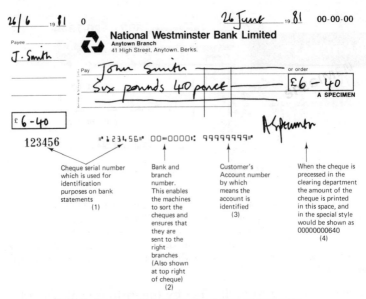

Cheque serial number which is used for identification purposes on bank statements
(1)

Bank and branch number. This enables the machines to sort the cheques and ensures that they are sent to the right branches (Also shown at top right of cheque)
(2)

Customer's Account number by which means the account is identified
(3)

When the cheque is precessed in the clearing department the amount of the cheque is printed in this space, and in the special style would be shown as 00000000640
(4)

The Clearing Departments of the banks have automatic sorters and cheque reading machines using magnetic ink characters on the bottom of the cheque.
The code line has 4 sets of figures known as E13B characters.
(1) is the serial number of the cheque which is also shown on the counterfoil
(2) is the number of the bank and branch
(3) is the account number of the customer
(4) is the amount of the cheque which is printed by the bank in a special style of figure and in an ink which can be magnetised.

Cheque coding.

generally three days.

If the drawer has paid out a cheque when he did not have enough money in the bank, when the cheque is returned to the branch on which it was drawn (as shown in the diagram), the branch would send it back to the payee's bank marked *refer to drawer* (R/D). This means that the payee should contact the drawer again for payment of the amount owed. When people talk about a cheque which 'bounces' they mean it is returned like this. Therefore, great care should be taken when accepting cheques from unknown or unreliable people and many businesses insist on cheques being backed by a cheque card.

Cheques can, however, be returned for other reasons:

- if the writer of the cheque omits a detail (eg signature or date missing)
- the amount in words and figures do not tally
- the drawer's signature differs from that in the bank's records
- an alteration requires signing

124

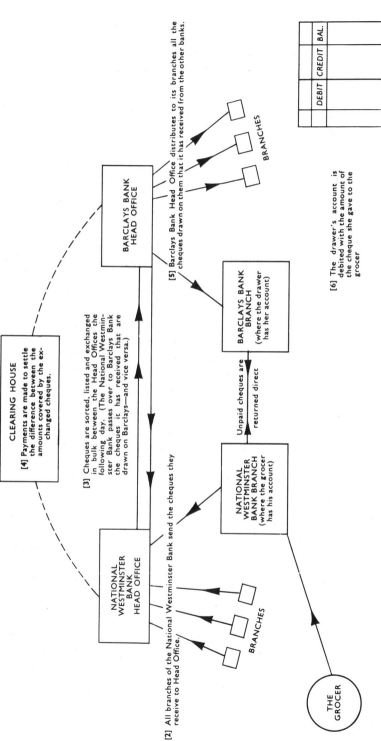

CLEARING HOUSE

[4] Payments are made to settle the difference between the amounts covered by the exchanged cheques.

BARCLAYS BANK HEAD OFFICE

BRANCHES

[5] Barclays Bank Head Office distributes to its branches all the cheques drawn on them that it has received from the other banks.

[3] Cheques are sorted, listed and exchanged in bulk between the Head Offices the following day. (The National Westminster Bank passes over to Barclays Bank the cheques it has received that are drawn on Barclays—and vice versa.)

BARCLAYS BANK BRANCH (where the drawer has her account)

[6] The drawer's account is debited with the amount of the cheque she gave to the grocer

NATIONAL WESTMINSTER BANK HEAD OFFICE

Unpaid cheques are returned direct

NATIONAL WESTMINSTER BANK BRANCH (where the grocer has his account)

[2] All branches of the National Westminster Bank send the cheques they receive to Head Office.

		DEBIT	CREDIT	BAL.

[7] Note: had there been insufficient money in the drawer's account to 'meet' the cheque, her branch would have returned it, by post, direct to the branch of the National Westminster Bank where it had been paid in.

BRANCHES

THE GROCER

[1] The grocer pays into his bank all the cheques he has received from his customers (including the cheque from the drawer, drawn on a branch of Barclays Bank.)

- the cheque is post-dated (therefore it cannot be paid until the due date)
- the cheque is 'stale' (ie more than six months' old)
- payment has been stopped by the drawer since writing the cheque
- notice has been received of the customer's death, bankruptcy, or insanity (the account is then 'frozen')
- forgery is suspected

Questions

(Some of these may best be answered after the study of Chapter 11, Means of payment)

1. An acquaintance has asked your advice on the desirability of opening a current banking account. Outline the procedure involved in opening an account and state what, in your opinion, are the main advantages of being a bank's customer. (SR)

2. The following are services provided by joint stock banks to current account holders. Describe any *four* of them in detail.
   (a) Loan   (b) Cheque card   (c) Night Safe
   (d) Overdraft   (e) Travellers' Cheques   (f) Status inquiries
   (MRED)

3. (a) Describe *two* advantages to a sole trader of having a current account in a commercial bank.
   (b) Explain *two* of the following:
      (i) a direct debit   (ii) a standing order   (iii) a paying-in book
   (c) Give a short account of how the night safe facility operates.
   (d) Why are night safes important for traders?

4. (a) What is the Bankers' Clearing House and which banks belong to it?
   (b) What is the advantage to the banks of using the Clearing House system?
   (c) What part does the Bank of England play in the clearing process?
   (d) State *one* advantage of making payments by cheque.
   (EA)

5. A retailer wishes to obtain a loan (or an overdraft) from his bank. What information should he give to his bank manager?
   (RSA)

6. What are the main functions of a clearing bank?

(RSA)

7. Give *five* reasons why a cheque may not be acceptable in payment of a debt.

(RSA)

8. (a) Name *three* important services which a banker is prepared to offer to a customer.
   (b) Explain *two* differences between a current account and a deposit account with a commercial banker.
   (c) Name the *three* parties concerned with a cheque.
   (d) What is a post-dated cheque?
   (e) What is a banker's draft?

(NI)

9. (a) What are the similarities and differences between the following:
   (i) Mortgage (ii) Bank Loan (iii) Bank Overdraft
   (iv) Bridging Loan (v) Personal Loan, other than from a Bank
   (b) From whom are they obtainable and how are they usually repayable?

(SW)

10. Name *five* different services which Joint Stock Banks offer to their customers which you would find useful now, or during the next six years. You should show clearly how each of the five services could be of benefit to you.

(SW)

11. Make out a Bank paying-in slip and pay into your account the following:

2 x £10 notes   mixed bronze £5.25   cheque for £27.10
5 x £5 notes   33 x £1 notes   7 x 50p coins
mixed silver £6.00

Clearly indicate the total amount you are paying in.

(RSA)

Special note

In 1981 the Bank of England Minimum Lending Rate was discarded. Individual banks can now decide on their own bank base rate.

The Bank of England has its own discount rate.

9

Finance for industry

Both large and small businesses are faced from time to time with the need to find finance from outside sources. Commercial banks provide short-term credit, but for many years, for a variety of reasons, there was difficulty in obtaining medium and long-term capital, especially for small businesses.

Over the last fifty years there has been a growth of financial institutions set up especially to fill this gap. More recently there has been strong and open competition for the opportunity to lend money and give financial advice to all sizes and types of companies. It should be borne in mind, however, that the criterion for financial aid is that the venture is profitable.

Government support, apart from the capitalised programmes of the nationalised industries already discussed (see Chapter 3) includes grants to companies setting up factories, help in development areas, finance for special projects in the aircraft and other industries, as well as general support for export, research and training.

Government institutions

The *Department of Industry* is responsible for industrial policy as a whole, and 1975 marked the devolution of certain responsibilities towards industry in Scotland and Wales. Northern Ireland has a Department of Commerce.

Under various Finance Acts the Department provides assistance for key industries. Financial and other aid is also available to areas of high unemployment, known as assisted areas. There are three types: special development areas; development areas; and intermediate areas, (see map). The Department of Industry provides regional development grants in all these areas for building factories, and in special development and development areas for plant and machinery. The grants may be used on projects creating employment or for improving or modernising existing factories. In addition, various forms of financial aid, including

128

THE ASSISTED AREAS

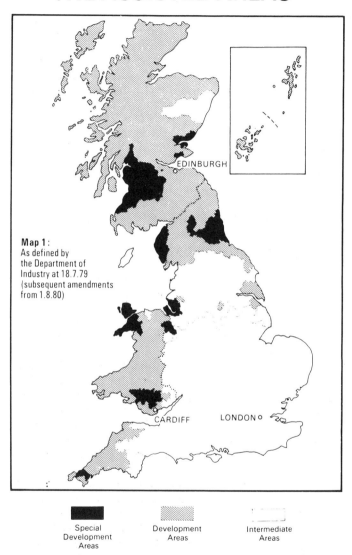

Map 1:
As defined by
the Department of
Industry at 18.7.79
(subsequent amendments
from 1.8.80)

EDINBURGH

CARDIFF   LONDON o

Special
Development
Areas

Development
Areas

Intermediate
Areas

low-interest loans, may be provided for projects creating employment. Other aid includes the provision of modern factories, free government training services, and grants to help key workers transfer to assisted areas.

Regional offices in the main assisted areas can make loans up to £2 million.

The Industrial Development Advisory Board, a statutory body made up of members of industry and the financial community, advise the Department of Industry on industrial opportunities and the provision of financial assistance. Regional Boards have been set up in 5 development areas. Similar duties are carried out by the Scottish and Welsh Development Agencies.

The National Enterprise Board (NEB) is a statutory body set up by the Government as a result of the Industry Act 1975. Its purposes are the

- development of or assistance to the national economy,
- promotion of industrial efficiency and international competitiveness, and the
- provision, maintenance and safeguarding of employment.

Among other things the NEB provides

- finance for industrial investment and restructuring, and
- assistance to companies in short-term difficulties.

The Development Agencies in Scotland, Wales and Northern Ireland carry out broadly similar functions.

There is close association between industry and the Government through such channels as the National Economic Development Council (NEDC), which is the main forum for consultation between the Government, management and the trade unions and the Economic Development Committees (EDCs) which cover particular industrial sectors. The EDCs bring together the representatives of all concerned to study, and make recommendations on, the efficiency and prospects of individual industries.

There is a growing number of local and central government services to help firms. Small Firms Information Centres may direct local enquirers to the Department of Industry's new Small Firms Counselling Service. This is staffed by businessmen who may provide channels for capital as well as give expert advice on how to run the business and make the most of the money.

There are also well-established regional and local organisations, one of the best known being the Council for Small Industries in Rural Areas (CoSIRA). CoSIRA's services include expert business consultants, secretarial and accounting services and purpose-built factories and workshops. CoSIRA is roughly paralleled in Scotland by the Highlands and Islands Development Corporation and in Wales by the Development Board for Rural Wales. Basically they were created to stop population losses in rural areas. They may not give money but can make life much cheaper.

Nowadays, however, they are finding that there is competition from inner city boroughs, who are looking at ways to get businesses back into communities with serious unemployment problems.

The National Research Development Corporation (NRDC), although an independent public corporation, is supported by Government loans through the Department of Industry. It is intended to speed up technological advance by investing money in British firms, on a joint venture basis, for the development of their own inventions and projects. Thus it provides a source of capital for private inventors as well as for Government laboratories and universities. The over-riding proviso is that there must be a technological innovation with a financially sound future, for the NRDC to provide help for the patenting of the invention, and money to finance its development, manufacture (under NRDC licence) and sale. Unlike finance house loans, the NRDC's levy scheme means that it charges a percentage levy on sales to get back its initial lendings. When success is assured, and a profit has been made on the investment, the NRDC withdraws leaving the whole company with the original owners.

Projects so far sponsored include antibiotics, insecticides, computers, packaging equipment, micro-electronics, diving and oceanological equipment, plastics and the hovercraft. The success of the hovercraft as a purely British development is a good example of the NRDC's aid. John Cockrell's prototype was described as looking like 'a hair dryer with a tin can on the end' when he first took it to the Corporation.

Financial institutions

To review the activities of the financial institutions it is convenient to divide them into two groups:

- those which form the short term money market, namely the joint stock banks, the discount houses and the merchant banks;

131

- the long-medium term or Capital market, consisting of the issuing houses (including merchant banks performing this function), the finance houses, the finance corporations, the insurance market and the stock exchanges.

All are linked to the Bank of England. The insurance market is discussed in Chapter 14.

The joint stock banks

These are considered in detail in Chapter 8, generally provide short-term loans, and may well be the first place a firm may contact should it require financial assistance and advice.

Discount houses

The London Discount or Money Market plays an important role in public and private finance operations. It is an institution which is unique to the City of London; its historical development has contributed considerably to the growth of London as an international financial centre.

The eleven discount houses borrow from the banks and other financial institutions at short notice or 'at call', and at comparatively low interest rates. As a result, banks are able to reduce to a minimum the amount of money they must keep available to meet customers' demands for cash and at the same time earn interest on surplus funds. If the banks require money they obtain cash from the discount houses by calling in part of their loans.

The Bank of England acts as lender of last resort to the discount houses. This facility is essential so that the banks can rely on being able to recall the money they have placed with the discount market.

A large part of the money borrowed by the discount houses is invested in British Government stocks and Treasury bills, local authority bonds and commercial bills of exchange.

It is understood that the discount houses should meet the needs of the Government by buying up the Treasury bills offered on tender weekly.

Dealing in commercial bills requires a detailed and up-to-date knowledge of the credit-worthiness of thousands of customers in many trades. The importance of the work of the discount houses in commercial bills can be seen in the fact that, while trade is largely financed today in other ways, their holdings in commercial and other bills increased from £70 million in 1958 to over £1100 million in 1974.

Merchant banks

These are specialised banks which help industry and commerce in particular ways. They are found almost exclusively in the City of London. Some are descendants of the famous merchants of earlier centuries, who were among the early traders to set up overseas trading connections. Eventually they gave up trading, and because of their good financial reputation, and their undertaking to pay bills on behalf of other people (ie, accepting bills of exchange), documents signed by them were handed from person to person in payment of debts.

Today the merchant bankers are also engaged in other aspects of trade:

* that of raising capital for new companies, for the expansion of existing companies, or for private companies wishing to become public concerns, as well as the raising of loans for overseas borrowers.
* They are concerned in arranging terms for mergers and take-over bids between companies.
* They act as agents for British companies by registering shareholders and paying dividends.
* They arrange the investment of funds;
* the safe custody of securities; and
* the administration of pension funds.
* Their expert advice and assistance is sought on the problems of exporting and importing, the insurances involved and on foreign exchange problems; and on the effect of taxation on investment decisions.

The merchant banks must not be forgotten as possible sources of money. By and large they are interested in medium to large companies and prefer to lend for longer periods of time, with specially tailored financial packages. They fall half-way between the joint stock banks and the finance houses but the edges are sometimes blurred.

Accepting houses

These also deal with bills of exchange. They do not actually lend money, but lend their names so that the bills which they accept may be readily discounted (money advanced on them). Because of their high reputation, their acceptance of a bill indicates that it is a first-class security. Accepting houses have also entered other areas of finance, and they are particularly esteemed as advisers on the administration of various funds, such as pension schemes, and as organisers of large-scale, long-term finance for major projects.

The new issue market—issuing houses

When a company wishes to introduce a new issue of shares on to the market, it will use the services of an issuing house. Its experienced staff will be able to advise on the best time to issue, draft the announcements and handle all clerical work. There is strong competition to launch new issues, and an Issuing Houses Association has been formed by merchant bankers and specialised issuing houses.

Under the Companies Act, any issuing house whose issue does not reach a certain level must return the funds collected to the applicants. The minimum set is the amount required to ensure a successful start to the proposed project. To avoid returning funds, the issuing house will itself underwrite or arrange for the underwriting of the issue, so that all the shares will be taken up even if the amount bought by the public falls short of the total issue. Issuing houses will investigate thoroughly the affairs of a company before they will accept the handling of a new issue.

The issuing houses were represented on a working party which prepared 'The City Code' to regulate take-overs, and are on a panel which oversees the application of the code. Their advice is increasingly sought on the structure of mergers, and on how to resist a take-over bid, or to get better terms for shareholders.

Finance houses

Many special financial facilities, which are supplementary to the credit facilities of the banks, are provided through institutions outside the banking system. These include hire-purchase finance companies which are in fact money-lending businesses. They specialise in lending money, in the financing of hire-purchase and for other instalment credit transactions. They lend money to individuals for the hire-purchase of cars, household and other goods. In recent years there has also been a tendency for industry to turn to finance houses for money for its investment in machinery and plant, and for raw material stocks.

There are almost 2000 firms engaged in financing credit transactions and about forty of these constitute the Finance Houses Association which accounts for about 90 per cent of all finance house business. The finance houses are subject to controls affecting minimum deposits and maximum repayment periods.

Some of the finance houses are competing with the commercial banks by opening **Moneyshops** in the high street where cheques can be cashed, and loans arranged. To counteract this, the clearing banks have acquired substantial interests in finance houses.

In addition, new schemes have been devised to suit the needs of industry, and the leasing of plant and equipment has been one of the most important. This allows companies to make use of productive machinery without owning it. The latest machinery is thus available and capital has not been tied up.

Stock exchanges

People who invest money in public companies (see Chapter 2) may wish to secure a steady income from safe investments, or may wish to have a share in large profits made by successful industrial and commercial companies. In either case, they would be unlikely to invest if they could not be sure of getting back their money if they needed or wished to. When shares are bought, they cannot be resold to the company itself, but they can be sold to other investors.

A Stock Exchange is the means of bringing together those who have shares to sell and those who want to buy them. It is a market.

The stock exchanges of the United Kingdom and Eire amalgamated in 1973, so that firms, wherever situated, could trade on equal terms. The main exchange and central administration are in London. The London Stock Exchange, which has been rebuilt and housed in modern premises, is in Throgmorton Street and can be visited by the public on weekdays. They can watch the proceedings from the visitors' gallery, though they themselves cannot buy or sell. As in all markets, prices are fixed by supply and demand.

There are two kinds of members of the Stock Exchange, jobbers and brokers. **Brokers** are the agents with whom the public deals. People who wish to buy or sell shares must consult their stockbroker, who will charge a percentage commission.

A **jobber** does not deal with the public, only with brokers. He will have lists of prices of securities in which he deals, and acts like a merchant in that he buys shares from one broker selling on behalf of a client, and selling to another broker buying for other clients. Senior clerks, known as authorised clerks, actually carry on the business; and unauthorised clerks, distinguished by blue badges, get quotations or prices. The broker or his clerk will ask a jobber the price of the shares in which his client is interested, and the jobber will give him two prices. One is the price at which he is prepared to buy, and the second at which he is prepared to sell. The difference between these two prices is known as the 'jobber's turn', and it is from these sums, multiplied many thousands of times each day, that the jobber makes his living. The broker will go from jobber to jobber to find the most satisfactory price. The deal is jotted down in a notebook, but nothing else is done on the spot. The whole transaction or 'bargain' is a spoken one.

The clerical work is done largely in Brokers' offices. The Settlement Office of the Stock Exchange is like a bankers' clearing house, matching buyers to sellers. Documentation, ie the transfer forms and share certificates and the payment for bargains, is centralised through the Central Stock Payments Office of the Stock Exchange. Much of this is computerised.

Value and prices of shares

The capital of a public company is divided into a number of shares which are available to investors when the company is formed. The value of a share when first issued is known as the **nominal value**. Thus, a £1 share has a nominal value of £1. When shares are bought at their nominal value they are said to be bought **at par**. However, the price at which shares are bought and sold fluctuates, and the price quoted on the Stock Exchange may be higher than nominal value (**above par**) or it may be lower (**below par**).

If a company is successful and making good profits, it will be expected to declare a high dividend, and its shares will be in great demand. The price at which the shares can be bought will rise, and a jobber will quote a price well above the nominal value. Conversely, a company not doing well will find that its shares are not in demand, and the price quoted may be below par.

Because of the rise and fall in the price of shares, it is possible to make a profit out of buying or selling at the right moment. **Speculators** are people who attempt to do this on a large scale. They may be divided into two groups, known as 'bulls' and 'bears'.

Bulls will buy extensively when shares are low in price, hoping to make a profit by re-selling when prices rise quickly. If it rises quickly enough they will be able to re-sell before the time has come to pay for them.

Bears, on the other hand, sell shares when prices are high, expecting the price to fall. If they are right, they can buy more shares than they had originally for the money they obtained. A bear may even sell shares he does not actually possess, expecting that by the time he has to transfer the shares to the person who has bought them from him, he will be able to buy them at the reduced price.

This kind of speculation is not the purpose of the stock exchange, which exists to allow people who wish to invest freely to buy and sell shares. In addition to industrial shares, there are stocks and shares in such things as property, hire-purchase, Commonwealth Government Stock and Public Boards.

'Gilts' or gilt-edged securities are Government Stock, securities issued by the British Government, the state-owned companies and the Commonwealth governments. Although they are 'safe' as an investment, they pay low rates of interest compared with high rates of dividend paid on some industrial shares.

Industrial shares vary very much in the security they offer. Those of well-known and reliable companies are known as '**blue chip**' investments. It should be remembered, however, that where the dividend is high the price of the shares will have risen. If, therefore, the dividend were 35 per cent you may well have had to pay £2 for a £1 share. This means that you will receive 35 per cent of £1 (ie 35p) for your investment of £2, so that your return is $17\frac{1}{2}$ per cent of your investment. This actual return is known as the **yield**.

Of course, a company can only pay dividends on its shares when it makes a profit. You may wonder why anyone should want to invest money in ordinary (equity) shares which do not regularly each year bring in the same dividend and which run the risk of paying no dividend at all. People are prepared to take the risk and buy these shares either for an unexpectedly high dividend or for a rise in price which will allow them to sell their shares at a profit (capital appreciation).

Investors who want a regular fixed income will buy preference shares or Government Stock ('Gilts').

Investment trust companies and unit trusts

These are two different types of organisation forming part of the complex machinery of the capital market. Their function is to raise capital from the public and help to direct it into profitable investment channels. They enable the individual investor with a limited amount of capital to spread his risks, both industrially and geographically, under skilled management and over a wide range of securities. They are, therefore, of particular benefit to the small investor with little experience of the stock market as these institutions specialise in balanced portfolios of shares to give a reasonable yield with maximum safety. Excessive profits probably would not be made, but neither would there be high losses.

The investor in an investment trust can only recover his capital by selling his stock through the normal stock exchange channels. The word 'trust' is really inappropriate in the case of Investment Trusts and these should be considered as investment companies. They are limited liability companies and issue debenture, preference and ordinary shares.

The investor in a unit trust, on the other hand, is entitled to recover his capital at any time by applying to the management for repayment, which will be based on the selling price of the units at that time. Unit trusts give the small investor the interest of holding 'shares' in some of the great industrial companies, and the feeling of speculation without the risk attached to buying on the stock market with no specialised knowledge.

Institutional investors

All kinds of investors bring in necessary capital to industrial and commercial firms. In addition to finance corporations and companies, pension funds and the unit trust movement, big institutions such as the Post Office, building societies and insurance companies, into which small savers put their money for safety, are themselves some of the largest investors on the stock exchange. So, too, is the Government. Investments allow the Government and other institutions in their turn to pay interest to their investors.

In this way the money of small savers, whose individual savings are too small to warrant buying stocks and shares on the stock exchange, finds its way to industry and commerce.

Finance corporations

As already shown, business enterprises needing to re-equip, develop or expand usually obtain the necessary finance from the banks as loans or in the form of new capital issues through the stock exchange. The banks provide temporary or floating capital, while the new issue market provides 'permanent' long-term capital. When medium or long-term capital is not readily available from these sources, specialised financial institutions have been established to cover the need.

Finance for Industry Ltd (FFI)

This is the best known of these finance corporations. It was formed in December 1973 by the merging of the Finance Corporation for Industry Ltd (FCI) and the Industrial and Commercial Finance Corporation Ltd (ICFC). Both companies, however, maintain their separate operations. They were formed originally in 1945 by the clearing banks and the Bank of England, and the Finance Corporation for Industry can provide substantial amounts of medium and long-term money, on normal commercial terms, including both share and loan capital.

ICFC provides both capital and related facilities, including advice, management consultancy and computer services, to small and medium companies, especially those concerned in technical development, which can put up a sound case that the funds will be put to profitable uses.

The Finance for Industry Ltd, together with insurance companies and investment trust companies, holds shares in a specialist long-term institution, Equity Capital for Industry (ECI), better known as the Equity Bank, whose purpose is to provide equity or equity-type capital for deserving companies when all other sources have failed.

The Commonwealth Development Finance Company (CDFC)

As its name implies this was originally set up to help finance private development in Commonwealth countries. It is no longer confined in its activities to the Commonwealth, but supports business enterprises covering a wide range of industries in forty countries.

The Agricultural Mortgage Corporation Ltd

This was established to make loans to farmers. These are in the form of first mortgages on lands and buildings, and are repayable usually on forty year terms. A similar function in Scotland is provided by the Scottish Agricultural Securities Corporation Ltd.

When searching for money there is always the possibility of finding a capitalist with some money to invest; and enquiries could be made of local solicitors, accountants and insurance brokers, as people with money to invest often approach these professions. An **entrepreneur** is an individual who is willing to back an enterprise. He knows the risks from his own experience and knows what is necessary for success. The entrepreneurial backer will want a good return on the money he puts into the business; he is going to want to share in the profits and the growing assets of the business as his return for taking a chance.

The Euro-currency market

The development of this so-called market has provided a new source of finance for private or national capital projects. The market, which dates from 1958, is unique in that transactions take place outside the country whose currency is used. Euro-Dollars are dollar denominated deposits or loans outside the United States. An American banking control (Regulation Q) limited the interest rate which banks could pay in the US, at the same time as the American balance of payments deficits left millions of dollars in overseas hands. These could be lent and re-lent more profitably outside the US, and the Euro-currency market was established.

Today any convertible currency is used, so that there are Euro-Sterling, Euro-Francs, Euro-Marks and even Euro-Yen. The market involves every money centre in Europe, but is concentrated in London, and it attracts funds because it offers higher rates of interest than the country of origin of the currency, freedom from exchange control, and a wider range of investment possibilities than other short-term capital markets. Costs are low because banks and firms using the Euro-currency are already well-established. By its use, large enterprises gain access to a range of banks in several countries.

Most of the funds are lent for commercial or industrial transactions. Demand often comes from multi-national companies including those catering for undertakings with a high risk content, such as oil or aircraft finance. The British Gas Corporation raised $250 million in Euro-Dollars as a seven-year floating rate loan to develop pipe-lines and terminals in the North Sea.

GOVERNMENT:

Department of Industry	Government department for industrial policy as a whole
NEDC (National Economic Development Council)	Main forum for consultation between Government, management and trade unions—Chaired by the Prime Minister
NEB (National Enterprise Board)	Public corporation set up to give selective assistance to industry particularly for re-development
NRDC (National Research Development Corporation)	Assistance for development of technology, especially new inventions, processes and products
Small Firms Counselling Service	Department of Industry service to which enquiries may be directed by local Small Firms Information Centres
CoSIRA (Council for Small Industries in Rural Areas)	Encourages development of industry in rural areas

---

FINANCIAL INSTITUTIONS:

Joint stock banks	Commercial banks offering payment services, financial assistance and advice (short term loans)
Merchant banks	Specialists in finance, aid and advice to industry and commerce
Accepting houses	Bills of exchange accepted so that they may be 'discounted'
Discount houses	Commercial bills of exchange discounted

Issuing houses	New issues of shares introduced and arranged on to the market
Stock exchanges	Market for the buying and selling of shares—members act on behalf of the public
Finance houses	Money-lending, hire-purchase companies

FINANCE CORPORATIONS:

FFI (Finance for Industry Ltd)	Capital for industry—medium and long-term
ECI (Equity Capital for Industry)	Last resource for equity-type capital for companies
CDFC (Commonwealth Development Finance Co)	Financial support for business enterprises—no longer confined to the Commonwealth
The Agricultural Mortgage Corporation Ltd	Long-term loans to farmers

THE EURO-CURRENCY MARKET	Source of loan and investment in foreign currencies

Glossary of terms

Authorised capital The capital which a company is allowed to issue (the total value of shares). Sometimes called **nominal** or **registered** capital.

Bear A speculator who, believing that share prices will fall, sells with the idea of buying them back more cheaply.

Blue chips Industrial shares of great reliability.

Broker A member of the Stock Exchange who negotiates with Jobbers to buy and sell shares on behalf of his clients.

Bull A speculator who buys shares at a low price with a view to selling them when the price rises.

Capital The financial resources of a company.

Commission Earned by brokers for acting as agents in the buying and selling of shares. The Stock Exchange Council fixes the scale.

142

Contract note Settlement of deals in gilt-edged securities is in cash and the client is expected to pay on receipt of the contract note, normally the day following the date of the bargain.

Daily list A list issued officially by the Stock Exchange showing quotations for stocks and other securities.

Debenture A loan to a company as opposed to buying shares in the company. Holders are entitled to interest before profits are distributed, and have a prior claim before ordinary creditors (people to whom money is owing) should the business fail. A very safe type of investment.

Deferred shares (or Founders' Shares) These are shares very often issued to the founder of a firm who sells out to a company. He agrees to defer any dividend due to him until the other shareholders have had a reasonable dividend. The deferred shareholder may then be entitled to all or a substantial part of the remaining profit which the directors wish to distribute, the exact terms having been agreed when the company was formed. To agree to be paid partly in deferred shares shows that the vendor has confidence in the business he is selling. The ordinary shareholders must be paid before the deferred shareholders.

Dividend That portion of the company's profits which is approved for distribution to the shareholders. It is generally expressed as a percentage of the nominal value of the shares. The amount of the dividend is recommended by the Board of Directors and approved at the Annual General Meeting of the company by the shareholders. All shareholders are entitled to attend Annual and Special or Extraordinary General Meetings.

Equities Ordinary shares; holders take the risk of high or low dividends, or none at all in a bad year. Not recommended for timid investors.

Gilt-edged Government or local authority stocks. Sound investment, with little risk attached, but comparatively low interest.

Interest Money paid regularly, at a fixed rate, to those who have lent money.

Investment trust Institutional investors who specialise in balanced portfolios of shares for investors who do not have sufficient experience of the Stock Market themselves. Secure, with reasonable yields.

Issuing house A banking house specialising in the new issue of shares.

Jobbers They buy from, and sell shares to, brokers who are acting on behalf of the public. There are jobbers who specialise in particular types of share.

Minimum Lending Rate (MLR) or Bank Rate   Replaced in 1981 by the Bank of England's discount rate—the rate at which it lends to the London Discount Market. Commercial banks fix their own base rate for interest charges.

Nominal capital   See Authorised Capital.

Nominal price   The face value (or par value) of a share given to it when it was issued. The nominal value remains static throughout its life although its actual value varies with the supply and demand.

Ordinary shares   Or equity shares. Ordinary shareholders have no guaranteed claim on the profits of a company. If business is good—substantial dividends; if business is poor—little or no dividends.

Par value   The nominal value of a share. If a share is said to be 'at par' then its market price is the same as the nominal value.

Portfolio   A collection of securities, by one investor, or by an institution.

Preference shares   Holders enjoy preferences over ordinary shareholders. Shares carry a fixed rate of dividend provided there is sufficient profit, and this is paid before ordinary dividends but after interest has been paid to debenture holders. Holders of **Cumulative preference shares** never lose the right to a dividend. If there are insufficient funds from which to pay their fixed dividends, the arrears will be made good from profits in later years. **Participating preference shareholders** are not only paid a fixed rate of income before dividends on other types of shares are paid, but also share in excess profits after the ordinary shareholders have been paid the agreed dividend.

Settlement (or account) day   Accounts, which usually last a fortnight (occasionally three weeks) are usually completed on the second Tuesday following the end of the account. This is Settlement Day, when securities purchased during the account are delivered to the client, and paid for.

Share capital   Money which the public will subscribe to a business which is run as a limited liability company.

Share certificate   The legal document issued to a shareholder certifying ownership of a part of the company concerned. This is known as security.

Subscribed, or issued capital   That part of the capital which a company sells to shareholders.

Take-over bid   An offer to the shareholders of a company, by an individual or a firm, to buy their shares at a price above the present market price with a view to securing control of the company.

Take-over code A code of conduct drawn up by the City Working Party on Take-Overs and Mergers, initiated by the Bank of England with representatives of various bodies in the City interested in the securities industry. This representative body supervises the code, sees that the principles are understood and its rules observed.

Treasury bills Short term securities issued by the Government, normally repayable after ninety days. The discount houses accept as a formal responsibility that they should cover the Government's need to borrow on Treasury bills which are offered on tender each week. In this way, the Government can raise funds it needs which are not immediately forthcoming from other sources.

Turn The jobber's 'turn' is the profit margin he hopes to earn and is the difference between his buying and selling price.

Underwriters Men who ensure the issue of new shares by agreeing to buy what the public does not buy. Directors often underwrite new issue in order to make sure that a new project goes ahead.

Unit trusts Offer a balanced portfolio to members of the public who are not willing to run the risks of buying and selling on the stock exchange. By buying units of small values, the small investor subscribes his funds into a pool which the unit-trust managers then use to buy a balanced portfolio of shares. The return to the investor comes partly in dividends and possibly in the appreciation of his units should he decide to sell them. By the spreading of his investments the investor is unlikely to incur heavy loss.

Yield The true return to an investor on his investment. The rule for calculating yields is

$$\frac{\text{par value}}{\text{market price}} \times \text{ rate of dividend per cent}$$

Questions

For some questions it will be necessary to have studied Chapters 2 and 3, Private and Public ownership, and Chapter 10, Capital.

1. (a) Why is a stock exchange necessary?
   (b) Explain, with reference to the Stock Exchange, *two* of the following:
       (i) account   (ii) settlement day   (iii) contract note

    (c) What is a unit trust?

    (d) Why is a unit trust considered to be attractive to the small investor?   (EA)

2. You have inherited £1000 and decided to invest in shares on the Stock Exchange

    (a) What would influence your choice of shares?

    (b) Describe the steps by which these shares would become your property.   (EA)

3. Describe briefly the main differences between:

    (a) a public company and a private company

    (b) a broker and a jobber

    (c) shares and debentures

    (d) the memorandum of association and articles of association

    (e) bears and bulls

4. Three years ago, I applied for and was issued with one hundred Ordinary shares of £1 each in a newly formed public limited company. Two years ago the shares were quoted on the Stock Exchange at 115p, a year ago at par, and today at 70p. What do these prices mean and what factors could have caused the changes in them?   (YR)

5. Describe the main methods by which a large firm may obtain capital. Reference may be made to:
Commercial banks; Shares; Debentures; Profits; Finance Houses; Hire Purchase; Industrial and Commercial Corporations.   (AL)

6. John Smith has invented a new improved type of car exhaust system and wishes to produce and sell this new product. What sources of capital are likely to be available to him in order to proceed with the venture?   (RSA)

7. A large public company is in need of further capital for expansion. Describe three different ways in which it might try to raise this money, indicating what considerations might influence the final decision.   (RSA)

10

Capital

The word **capital** is used in a number of senses.

Fixed capital

You have seen in Chapter 2 that when a business is run by a single (or sole) trader, or by a partnership, the money required to run the business is supplied by that man, or those men and women themselves, possibly with help from their family or friends, or loans from the bank. This money they call their **capital**. But their warehouses, shops, vans, barrows and stalls, and the stock which they have for sale is also their capital. So are the debts owing to them, and the money in their banks.

The expression 'capital or fixed assets' is the name given to such items as building, furniture and fixtures, motor-vans and equipment bought for running the business,but not for resale. This is **fixed capital**—it remains unchanged until it needs replacement.

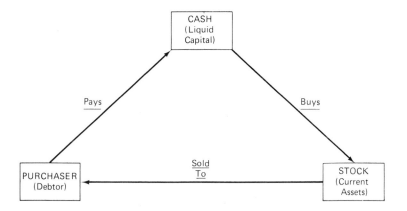

Circulating capital

This is sometimes called the **working capital** of a business and is that part of the capital used to finance day-to-day trading; and since it includes all goods in stock awaiting sale, all sums of money owed by customers buying on credit, cash in the till and money at the bank, it is constantly changing. The working capital in fact is the amount by which current assets exceed current liabilities, and so is readily available for running the business.

Liquid capital

This is the term used for that part of working capital which is readily available, such as cash or money owed by debtors. Every normal trading transaction (whether buying or selling stock or paying expenses) will affect the liquid capital.

The amount of circulating capital required by a business therefore depends very much upon the amount of business being done. If more goods are being sold it is very likely that more 'working' capital will be required. Profit, as it is earned, will increase the fund of working capital unless it is withdrawn by the proprietor for private spending or used in the business for fixed capital. 'Ploughing back the profits' means leaving the profits in the business to increase the capital employed.

Share capital

This expression is used to describe the money which the public will subscribe to a business which is run as a limited liability company, registered under the Companies Acts of 1948 and 1967. You will remember that there are public and private companies, both with shareholders. In the case of public companies, the shareholders are invited by **prospectus**, often advertisements in the press, to invest their money (buy shares in) the company. You will notice that we do not say 'lend' their money to the company, because when you subscribe to, or buy shares in, a company, you cannot get the money back from the Stock Exchange. You are in fact a 'part owner' of the company. This is discussed in Chapters 2 and 9.

When you invest money in a company, you receive a share certificate which represents your share of the company. This is known as a security. As you see from the diagram on page 149, capital which the company is allowed to issue (the total value of shares) is called its **authorised capital**. That which it actually

148

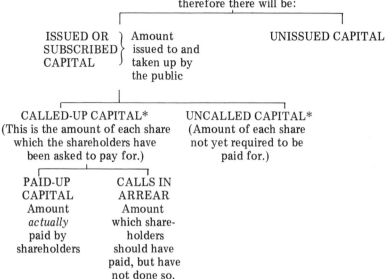

AUTHORISED, NOMINAL OR
REGISTERED CAPITAL
that which the company is permitted to
register. It need not all be issued at once
therefore there will be:

ISSUED OR
SUBSCRIBED } Amount issued to and taken up by the public
CAPITAL

UNISSUED CAPITAL

CALLED-UP CAPITAL*
(This is the amount of each share
which the shareholders have
been asked to pay for.)

UNCALLED CAPITAL*
(Amount of each share
not yet required to be
paid for.)

PAID-UP
CAPITAL
Amount
actually
paid by
shareholders

CALLS IN
ARREAR
Amount
which share-
holders
should have
paid, but have
not done so.

*Nowadays normal practice is to ask for full payment of the share on issue.
Therefore uncalled capital is a rarity.

sells to shareholders is called the **issued or subscribed capital**. A company is not obliged to issue all its capital at once. It may keep some back to issue at a later date. When the capital is issued, a shareholder is usually asked to pay the whole amount on application, but in a few cases he may have to pay a small amount on application. For instance, on a £1 share, an investor could pay 15p on application, 50p on allotment, and 35p on first call. When the investor agrees to buy the shares, he contracts (legally agrees) to pay the full amount, and this is in fact all that he is ever under any obligation to give to the company. This is what is called his '**limited liability**'; he is only liable to the company for the full value of his share, no matter how badly the business fares. As already explained in Chapter 2, this is different from the position of the sole trader or the partners, whose personal assets may be brought in to help provide money owing by the business.

Sources of finance for businesses are discussed in Chapter 9 but **short-term capital** may be obtained by bank overdrafts or

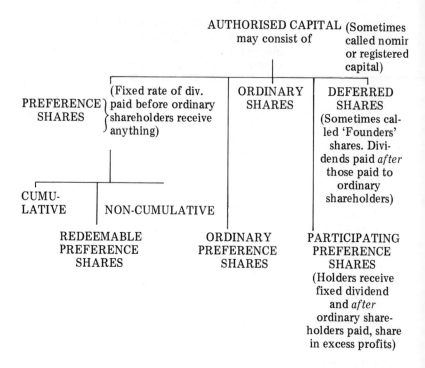

AUTHORISED CAPITAL (Sometimes
may consist of called nomir
or registered
capital)

PREFERENCE (Fixed rate of div.   ORDINARY   DEFERRED
SHARES paid before ordinary   SHARES   SHARES
shareholders receive   (Sometimes cal-
anything)   led 'Founders'
shares. Divi-
dends paid *after*
those paid to
ordinary
CUMU- shareholders)
LATIVE   NON-CUMULATIVE

REDEEMABLE   ORDINARY   PARTICIPATING
PREFERENCE   PREFERENCE   PREFERENCE
SHARES   SHARES   SHARES
(Holders receive
fixed dividend
and *after*
ordinary share-
holders paid, share
in excess profits)

loans, hire-purchase, expansion by ploughing back profits, or, in emergencies, by running down stocks and building up credit with suppliers.

Long-term capital may be raised by long-term loans, or again by ploughing back profits with a view to expansion. Businesses could also attract more capital by inviting partnerships or forming a company (private or public). Public companies could attract long-term capital by issuing more of its authorised capital on to the market.

All registered companies are required to produce annual audited accounts and these are submitted by the Directors, usually with an Annual Report, to the Company's Annual General Meeting. Shareholders receive a copy and are invited to attend the AGM. A **balance sheet** gives a picture of the financial standing of a company at a given time. The left-hand side shows **Liabilities** (items for which the business is liable, eg capital provided by shareholders or banks, management expenses, income tax liabilities), and the right-hand side shows **Assets**, eg value of fixed assets and of stock, moneys owed by debtors, cash in hand and at the bank, interest from investments, etc.

Issued share capital consists of different kinds of shares: look at the diagram on page 150.

You will see that the diagram shows preference, ordinary and deferred shares, and that there are several kinds of preference shares. These are described in Chapter 9, The Stock Exchange, and in the glossary of terms at the end of that chapter.

Turnover and profit

The money which is received from shareholders is used to buy buildings and stock, and generally to develop the business. Dividends may not be paid from it, but only from profits.

Profits are made from the circulating capital. The business buys stock for sale. A selling price is fixed that will make a profit after covering the cost of selling the goods, which includes the cost of rent, rates and light and heat, known as the overhead expenses, and such costs as wages. While the sales may go up and down, the overhead and other expenses need not do so. The greater the number of sales, therefore, the higher the profit will be.

A trading business aims to make its profit from the purchase of goods and their resale at a higher price.

The difference between the price at which the goods are bought and that at which they are re-sold is the 'gross profit', or 'profit margin'. In comparing the profitability of different articles the business man thinks of the profit margins as percentages, either of a buying price or of the selling price. The percentage he adds to the cost of an article to arrive at the selling price he calls the '**mark-up**', and the percentage of the selling price which represents the profit margin he calls his 'percentage on sales'.

For example, a trader buys an article for £1.00 and sells it for £1.50. The profit margin is £0.50 and, as percentages, the mark-up is 50 per cent and the percentage on sales is $33\frac{1}{3}$ per cent.

The total gross profit for the year will depend not only on the profit margin on each article sold but also, of course, on the total quantity sold.

Goods are bought and placed into stock awaiting sale. Every day some of these goods are sold from stock and must be replaced by buying more goods. In time all the original articles in stock will have been sold and replaced by fresh goods. It is said that the stock has been 'turned over'. The number of times this happens during a year, or the *rate* of stock turnover, depends on the type of business. A fishmonger must obviously clear his stock and replace it almost every day—the business has a high rate of stock turn. A furniture dealer may have articles in his stock for weeks or months before they are sold—a slow rate of stock turn (or rate of turnover).

From this idea of stocks being 'turned over' comes the use of the word **'turnover'** to express the total quantity or value of goods sold during a trading period. Therefore, the terms 'sales' and 'turnover' are interchangeable.

Example. A trader always keeps up a stock of goods which cost him £1000. He 'marks-up' his goods $33\frac{1}{3}$ per cent to get his selling prices; his percentage on sales therefore will be 25 per cent.

If, for the year, his total sales, or 'turnover', amounts to £12 000 then:

his gross profit for the year will be £3000 (25 per cent of £12 000);

the cost to him of the goods sold will be £9000 (£12 000 less £3000);

his rate of stock turn will be 9 times (£9000 divided by £1000).

Out of this **gross trading profit** the trader will have to pay his **overhead expenses**. These are all the other expenses of trading, such as assistants' wages, the rent of the shop, rates, the cost of lighting, heating, postages, etc. Thus his actual *net* **profit** for the year will be very much less than the gross profit.

Some of these expenses may depend on the quantity or value of the goods sold; such as salesmen's commission or the cost of wrapping or delivering goods sold. This type of expense is said to be **'variable'**, ie it will vary with the turnover of the business. Other expenses, such as rent, will not be affected by variations in the turnover; they are said to be **'fixed** expenses'.

Example. A trader making a gross profit of 20 per cent shows the following figures for two years' trading.

	YEAR 1 £		YEAR 2 £	
SALES turnover		40 000		80 000
STOCK held Jan. 1 at cost	6000		8000	
GOODS PURCHASED during the year	34 000		66 000	
	40 000		74 000	
less STOCK held Dec. 31 at cost	8000		10 000	
COST TO TRADER OF GOODS SOLD during the year		32 000		64 000
GROSS PROFIT FOR THE YEAR		8000		16 000
deduct SUNDRY EXPENSES:				
variable	1000		2000	
fixed	4000		4000	
total expenses for the year		5000		6000
NET OR REAL PROFIT for the year		£3000		£10 000

From the above figures you can calculate:

average stock held during the year $\left(\dfrac{6000 + 8000}{2}\right) = \pounds7000$ $\qquad \left(\dfrac{8000 + 10\,000}{2}\right) = \pounds9000$

rate of stock turn $\left(\dfrac{32\,000}{700}\right)$ $\qquad \left(\dfrac{64\,000}{9000}\right)$

about $4\frac{1}{2}$ times $\qquad$ about 7 times

percentage mark-up $\left(\dfrac{8000}{32\,000} \times 100\right)$ $\qquad \left(\dfrac{16\,000}{64\,000} \times 100\right)$

= 25 per cent $\qquad$ = 25 per cent

Turnover and gross profit have doubled in year 2 but net profit has increased $3\frac{1}{3}$ times. This is because expenses include a high proportion of 'fixed' expense which has not increased with the turnover and gross profit.

Now answer the following questions using the figures from the above example:

1. If sales in year 2 were £120 000 instead of £80 000, goods purchased in year 2 were £90 000 instead of £60 000, and stock

153

at December 31st was £11 000 instead of £10 000, calculate:

(a) gross profit for the year
(b) average stock held during year
(c) approximate rate of stock turn

2. Using the details given in Q.1, calculate:

(a) variable expenses
(b) net profit for the year

Note: be careful to distinguish between (a) 'turnover' and (b) rate of stock turn or rate of turnover.

The sole trader and partnerships, after paying their overhead and other expenses, and deciding how much of their profit they wish to put back into their businesses, have no obligations to anyone but themselves, and pay the profits to themselves.

Private companies and public companies declare a dividend and pay the profits in the form of dividends to preference and other shareholders. They should, of course, in the interests of their shareholders, put an adequate sum aside as reserves to ensure that the business is adequately run, and the directors of a public company cannot reward themselves unknown to the shareholders, although they may receive salaries and they will be among the shareholders to whom dividends are paid.

In the case of Co-operative Societies, the distribution of profits is made differently. Share capital receives differential rates of interest: 3 per cent up to £50 invested, 5 per cent between £50 and £100, and $7\frac{1}{2}$ per cent above £100. The traditional 'dividend' was based on purchases and not on share-holding, and until recently members' purchases would be totalled half-yearly, and surplus money after meeting expenses would be returned to customers/members in amounts proportionate to their purchases. It could be withdrawn or left as interest-earning share capital. Today, dividend is returned as goods are purchased in the form of trading stamps. Books of stamps may be redeemed for cash, or exchanged for goods, or placed as a deposit in a share account.

The surplus, if any, made by the State trading bodies such as the National Coal Board, the Electricity and Gas Boards, is eventually paid into the Bank of England and the Government's consolidated account. If these bodies run at a loss, as some of them have done, the Government is obliged to finance them.

Questions

1. Compare fixed and circulating capital and give two examples of each.
2. What is meant by liquid capital?
3. Explain the meanings of the following.

    share capital; authorised capital; issued capital.
4. Among a firm's assets are listed cash, delivery vans, furniture and fittings; stock-in-trade and trade debtors. Of these the current assets are

    (a) cash, trade debtors, and stock-in-trade.

    (b) cash only.

    (c) none of those listed in this question.

    (d) delivery vans and furniture and fittings.

(RSA)

5. **Either**

    (a) Explain fully the meaning of *each* of the following terms and by illustration show the ways in which they are interrelated when applied to a retail business.

    (i)   Gross Profit.   (ii) Net Profit.

    (iii) Capital   (iv) Turnover.

    (v) Stock.

or

   (b) Below is the Balance Sheet of Cornish Craftsmen Limited, a business which manufactures and sells hand-produced art and craftwork.

BALANCE SHEET

Authorised capital		Land and buildings	88 000
250 000 ordinary shares		Plant and machinery	4800
of £1 each *£250 000*		Stock in trade	17 200
Issued capital		Sundry debtors	48 700
150 000 ordinary shares			
of £1 each fully paid	150 000	Bank	2100
Profit and loss account	8700	Cash	200
Sundry creditors	2300		
	£161 000		£161 000

In what ways and for what reasons might the company increase:

   (i) its long-term capital; and

   (ii) its immediate capital?

(SW)

11

Means of payment

When goods and services are required by a consumer, money is the essential item. It is money which gives the power to purchase, and in a civilised community this power can be postponed, transferred and even passed on after death. Money may be regarded as the most important tool of civilisation, at the same time providing a means of storing wealth, a measure of value, and a title to goods and services.

Payment is almost always made in money; and while it is frequently made in cash, in this country the facilities of the banks and the Post Office may be used.

Money

The money we use today is known as 'token money', as the paper notes and metal coins have no value in themselves.

Before money was evolved, primitive man used **barter** to pay for things he wanted but could not produce for himself. If he needed arrow-heads he might offer pottery or wool. Occasionally barter is still used; children still barter or 'swop', and in rural communities vegetables may be bartered for fruit or home-made wine. The drawback of barter is that a **coincidence of wants** has to exist.

Because of this inconvenience, various forms of money evolved, ranging from beads, shells, teeth, stones, salt and ivory tusks to gold and silver. It had to be something that could be counted or measured out, generally acceptable in its own society, and, if possible, in another society.

It can be seen, then, that money needs to be **acceptable**; that it should be capable of being divided in various sized units (**divisible**); that it can be carried around (**portable**); that it will last (**durable**); and, in order to have some value, it should not be too easily obtainable (**scarce**). Its value should be reasonably steady and not fluctuate (**stable**).

Gold and silver became popular even in very early civilisations. They were in sufficiently short supply to be desirable, could be worked easily into various sized units, and did not rust, decay or diminish in size or weight. The making of coins was a natural step, in pre-determined weights, and impressed with symbols to show their value and the likeness of the ruler who authorised their issue. At that time the value of a coin was determined by its weight, and in spite of severe penalties the edges of coins were continually 'clipped' or 'trimmed'. The 'trimmings' were melted down. This practice was halted by the invention of milled edges for coins. Today, precious metals are not used for coins for general issue. 'Silver' coins are made of cupro-nickel, and gold sovereigns are not generally available, their actual value being very much more than their face value.

Paper money was developed by the early goldsmith bankers when they began to issue notes for fixed amounts (£10, £50, and so on) instead of receipts to named individuals in respect of gold deposited with them. These 'bank' notes could then be passed from hand to hand, with the bearer being able to claim the gold if need be. Gold backing for present-day money is discussed in Chapter 8, Banking.

Cash as a means of settling debts

Bank notes and coins of the realm are **legal tender**, and, as such, must be accepted by citizens of the state concerned. Notes are legal tender up to any amount but coins need not be accepted in large quantities. The maximum legal tender for coins is:

> £10 of the seven-sided 50p coins,
> £5 of cupro-nickel ('silver'), and
> 20p of decimal bronze.

The limit on coin as legal tender does not mean that the person who is being paid may not take more than that amount, but he is not obliged to do so.

The advantage of cash as a means of payment is that it is of immediate value to the receiver. Its disadvantages are that:

- it is at risk when kept or moved in large quantities
- special and costly security arrangements become necessary
- cash sent by post is required to be registered
- receipts are usually required
- it could prove a temptation to staff

157

Settling a debt immediately, say over a shop counter, is known as a **cash transaction** and some sort of receipt or proof of payment is provided (a till receipt for example).

If goods or services are provided and payment made at a later day it is known as a **credit transaction** and this is usual between suppliers and their regular customers when bills are sent out and paid monthly. New customers wishing to receive goods on credit on a regular basis may quote their bank, or an existing trader with whom they deal, to vouch for their credit worthiness. It should be noted that many householders receive goods and services on credit, including milk, bread and newspaper deliveries, gas, electricity and telephone supplies. Credit transactions when payments are made by instalments are discussed in Chapter 12, Credit.

Bank payment services

Bank services in general are discussed in Chapter 8, but the payment services covered in detail in this chapter include the use of cheques, bank giro credit (credit transfer), direct debit, standing orders, bank drafts and bills of exchange.

Cheques

There are 3 parties to a cheque:

- the **drawer** (the one who signs it);
- the **drawee** (the drawer's bank, the bank on which it is drawn); and
- the **payee** (the person to whom the cheque is payable).

An open order cheque.

158

A cheque is a written order on the bank to pay, on demand, a stated sum of money, and bears the name of the person to whom it is payable. It must be signed and dated by the drawer.

Cheques can be either **open order** cheques, or, more usually **crossed** cheques (indicated by the fact that they have two parallel lines drawn across them).

The cheque above is an **open order** cheque. It can be cashed over the counter of the branch where the person signing it (the drawer, A Specimen) has his account, and no other branch except by prior arrangement. The payee (the person named on the cheque, Albert Brown) must endorse it by signing his name on the back before he can receive the cash. The endorsement must agree with the name on the front. Such a cheque should not be endorsed before arrival at the bank or being handed to a reliable person, for if it falls into the wrong hands after endorsement, the bank will cash it.

If the payee (Albert Brown) has a bank account and does not wish to cash the cheque he can, of course, pay it into his account and should, as a safety measure, 'cross' the cheque upon receipt.

A crossed cheque.

The above cheque is a **crossed** cheque, and it cannot be cashed over a bank counter by anyone but must be paid into a bank account. A crossed cheque need not necessarily be paid into the payee's account: she may not have a bank account, or she may wish to use it to settle a debt. It can be paid into any bank account, but before passing it on she must first endorse it on the back. This is not necessary if paid into her own account. As a crossed cheque must always pass through a bank account, it can be traced, and this prevents dishonest people from using cheques not intended for them. For safety, cheques should be crossed if they are being sent by post.

An additional safeguard for a crossed cheque is to write the words 'Account payee only' or 'Not negotiable' within the crossing. An example of such **general crossings** is shown below.

A cheque with general crossings.

The two remarks do not mean exactly what they seem to mean: 'account payee only' sounds as if that cheque could be paid only into the named payee's account, and the words 'not negotiable' seem to indicate that this cheque cannot be passed to anyone else. This is not the case. Cheques bearing these words can in fact be paid into anyone's bank account but the words 'account payee only' will cause the collecting bank to look with extreme suspicion and exercise great care if the person paying in the cheque is not the named payee. The words 'not negotiable' mean that if the cheque gets into the wrong hands anyone to whom it is subsequently given has no right to the money for which it stands, even though the cheque was acquired honestly.

Special crossings (see examples below) are even safer because the name of the banker is written within the crossing, and if it is paid into an account other than that of the person named, then the bank will make enquiries. Adding 'not negotiable' to a cheque that bears a special crossing means that the cheque can only be cleared into the account of the payee at the bank named. To use a special crossing the drawer must, of course, know the name of the payee's bank.

To draw cash out of a bank account, the drawer makes a cheque out to 'Self', or 'Cash'. If a cheque book has only crossed cheques in it, the holder can 'open' the cheque by adding the words 'pay cash' and signing his name within the crossing, although this cancelling of the crossing is no longer considered essential. If the drawer is cashing a cheque himself it is safer not to sign it until he gets to the bank.

160

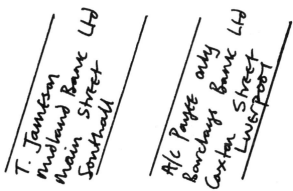

Examples of special crossings.

A crossed 'self' cheque.

A **blank** cheque is one that has been signed and dated by the drawer but the amount and/or name of the payee has been left blank, to be filled in later when the amount and/or name of the payee is known. Obviously it is a risky practice as it could fall into the wrong hands. There is a slight safeguard if the amount of the cheque is 'limited', that is by writing across it as shown on the cheque below.

The possession of a cheque book is a responsibility, and the following points should be remembered:

- Keep your cheque book with you or in a safe place.
- Do not put your signature on the cover, or keep with it anything showing your signature (eg, cheque card, credit card).
- Never give blank cheques to strangers.
- Notify the bank at once if you lose your cheque book—by telephoning, and then in writing. They will then 'stop' the cheques concerned.

- When writing a cheque, use ink. Begin writing as far as possible over on the left-hand side, and do not leave spaces into which unauthorised words or figures could be added.
- Sign any alterations made.
- Always use the same signature as the specimen held by the bank.
- Do not lend a cheque to a friend as the account number, not the name, is used to debit accounts.
- Fill in the counterfoils so that you can check your own record of spending against your bank statement.

A blank cheque.

A correctly written cheque should look like this—

A correctly written cheque.

and **not** like this.

An incorrectly written cheque.

Cheques as a means of settling debts Cheques are a convenient and safe way of settling debts. They can be sent via the normal postal system; they provide a record and proof of payment; and a cheque book is easier and safer to carry around than large amounts of cash.

To complete a cheque the drawer merely writes in the date, the name of the payee, the amount in words and figures, decides whether any special crossing is needed, and signs it.

The payee can, upon receipt, pay it into his own bank account or, if he wishes, can pass it on to another person (for cash or perhaps in payment of a debt) after endorsing it on the back with his/her name as shown on the front of the cheque.

It is not quite so convenient if the payee does not have a bank account. The drawer then has two choices: he can give an 'open' cheque which means the payee can claim cash—but usually only from the drawer's bank and branch unless special arrangements have been made, or alternatively the drawer can send a crossed cheque and rely on the payee being able to pass it on to someone with a bank account who will let him have the money for the cheque.

As a safeguard against the misuse of funds, many organisations require cheques to carry two signatures; for example the Chairman and Treasurer, or Secretary and Treasurer, or Managing Director and Accountant.

Where large numbers of cheques are made out each month, business organisations have cheques in sheets instead of in books, and carbon backing provides a record for the book-keeping system. Typewriters are also available with a special pin-point typing unit. The fine points pierce the paper, thereby preventing fraudulent alteration. Cheque-signing machines,

163

which impress facsimile signatures can be used for multiple signings. These machines are lockable and naturally must be locked away when not in use.

The clearing of cheques through the banking system, reasons why a cheque may be returned by the bank as not payable, and the use of cheque guarantee cards are discussed in Chapter 8, Banking.

Bank Giro credit

As well as dealing with cheques, banks deal with credit transfers (Bank Giro). By this method:

1. A bank customer can pay cash, cheques and postal orders into any branch of any bank to be credited to his or any other person's bank account. If the money is to be credited to some-one else's account then the payee's bank, branch and account number need to be known.

It has become usual for the bank giro credit form to be a detachable part of bills (eg gas, electricity, telephone, rates). The slip is pre-printed to include all the necessary details so that the money can be transferred to the correct account and the customer identified. If the bill is taken into the bank with the credit slip the bank will date-stamp it as a form of receipt.

There is no special charge for this service and, of course, there are no postage costs involved. It is a convenient, safe and economical way of settling bills.

Date_____	**bank giro credit** ✧		pounds	pence
Cashier's stamp and initials	Destination Branch Code number	£5 notes and over		
	99-99-99	£1 notes		
		50p coin		
		Other silver		
	National Westminster Bank	Bronze coin		
	Branch	Total cash		
	Anytown	Cheques, P O's etc. (see over)	£	
	Account Name (Block Letters) & A/c No			
	A Specimen	99999999		
Paid in by	Details for advice to recipient			

A Bank Giro credit slip.

2. A customer can also give the bank instructions to make any number of payments by bank giro, and either issue one cheque made payable to the bank for the total amount being trans-ferred, or instruct the bank to debit his account. Business

164

organisations can settle a number of bills or company salaries in this way. Special stationery is available incorporating gummed labels so that, with the use of carbon paper, the credit slips, summary sheet and office records can be completed with one writing. This arrangement saves clerical work.

Again, settling monthly bills in this way saves on postage costs, and the direct crediting of employee's bank accounts with their pay overcomes the problems of safety and security.

National Westminster Bank Limited ⌘

To be completed in duplicate if a receipt is required.

To ___DONCASTER, KINGSGATE_____ Branch

Date____1st November 137-_____

Cashier's Stamp	**Bank Giro Credits - Summary List**
	Please distribute the undermentioned sums in accordance with the __6__ bank giro credits attached as arranged with the recipients.
	Our cheque for £ 260-50 _____ is enclosed. E Drewery
	Signature(s)

Code Number	Bank and Branch	Account and Account Number	Amount
60-06-52	Nat West, Kingsgate, Donc.	Taylor & Colbridge 6010654	£51.00
20-75-14	Barclays, Scunthorpe	Mrs T B Holden 7048 3036	£10.50
50-33-17	Lloyds, Doncaster	YEB 5512345	£75.80

From
National Westminster Bank Limited ⌘

DONCASTER, KINGSGATE

bank giro credit ⌘

Date 1 Nov. 197-

Branch

Destination Branch Sort Code	20-75-14	£ 10.50
Bank	BARCLAYS	
Branch	SCUNTHORPE	
Account & A/c No.	Mrs T B Holden 7048 3036	
By order of	Sutton & Drewery Ltd	

To

NWB 1803-1-2-72

1 Nov .19]- 0

1 November .19]- 00-00-00

Payee Nat West Bank Ltd

National Westminster Bank Limited
Anytown Branch
41 High Street, Anytown, Berks.

Sundry Traders' Credits

Pay National Westminster Bank Ltd or order
Two hundred and sixty pounds 50 pence
£260 - 50

E Drewery

£260 - 50

123456   ⑈123456⑈ 00⑈0000⑈ 99999999⑈

Settling a number of bills by a Bank Giro credit.

Direct debit

More recently banks have introduced direct debiting and collection accounts for business account holders. This means that if individual customers sign an authorisation, firms will send their invoices straight to the bank concerned, and the bank will debit (ie take money out of) the customer's account and credit the firm's account with the money. All payments intended for a particular firm can be collected at a pre-arranged collection account centre, usually the London headquarters of a bank.

This is a useful, time-saving and economic way of settling and collecting debts. The debtor knows his debts will be settled with no further action beyond the original authorisation, and the creditor is sure of payment on the due date. There is no checking of ledgers to see whether accounts have been settled and no sending of reminders, which cuts out clerical work and costs.

A direct debit transaction.

This service can be used either for the collection of varying amounts from regular customers (eg a wholesaler from a retailer) or for the collection of the same sum at set dates (eg, insurance premiums and subscriptions). The debtor should, of course, only sign authorisations for organisations of repute and he can, should a dispute or query arise, stop payment at the bank.

Standing orders

A bank customer can, with no special charge being made, ask his bank to make regular payments from his account of the same amount, on a given date, to the same person, club, com-

To
National Westminster Bank Limited   **Standing Order**

_____ Branch

Please pay on _____ to _____ Bank
           (date of first payment)

_____ Branch,   Code No. _____

the sum of £ _____ (say _____)

for credit to account of _____

Account no. (if known) _____   quoting reference no. _____

and make similar payments _____   on the _____
                          (state frequency)

up to and including * _____   or until this order is cancelled in writing

charging such payments to my/our _____ account numbered _____
* If this order is to terminate on a specific date insert
date of last payment but if not applicable please delete.

For Bank Use Only
Data submitted to computer
Print-out checked
NWB 1320

Signature _____

Date _____

An authorisation for standing order payments.

pany or firm, eg for insurance premiums, subscriptions, hire-purchase instalments, mortgage repayments, and rentals. This is called a standing order, or **banker's order**.

The advantage of this is that, as with direct debiting, debtor and creditor know that these regular payments will be met. There is also the possibility that a firm may reduce payments when paid by a standing order.

Although quarterly gas and electricity bills are of varying

amounts, the boards will accept a regular monthly payment from users, with an adjustment being made at the end of the year for any underpayment or overpayment. This allows users to spread payments over the whole year rather than have to meet heavy bills during the winter period. Local authorities will also allow householders to pay their rates by monthly instalments instead of half-yearly.

It has been the custom to pay regular set sums by standing order, but organisations are now changing to direct debit collections, so as to save paper work by claiming in bulk from banks, rather than have banks send them individual payments, which then have to be checked.

Bank draft

A bank draft is, in effect a bank's own cheque paid on behalf of a customer to pay that customer's debt. It is considered to be as good as cash since it is backed by the bank, and is obviously preferable to the customer's own cheque in cases where his credit worthiness is unknown or uncertain. This is especially so when large sums of money are involved, as in property deals, or payment is required in another country. The draft can be drawn on a bank in the foreign country, in the appropriate currency, and the money is immediately available to the payee.

The bank requires to be paid in advance by the customer.

Bills of exchange

A bill of exchange (B/E) is frequently used for obtaining payment for goods sold both in this country and abroad. The seller draws up a bill for the cost of the goods sold and states a time within which the money is payable: this may be on demand or at a future date. The buyer or his agent signs the bill as acceptable.

The seller may ask the bank to advance money on bills of exchange and the bank may do this for a 'discount'. This is called 'discounting bills of exchange' as mentioned in Chapter 9, Finance for industry.

A bill of exchange is a useful form of payment particularly to overseas buyers as it enables them to make sure that goods have arrived satisfactorily before payment need be made. It also enables suppliers to raise money on debts owing instead of waiting for payment. An illustration of a bill of exchange can be seen in Chapter 5, Trading overseas.

Air mail or cable transfers

A bank can make arrangements, either by air mail or cable, for funds to be paid through a bank abroad to a particular person on application and after identification. This bank service is an alternative to Post Office telegraph money orders payable abroad.

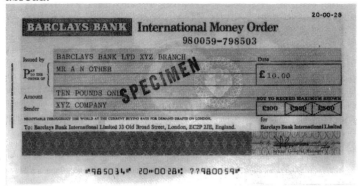

International money order

Financial telecommunications

Payments can be made by computer through the international telecommunications network. This system is being developed by the Society of Worldwide Interbank Financial Communications and it is known as SWIFT. At present the system is limited but it is likely to expand to cover all the world's banks in the next few years. A buyer in the UK, wishing to pay a supplier overseas, makes money available from his account. The computer at the UK bank makes contact with the computer at the appropriate overseas bank and the transaction is processed. The accounts can be adjusted in as little as half an hour if there are no queries on the accounts.

Credit Cards

By using credit cards, holders can shop, eat out, drive or travel by rail or air either at home or abroad, without paying at the time, wherever the credit card sign is displayed. In this country the best-known credit cards are Barclaycard and Access, and these are discussed in detail in this chapter.

Other credit cards include American Express and Diners Club and with these, once membership has been accepted, there is no upper credit limit as there is with Barclaycard and Access. These are, however, really charge accounts as payment is

169

expected in full on receipt of the statement of account, whereas payment can be made in instalments with the use of Barclaycard and Access cards. Also, an annual membership fee is required.

Credit cards were an American concept and are now part of the American way of life. Barclay's credit card, the Barclaycard was introduced in this country in 1966. In 1972 the Access card was launched by a group of banks including National Westminster, Midland and Lloyds Banks, together with Williams and Glyns and the Royal Bank of Scotland. To illustrate the growth and acceptance of the credit card system, there are at present some 8 million of these plastic cards in circulation, with many new cardholders being recruited each month.

Abroad, Barclaycard is accepted wherever the blue-white-gold VISA emblem is displayed, while Access is linked with Eurocard and Master Charge (the Interbank card). Between them the major credit card companies have a network of over 2 million outlets in 156 countries.

Examples of credit cards.

Credit cards are available free to all creditworthy persons over eighteen years, and additional cards are available for a cardholder's family. There are credit limits (the maximum amount the holder can spend using his card) and these range from £100 upwards. Cards are also available for companies, and these enable business travel and entertainment expense accounts to be simplified. Instead of executives having to submit expense claims, the company receives a monthly itemised statement for each cardholder, together with a summary statement showing

170

ACCESS APPLICATION

Access

PLEASE COMPLETE ALL SECTIONS IN BLOCK CAPITALS AND TICK (✓) WHERE APPLICABLE.
WE MAY ASK FOR REFERENCES.

Surname	First Name	Other Initials	Mr Mrs Miss	Are you:	
				Married	A Houseowner
Address	Time at this address	Years	Months	Single	A Tenant
				A Widow/er	Living with Parents
Town				Date of birth	/19
County	Post Code			Private Telephone No STD Code	Number
Give previous address if less than 3 years at present address		Years	Months	No. of dependants (exclude husband/wife)	
Name of your Bank				Do you have a	
	Time with Bank	Years	Months	Current A/C	Cheque Card
Branch Address (in full)				Deposit A/C	American Express
				Loan A/C	Diners Club
				Other A/C	Barclaycard
	Account Number			Barclaycard Number	
Employer's Name	Nature of business			Business Telephone No STD Code	Number
Business Address (in full)	Present position			Time with Employer	Years Months
				Gross annual income £	Is position pensionable Yes No
Service No. (H.M. Forces only)				Net pay per month £	Paid Weekly Monthly
Give name and address of previous employer if less than 3 years with present employer		Years	Months		

------------------------ PLEASE FOLD ALONG THIS LINE BEFORE SEALING ------------------------

House Mortgage with		Estimated value of house £		Monthly Mortgage Repayments	FOR ACCESS USE
Branch Address		Mortgage outstanding £		£	
Rental		If your property is rented please give monthly rental		£	

Hire Purchase Bank or Other Loans	Name	Address	Balance Outstanding	Account Number	Total HP/Loans repayments each month
			£		£
			£		
			£		

If married give details of husband/wife	Name	Date of birth	Gross annual income
	Employed by	Occupation	£

Additional Cardholder
(must be over 18)

Surname	First Name	Other Initials	Mr Mrs Miss

I accept and agree to be bound by the Access Conditions of Use as set out overleaf and as may be amended from time to time.

Additional Cardholder's Signature _____

I confirm that I am not less than 18 years of age and the information given above is true and complete and that I have read and agree to be bound by the Conditions of Use as set out overleaf and as may be amended from time to time. Where requested above I hereby authorise you to issue in accordance with the Conditions of Use as set out overleaf and as may be amended from time to time, an additional Access Card to the person named above who is not less than 18 years of age for use on my Access account.

Date _____ Signature of Applicant _____

AS 78-6

A credit card application form.

the total amount due.

Procedure

When the card is used, the trader makes out a sales voucher, entering the date, price and a description of the goods or services. He then uses an imprinting machine to impress the name and number on the card, together with his own firm's name and address, onto the voucher. The customer then signs the voucher as correct. The trader must inspect the card to compare the signatures, and make sure that it is a current issue, and not out of date. Most establishments have what is known as a 'floor limit', and if the purchase price exceeds this limit, the trader must telephone the cardcentre for authorisation. The cost of such telephone calls is refunded by the cardcentre. When the trader is satisfied that everything is in order he gives one copy of the voucher to the customer.

A credit card sales voucher.

The trader must deposit a copy of the voucher with the bank within three days, and his account is immediately credited. However, he does not receive the full selling price for the goods he has sold. Between 2 per cent and 5 per cent is charged by the cardcentre, and he receives a monthly statement showing how much he owes. The cardcentre claims payment by direct debit from the trader's bank account.

172

From
National Westminster Bank Limited

bank giro credit
Date 23-1-78

Branch

Destination
Branch
Sort Code   00 - 00 - 00

£ 72-71

To

Bank   Anytown Bank

Branch   Millingham Branch

Account
& A/c No.   WILMANS LTD

By order of   M Cohen

NWB 1813

Credit card deposit voucher etc. . . .

The customer can use his copy of the voucher to check the monthly statement sent to him by the cardcentre showing how much he owes for various sums paid to traders on his behalf. He has twenty-five days to pay, and can either pay in full or a minimum amount £5 or 5 per cent of the total, whichever is the greater) which is shown on the statement. He will be charged interest on amounts outstanding.

Advantages of a credit card to the cardholder

- Convenience—saves carrying cash or making out individual cheques
- Record of expenditure provided by copy vouchers
- Credit facilities (buy now—pay later)—there is a delay before payment is required
- Higher priced goods may be bought than a cheque guarantee card allows
- Payment may be made in monthly instalments, without hire-purchase formalities, if minimum sum is paid

173

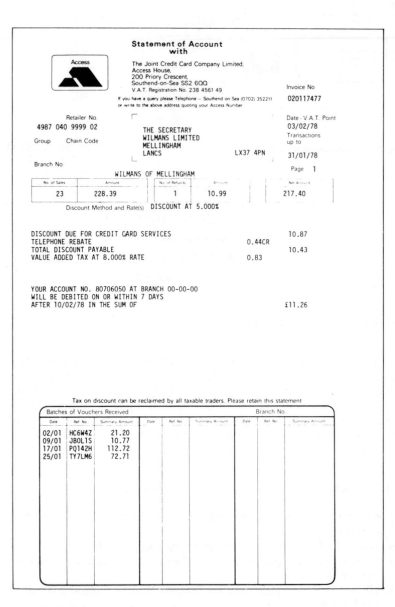

Statement of Account
with

Access

The Joint Credit Card Company Limited,
Access House,
200 Priory Crescent,
Southend-on-Sea SS2 6QQ
V.A.T. Registration No. 238 4561 49

If you have a query please Telephone — Southend-on-Sea (0702) 352211
or write to the above address quoting your Access Number

Invoice No
020117477

Retailer No.
4987 040 9999 02

Group   Chain Code

Branch No.

THE SECRETARY
WILMANS LIMITED
MELLINGHAM
LANCS   LX37 4PN

Date - V.A.T. Point
03/02/78

Transactions
up to

31/01/78

Page   1

WILMANS OF MELLINGHAM

No. of Sales	Amount	No. of Refunds	Amount	Net Amount
23	228.39	1	10.99	217.40

Discount Method and Rate(s) DISCOUNT AT 5.000%

DISCOUNT DUE FOR CREDIT CARD SERVICES   10.87
TELEPHONE REBATE   0.44CR
TOTAL DISCOUNT PAYABLE   10.43
VALUE ADDED TAX AT 8.000% RATE   0.83

YOUR ACCOUNT NO. 80706050 AT BRANCH 00-00-00
WILL BE DEBITED ON OR WITHIN 7 DAYS
AFTER 10/02/78 IN THE SUM OF   £11.26

Tax on discount can be reclaimed by all taxable traders. Please retain this statement

Batches of Vouchers Received						Branch No.		
Date	Ref. No.	Summary Amount	Date	Ref. No.	Summary Amount	Date	Ref. No.	Summary Amount
02/01	HC6W4Z	21.20						
09/01	JBOL1S	10.77						
17/01	PQ142H	112.72						
25/01	TY7LM6	72.71						

A trader's statement of account.

- Only single payment required for monthly expenditure, either by post or by bank giro credit slip over bank counter
- Card can be used internationally—for holiday or business expenses when travelling
- Growing acceptance by advertisers and mail order firms—card number may be quoted on orders
- Cash advances can be obtained from any participating bank to limit of cardholder's credit—these incur a service charge or immediate interest charges
- Barclays Bank customers may use Barclaycard as a cheque card, guaranteeing cheques up to £50. (Other banks issue separate cheque cards.)

Disadvantages to cardholders

- Temptation to buy on impulse and overspend
- Interest must be paid on outstanding debt each month
- Risk of loss—holders may be liable for mis-use of card up to the time the loss is reported to cardcentre.
- Signature on card means that it must be kept safe and not kept with a cheque book

Advantages to the trader
- Encourages customer spending
- Encourages buying of higher priced goods
- No risk involved—payment immediate and guaranteed
- Clerical work of arranging instalments cut out, and no bad debts
- Safer than handling cash

Disadvantages to the trader
- Discount on goods sold paid to cardcentre
- Sales procedure slowed down—sales voucher must be made out, card checked and credit worthiness of customer often has to be established by telephone

Post Office Remittance Services

The Post Office offers facilities for transmitting payments from person to person by post or telegraph, to inland and overseas addresses including to HM Forces and merchant ships. It has also set up a banking and money transfer service, the National Giro bank service.

It should be remembered that if coins, notes, open cheques and anything of monetary value are sent by post then they should be sent by **registered post** as mentioned in Chapter 7, Communications and the Post Office. In that chapter also are details of the **cash on delivery** (COD) service which is one way of paying for goods sent through the post as the Post Office, upon delivery, collects the amount specified and remits this sum to the sender.

The Post Office remittance services are of two types: the postal order and the telegraph money order or overseas money order.

Postal orders

Postal orders may be purchased, and are payable, at most post offices throughout Great Britain and Northern Ireland and are useful for sending small sums through the post. They are available in certain fixed values from 10p to £10, and postage stamps can be affixed to make up the amount required. A small fee is charged in addition to the cost of the postal order.

The sender should fill in the postal order with the name of the payee and the post office where the order is to be cashed. He should also complete and retain the counterfoil attached to the postal order. This is his record and would be needed if application had to be made to the post office in the event of loss, damage or destruction of the postal order.

To obtain cash the payee signs the postal order and hands it over the post office counter. Postal orders can be crossed for safety and then can only be paid through a bank account.

There is an overseas postal order service.

Inland telegraph payments

A telegraph money order may be obtained from post offices for any sum not exceeding £100. There is a fee plus a fixed charge for the standard telegram of advice. Should the sender wish to include a private message, payment for each additional word is required. Value added tax is payable on the fees charged.

The sender fills in a requisition form which requires his own and the payee's names in full; he is given a certificate of issue as his receipt.

The telegraphed money order is cashable at the payee's nearest post office unless the sender requests otherwise. Before payment is made the payee has to sign the order and give the name of the remitter correctly. The paying post office checks these details with its records to see that all is correct before handing over the money.

Although costly, telegraph money orders are a safe and speedy way of remitting money, they can be crossed for payment into a bank account and are valid for six months. For a supplementary fee the sender will be informed of the date of payment of the order.

Overseas money orders are also available and the Post Office Guide should be studied for the special conditions affecting the various destinations and countries.

National Giro bank

National Giro is a banking system operated by the Post Office. All the accounts are kept at the National Giro Centre, Bootle, Merseyside, which houses one of the largest computer complexes in Europe. There are some 21 000 post offices throughout the country which transact Giro business. Giro is essentially a money transfer service by which payments are made and received from one account to another, in this country and overseas, without cash being handled. Although postal giro has been spreading across Europe for the past ninety years, the British National Giro system was established as recently as 1968.

There are two kinds of account: a business account and a personal account (for anyone over the age of fifteen). If a personal account holder has his pay credited direct into his Giro account he has many concessions concerning service charges and fees, and a **guarantee card** is available, guaranteeing payments by Girocheque up to £50 for across-the-counter purchases. Every account holder has an account number and a directory of Giro business account holders is available.

The services offered by the Post Office National Giro are similar to those offered by the banks and these are being extended so that now National Giro offers **deposit accounts**, paying interest on the amount held, and **budget accounts** aimed at smoothing out payments over the year. However, the procedure is somewhat different from the banks in that most transactions are dealt direct with the Giro Centre at Bootle through the post (postage-paid envelopes are provided which travel by first-class mail). The post offices handle cash transactions (cash inpayments, cash transfers and the cashing of Girocheques).

Other services provided are: **credit transfer, direct debiting** (Automatic Debit Transfers, ADT for short), and **standing orders. Statements,** showing transactions in and out of the account and the balance in hand, are supplied. **Personal loans** and **bridging loans** can be arranged but only limited overdrawing is allowed to guarantee card holders and then any amount overdrawn must be cleared by the next pay credit. **Girocheques** are provided either for withdrawing cash at a nominated post office, or for paying someone who does not have a Giro account. (The transfer system is used for payments between account holders). A Girocheque can be crossed for payment through the banking system, or left uncrossed for the payee to cash at a named post office. An uncrossed Girocheque must, however, be sent to the Giro Centre where it will be authenticated and sent on to the payee. **Foreign currency** and travellers cheques can be bought direct from Giro.

Many business organisations now include a National Giro transfer form as part of their invoice: this can be used over the post office counter when paying by cash, or sent to the Giro Centre if a transfer between accounts is required. Mail Order companies are now customers, which means that agents can pay in their collections over the post office counter instead of sending money through the post. Government departments have Giro accounts and benefits are paid out by Girocheque, so that sickness benefits for example are received by cashing Girocheques at a post office.

There are sixteen million account holders in Europe and so payment to them can be made by **international Giro transfer.** Payments can also be received from those accounts direct into a Giro account held here. It is also simple to accept payments from people with accounts with other banks throughout the world.

STATEMENT OF ACCOUNT			NATIONAL Girobank	HA 147985

Summary			Transaction	DEBITS	£
previous balance	4JAN79	£173.00	6JAN G 000059 SELF		30.00
total debits		70.90	9JAN S 6139627 TV RENT CO		3.40
total credits		66.35	9JAN T 6130008 NW ELEC CO		14.50
current balance	11JAN79	£168.45	10JAN T 2143211 T DAY LTD		8.00
			10JAN G 000061		15.00

MR J ASHTON   CREDITS
365 GREEN MOUNT   11JAN T WAGES   52.10
MANCHESTER   11JAN T 442004001 WOODS 4.25
M19 4ZZ   11JAN D SELF   10.00

A private account holder's statement.

NATIONAL Girobank
Bootle Merseyside GIR 0AA

Transfer/Deposit

Paying other people who have Giro accounts

1. Using your own Giro transfer/deposit form

Make these entries on a Transfer/Deposit form:
1 date
2 account number of the person or organisation you are paying
3 amount in figures
4 amount in words
5 your signature

10A 21D	Credit Account number	Amount No fee payable at the counter	

Credit Account number: 613 0008
Amount: £ 19-20
27th Nov 19 78

Amount: Nineteen pounds 20p only

MR J ASHTON
365 GREEN MOUNT
MANCHESTER
M19 4ZZ

Signature: 66 199 7308
g. Ashton

Please do not write in the space below

661997308

6 If appropriate write (on the back of the form) the reference number of the bill you are paying or other information which will identify the payment to the person or organisation you are paying.
Post to the National Giro Centre in one of your Giro envelopes. The form will be sent to the person or organisation you are paying after your account has been debited.

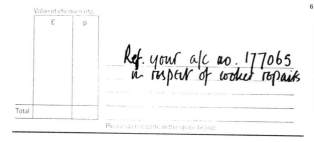

Value of cheques etc.

	£	p
Total		

Ref. your a/c no. 177065 in respect of cooker repairs

Please do not write in the space below

The TRANSFER/DEPOSIT form is also used for:

Paying cash in your own account — over a Post Office counter

Paying cheques etc. into your own account — by posting to the National Giro Centre

G⊐ the Post Office
National Giro
Bootle Lancs, GIR 0AA
credit Giro account number

credit Yorkshire Electricity Board PBXG2
Limewood Approach, Leeds LS15 8TB

604 5006

00 7557 144585
amount £ 10-61
by transfer from Giro account no. 613 0008

13PX 20BX	

3

signature A.Sprunitii

The space below this line must be left clear for machine processing at the National Giro Centre.

7006045006

Paying other people who have Giro accounts

2. Using the form supplied by the people you have to pay

1 your name and address (if required)
2 your own account number
3 amount in figures
4 your signature
5 date

Tear off the Giro form and post it in one of your Giro envelopes to the National Giro Centre. The form will be sent to the organisation you are paying after your account has been debited.

179

National Girobank

Application for a Personal Loan

PLEASE USE BLOCK LETTERS

Surname (Mr / Mrs / Miss*) _____

First name / s _____

Age _____ *Single / Married

Number of dependent children _____

Postal address _____

_____

_____

_____ Postcode _____

Telephone
Home _____

Business _____
*Please delete as appropriate

Name and address of present employer _____

_____

_____

_____ Postcode _____

Current net income from main employment each month (after deduction of Income Tax, Social Security and Pension contributions).

Self _____ £ _____

Please enclose two most recent pay slips unless your pay is credited to your account.

Husband / Wife _____ £ _____
Please enclose the two most recent pay slips.

Other regular income
(excluding family allowance) £ _____

Details of existing hire purchase and loan transactions

Company

_____

_____

_____

Purpose of loan _____

_____

_____

To: Customer Credit Manager
National Girobank
BOOTLE Merseyside GIR 0 AA.

The information set out above is true to the best of my knowledge and belief and I authorise you to make any enquiries you think necessary to enable you to consider this application. I accept that you reserve the right to decline this application without stating a reason. I accept that if you make me a personal loan in response to this application, the conditions entitled 'National Girobank Personal Loan Conditions' shown on the back of the application form will apply. I am in good health.

Account number [ ] [ ] [ ]

Do you receive your pay through Girobank? *Yes / No

*Owner occupier—without mortgage / with mortgage
Rented accommodation—furnished / unfurnished
Lodger. Living with parents

How long have you lived at your present address? _____ years

Previous address if you have been less than 5 years at your present address

_____

_____

_____

_____ Postcode _____
*Please delete as appropriate

Profession / trade and position held _____

_____

_____

Length of time in present employment _____ years

Current expenditure each month

Mortgage / Rent £ _____

Rates £ _____

Total of existing
hire purchase and loan repayments £ _____

	Monthly repayments	Date of final payment
	£ _____	_____
	£ _____	_____
	£ _____	_____

Total expenditure involved £ _____

Amount of loan required £ _____

Period of repayment _____ months

Signed: _____

Date: _____

GIROBANK /L249/APRIL'79

A personal loan application.

NORTHERN BANK LIMITED
KING STREET, NEWTOWN

16-19-17

PAY _J. Rowlands_ OR ORDER

One hundred pounds only ————— £100———00

T. KENYON

DATE   19

J. Kenyon

⑈524312⑈ ⑈16⑈1917⑈ ⑈2049375⑈

Questions

1. Study the above cheque and answer the following questions:
   (a) Who is
       (i) the drawer,
       (ii) the payee,
       (iii) the drawee?
   (b) What has been omitted from the cheque?
   (c) Name *four* services provided by a commercial bank.
   (d) What do the words 'Not Negotiable' mean when written across the face of a cheque?
   (e) What is the main reason for crossing a cheque?

   (NW)

2. For each of the following situations write down the most appropriate method of payment to be used.
   (a) Mrs. Dryden, a mail order agent, sends her weekly remittance of £45 to Liverpool. She does not have a bank account.
   (b) Mr. Jonson of Taunton, whose son at Bristol University urgently needs £5. His son does not have a bank account.
   (c) Mr. Jonson's son, now having some cash, wishes to buy a book costing £1.20 from a Swindon firm.
   (d) Christopher Marlowe who has to pay 75p per week for his school meals.
   (e) John Milton, a Helston retailer, who has to pay the £365 he owes a supplier from Plymouth.
   (f) A small manufacturing firm wishes to pay twenty two accounts with different suppliers where the total amount outstanding is £4008.
   (g) Bill Blake, who does not have a bank account, wishes to send off his football pool stake money of 50p.

(h) Gerald Hopkins who has a bank account and needs to pay his mortgage repayments to his Building Society monthly.

(SW)

3. Explain how the services of a bank are used by a commercial trader in the following activities:
   (a) making regular monthly payments on equipment purchased on HP terms
   (b) paying weekly wages to employees
   (c) accepting cheques from customers in the shop.

(RSA)

4. Say how each of the following Post Office services may contribute to the effectiveness of a business engaged in buying and selling:

   Giro : registered postal packets: COD

(RSA)

5. (a) Explain how the National Giro system operates, and then
   (b) indicate some of the advantages and disadvantages of the system.

(RSA)

6. (a) What is a cheque and what information is necessary to be written on a printed cheque form? You may illustrate your answer if you wish.
   (b) If a cheque is said to be crossed what does this mean and what effect does this have on the payment of it?
   (c) Draw an example of a General Crossing and of a Special Crossing.

(SR)

7. (a) What is credit?
   (b) Explain briefly how the credit card system introduced by the commercial banks operates.
   (c) From the user's point of view, give *two* disadvantages of having a credit card.

(EA)

12

Consumer credit

Credit is the term used when goods or services are received but not paid for until a later date. This can apply to businesses or to private individuals who receive goods or services which are invoiced at the end of the month (see Chapter 4), as well as to those who enter into a contract to pay by instalments.

The rapid growth of sales of household and durable consumer goods has in fact been helped greatly by instalment credit facilities, and there was a 21 per cent increase in 1976 over credit extended in 1975.

Credit facilities are really loans to the buyer, and as the lender could be using the money in other ways, he charges for the money he lends. The finance is not always provided by the seller. Often he will have arrangements for someone else, such as a bank or finance house (see Chapter 9) to advance the credit. In 1976, 42 per cent of credit was advanced by finance companies.

Most credit instalment transactions are for durable (long-lasting) goods but credit also applies to non-durables. For instance, newspaper, milk and bread deliveries are obtained on credit if payment is not made until, say, the week-end; and gas, electricity and telephone charges are based on usage over the previous quarter.

Buying goods on credit has now become an accepted part of life, and does not carry the social stigma it once did, although 'getting into debt' is still a great fear for many people, and accounts for much of the remaining hostility towards consumer credit. Those contemplating and participating in credit schemes need to be fully aware of all their financial commitments, both actual and possible, in order to avoid the trap of living beyond their means.

- They must consider the full cost of the item, including any deposit and all interest and service charges, and not just look for the amount of the weekly or monthly instalments.

- They should read carefully any agreement and look to see if interest charges or payments can be increased.
- They should never sign a blank form since agreements are legally binding.
- They should also remember that as soon as the goods are out of the shop and used they only have secondhand value, and if resold are unlikely to reach the cash price, let alone the credit price.

Credit, however, can be advantageous in the modern consumer society. The kind of durables that will last long after the credit bill has been settled are likely to be worthwhile paying extra for, since they can give useful service from the time of the first payment. Car ownership has become widespread as people travel to work and wider afield. Credit facilities are used for buying most private cars, particularly by first-time owners. House ownership, by mortgage deed, is discussed in Chapter 13. Furniture is needed for the house and, generally speaking, is far too expensive to buy all at once for cash, and so again credit is required. Mass production means that a wide range of household durables is available to many: cookers, washing machines, refrigerators, deep freezers, television sets, stereo equipment, etc. Having furnished the house, there is then the need to cut down on annual expenditure. Double-glazing, roof and wall insulation may be contemplated to cut down fuel bills, and this may well involve even more credit being received.

As you can see, before long the householder is living on borrowed money, perhaps beyond his means. There is then a need for the wife to go to work to supplement the family income and, because many of the items are labour-saving, she has time to do this: and so it is a vicious circle. She needs to go to work to help pay for the higher standard of living she likes, and modern equipment gives her the time to do so.

There are many ways of receiving credit, including the following.

The Banks

(See also Chapter 8).

Bank overdraft A bank customer is allowed to overdraw current account up to an agreed limit. Interest is calculated on the daily balance overdrawn.

Ordinary loan These are available to bank customers holding a current account and may be granted with or without security. It is effectively an overdraft held on a separate account but for a fixed period.

Personal loan   These are available both to bank customers and non-customers and based on a lump sum loan without security, for an agreed period. The rate of interest charged is usually higher than for overdrafts or ordinary loans. Finance houses can also arrange personal loans.

Credit cards

These, for example Access and Barclaycard, are discussed fully in Chapter 11. In addition, the Trustee Savings Bank (see Chapter 13), as another step towards full-scale high street banking, has introduced a Trustcard in blue, white and gold—the colours of the international Visa system in which the TSB will be joining Barclaycard.

If credit card accounts are settled in full by the due date, no interest charges are payable. Under the Consumer Credit Act 1974 it is an offence to give out credit cards unless they have been asked for.

Trading checks

Credit here is provided by trading companies which issue vouchers that can be used at a number of shops. Some check-trading firms have their own shops. Payments are collected weekly by the 'tally-man', usually over a twenty-week period and a service charge is made which must, of course, be added to the price of the goods to find out their true cost. Names of credit check traders can be found in the Yellow Pages of the Post Office Telephone Directory.

If a credit card or trading check is lost the holder has no liability for its misuse after the issuer has been informed.

Hire purchase

Goods are paid for by instalments but the buyer does not become the owner of the goods until the final payment: until that time he is the 'hirer' and the goods belong to the shop-keeper or the lender of the money, although there are legal protections to prevent the goods being taken back without warning (see details below under the Consumer Credit Act). A hire purchase agreement has to be drawn up and signed. The goods cannot be sold by the hirer until the final payment has been made.

A conditional sale agreement

This is an agreement for the sale of goods or land wholly or partly by instalments, but with the ownership remaining with the seller until specific conditions as to the payment are fulfilled. Generally speaking, the provisions regarding HP also apply to conditional sale agreements.

Credit sales

A credit sale agreement is for the sale of goods where the purchase price exceeds £30 and is payable by five or more instalments, being similar to hire purchase except that the goods belong to the buyer from the first payment. This is because the price is treated as a debt payable by instalments. Sometimes credit may be offered when goods are bought by mail order.

Hire

Some goods are available for hire (notably television sets and video recorders) and therefore never become the property of the hirer. Before signing rental agreements the hirer should find out whose responsibility it is if the goods are stolen or damaged and, if it is his responsibility, he should consider having them insured. Unless the hiring is required as a temporary measure, it should also be considered whether, in the long run, it would be cheaper to buy. (Hire regulations are also covered by the Consumer Credit Act—see below.)

Credit facilities offered by stores

Stores, notably department stores, may issue their own plastic credit cards. These cards are produced in the store instead of cash and the customer's account is charged with the amount of the purchases. Increasingly it is possible to use a store's credit card at any of the shops in the same group. Thus a Debenham's card can be used in most of its shops around the country, including such well-known names as Harvey Nicholls and Swan & Edgar. Similarly, the John Lewis Partnership and House of Fraser have stores throughout the country at which their account cards can be used when buying merchandise.

The ways of paying for purchases fall into two main groups. *The Charge Account* Each month the customer receives an itemised statement of account. This may be paid in full, but

186

many stores also state the minimum payment required, and the balance is then carried forward to the following month. If the account is not settled in full, a service charge (of about $1\frac{1}{4}$ per cent) is added to the amount outstanding. However, some stores do not offer the choice of deferred payment and require full settlement of the account at the end of each month. This is referred to as a **monthly account.**

A budget, or subscription account   The customer pays an agreed fixed amount into his account each month, and may make purchases up to twenty-four times that amount. The account then remains available for additional purchases on a continuing basis up to the previously agreed limit. Therefore, if £5 a month is the payment agreed upon, the customer may spend up to the limit of £120. A service charge (of about $1\frac{1}{4}$ per cent in the pound) is made on the outstanding balance each month.

In addition to these accounts, **interest free credit** is offered by some stores, to enable customers who wish to purchase more expensive items to spread their payments over a period of time. This is usually six months. A deposit of one-sixth of the price is required at the time of purchase, followed by five equal monthly payments. Occasionally, as an added incentive to buy, the store offers interest free credit over a twelve month period, one-twelfth being the deposit, followed by eleven monthly payments. These schemes apply to selected areas of merchandise (eg furniture, household furnishings, electrical goods) for items totalling over £50 or £100. Since there are no interest or service charges payable, it is a popular way of receiving credit.

Stores also offer **extended credit sales** where minimum deposit rates and maximum repayment periods are subject to Government restrictions. There are interest charges on all Credit Sale accounts (see example below).

Example

You wish to buy various items of furniture costing altogether £400 and you decide to pay by Credit Sale over 30 months.

	£
Cost of goods	400
Deposit required 10 per cent	40
	360
Interest charged at 10 per cent per annum for 30 months	90
Balance to be paid by 30 monthly payments of £15	450

Shopping by credit is growing and it has been said that we are becoming a 'cashless society'. In addition to department stores, other big retailing groups are introducing credit facilities: Marks & Spencer, Dunn, Fine Fare, Lasky and Etam among them. As there is considerable expense and administration involved in starting up a credit card scheme, outside agencies are often employed. Barclaycard, for instance, has set up Barclaycare to give retailers their own card; and others have similar schemes.

Credit transactions

	Advantages	Disadvantages
to the BUYER	• he can enjoy possession of the goods before he has paid for them • because he knows outlay, he can budget for items out of earnings • time- and labour-saving equipment could release other members of the household for employment • a wider range of goods is available to him • higher standard of living through mass-produced goods • benefits by lower prices brought about by competitiveness between retailers • greater mobility for work and recreation through purchase of vehicles	• the temptation to over-spend • vulnerable to persuasive salesmen and advertising
to the SELLER	• increases turnover and trade	• competitive atmosphere may reduce profit margins
to the FINANCIER	• money loaned earns good interest • hire purchase, by earning higher than normal rates of interest, is a particularly lucrative field of financial investment	• risk of bad debts

| to the MANUFACTURER | • increased sales enable fully specialised systems of production, thereby improving efficiency and lowering unit costs | (see Chapter 1 where mass-production and specialisation is discussed in full) |

The Consumer Credit Act 1974

The Consumer Credit Act 1974, which applies to Great Britain and Northern Ireland, modernises, rationalises and extends the law governing credit and hire. It covers virtually every form of credit, including HP, instalment sales, cash loans, budget accounts and trading checks, for sums up to £5000 advanced to individuals, sole traders, partnerships and other unincorporated bodies (see Chapter 2). The £5000 limit applies only to the amount of credit advanced, and does not include any charges or any deposit or advance payment.

The Act is a framework, the details being filled in by Regulations made by the Secretary of State for Prices and Consumer Protection, and is being brought into force in stages. 1977 was the year when regulations under the Act started to become effective. When the process is complete the Act will repeal (ie delete from the statute book) earlier legislation relating to credit, some of which dates from the last century.

Formerly, different forms of credit had different rules, and the 1974 Act is intended to be comprehensive, and seeks to ensure that both traders and customers get a fair deal. It allows for stricter control of the various businesses that make up the credit industry, and entitles customers to more information. The Consumer Credit Act 1974 is a result of the Crowther Report, ie, the recommendations of the Committee on Consumer Credit, chaired by the late Lord Crowther (the Crowther Committee).

The **Director General of Fair Trading** is responsible for administering the Act, and is concerned with the interests of both traders and consumers. The Office of Fair Trading provides guidance on the main parts of the Act and the Regulations made under it as they come into force. Their leaflets, and help, are also available at local Citizens' Advice Bureaux, Consumer Advice Centres or Trading Standards Departments (in some areas called Consumer Protection or Weights and Measures Departments) of local authorities.

By its very nature the Act is bound to be complex, but the relevant points, as they affect the student of commerce, are as follows.

Licensing

Licensing of businesses offering consumer credit will curb unfair trading practices, and it is a criminal offence for consumer credit or consumer hire businesses to trade without a consumer credit licence. The various licence categories cover people who provide credit or hire from their own resources (such as banks, finance houses, TV rental firms and some high street shops); people who introduce others to sources of credit (including credit brokers, financial advisers, estate agents and those car dealers and shops that introduce customers to finance houses); and other categories including debt collectors and credit reference agencies, etc.

The Regulation came into effect on 1st October 1977.

The total charge for credit (TCC)

This is a measure of the total charges to the consumer when he borrows under a consumer credit agreement. This will include not only interest charges but, with certain exceptions, linked transactions, ie, any other contract which the borrower must make as part of the transaction; any contract for subsequent maintenance or security of equipment; or any charges arising out of the contract. For example, charges made under the agreement to service a washing machine sold on credit may be taken into account. If the buyer prefers to take out a maintenance contract with someone other than the seller, he is free to do so and such charges are not part of the TCC.

The exceptions mentioned above, which do **not** form part of the total charge for credit include any charge made to cash and credit customers alike (eg delivery charges on a new car); charges made against a creditor who defaults (fails to carry out his side of the agreement); and certain types of insurance premium.

The principle on which TCC is based is that there shall be 'truth in lending'—in credit advertising, in quotations and in written agreements. Under this consumers will be able to compare the actual cost of credit facilities offered by various businesses, and choose that which seems most suitable to them. It will provide an actual measure of the cost of obtaining credit.

Advertisements for credit must give detailed information, especially on the true rate of charge, as well as the total charge for credit. For instance, if you borrow £100 and pay back £109.50 in twelve monthly instalments, the flat rate of interest is $9\frac{1}{2}$ per cent, but this is not the true rate of interest, because

190

after the first monthly instalment you owe less than £100 and after each month's payment the debt is less. In fact, in this example, the true rate of interest is about $18\frac{1}{2}$ per cent (roughly equivalent to double the flat rate).

The Regulations, then, require that the rate of total charge for credit ('the **annual percentage rate of charge**'—APR) should be calculated on the basis of annual compounding—the effective annual rate.

Extortionate credit

If a customer considers that the terms of a credit agreement are extortionate, he may appeal to a County Court (Sheriff Court in Scotland). The Court may give relief to the debtor, and this will depend upon the whole of the credit agreement, including any transaction which affects the total charge for credit.

Agreements

Before signing an agreement for credit or hire the customer has to be given full details about the financial commitments (as outlined above) and must also be given a copy of the agreement. After signing, the customer can, for a small fee, receive further copies and ask for a statement of account. People who act as **guarantors** or give other security for credit agreements also have a right to obtain copies and other information.

The Act applies to **regulated agreements**, and these may be either consumer credit agreements, or consumer hire agreements.

Regulated consumer credit agreements These are agreements under which credit is provided to an individual for an amount not exceeding £5000 (excluding charges and deposits). There are certain exceptions, and among exempt consumer credit agreements is normal trade credit, and also low cost credit where the annual percentage rate (APR) does not exceed 13 per cent, or 1 per cent above Bank of England MLR (or bank rate) if this is higher.

The Act applies whether credit is provided as a fixed sum or on a running account basis and whether it is provided by the supplier of the goods or services or by a separate creditor (eg, a finance house).

Credit agreements regulated by the Consumer Credit Act in fact are divided into two kinds:

- Debtor-creditor-supplier agreements, and
- Debtor-creditor agreements. (See table below).

DEBTOR-CREDITOR-SUPPLIER AGREEMENTS
and
DEBTOR-CREDITOR AGREEMENTS

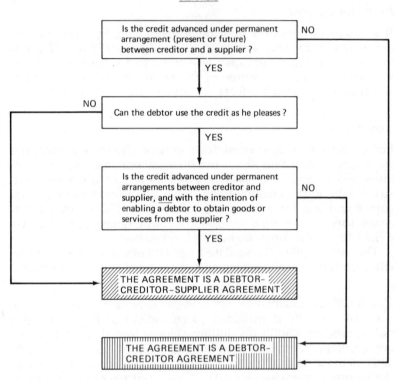

Start here

Is the credit advanced under permanent arrangement (present or future) between creditor and a supplier ? — NO

YES

Can the debtor use the credit as he pleases ? — NO

YES

Is the credit advanced under permanent arrangements between creditor and supplier, and with the intention of enabling a debtor to obtain goods or services from the supplier ? — NO

YES

THE AGREEMENT IS A DEBTOR-CREDITOR-SUPPLIER AGREEMENT

THE AGREEMENT IS A DEBTOR-CREDITOR AGREEMENT

An example of a debtor-creditor-supplier credit is a high street retailer arranging a personal loan for his customer from a finance house, for the purchase, say, of a washing machine. The use of a credit card or trading check in certain shops is also a debtor-creditor-supplier transaction, since there is a permanent agreement between the shop and the creditor. So far as the trader is concerned, these are cash sales, since he gets payment in full from the creditor, and the debt is then paid by the customer-

192

debtor to the creditor.

An example of a debtor-creditor agreement is an overdraft from the customer's bank to spend as he wishes.

Regulated consumer hire agreements These are those for the hire of goods (eg, apparatus, equipment, machinery) which satisfy five conditions:

- the hirer must be an individual
- it must not be a hire purchase agreement (which comes into the consumer credit agreement category)
- that the hiring can last for more than three months
- the payments must not exceed £5000
- it must not be an exempt agreement.

As mentioned before, goods on hire never become the property of the hirer.

Exempt consumer hire agreements apply only to meter or metering equipment for electricity, gas or water and for tele-communications apparatus where the owner is the Post Office or the Kingston-upon-Hull City Council (the only other body in the UK which runs a public telephone network).

Agreements signed off trade premises. If an agreement is signed at the trade premises of the seller, one statutory copy of the agreement is given to the customer, who then has no right to cancel the agreement. If the agreement is signed elsewhere (for example in the customer's home, or in a public house or restaurant, or in a car on the highway) the hirer must receive two statutory copies of the agreement, one immediately and another by post within seven days. Under this arrangement the debtor/hirer has a 'cooling-off period', since he has until the end of the fifth day following the date on which he received the second copy to cancel the agreement. Cancellation must be properly effected in writing.

If the goods have already been received, the debtor/hirer can retain them as surety against receiving any deposit he may have paid; and in any case he does not need to return them, but requires the seller to collect them. The customer is responsible for their safekeeping for twenty-one days, but his liability for them then ends.

Note that cancellation is not possible when there has been no personal contact between customer and salesman—eg by filling in a newspaper coupon to order goods. However, most reputable advertisers offer a money-back guarantee if goods are not satisfactory, and this should be looked for.

Termination of agreements   A debtor under a **consumer credit agreement** is entitled to terminate his agreement at any time by notice to the creditor and by paying all amounts due under the agreement. A minimum rebate, laid down by law, is allowed for early settlement.

Under a **hire purchase agreement**, or a conditional sale agreement, the debtor may terminate the agreement before final payment by giving notice. The debtor becomes liable to pay the sum necessary to bring his total payments up to 50 per cent of the total price, unless otherwise provided by the agreement.

Hire agreements may be terminated after eighteen months.

Default   If a customer breaks an agreement the trader must serve a 'default notice' before taking any action to enforce it. This notice will say how the customer has defaulted, and what must be done to put it right—giving at least seven days to do so.

Once a third or more of the total price has been paid on goods being bought on hire purchase or conditional sale, the trader cannot recover them without a court order. Neither can he enter premises for the repossession of goods without a court order. If goods are repossessed by an owner then the court may order repayment to the debtor of the whole or part of the money paid by him, and may order his release from the whole or part of the outstanding balance payable under the agreement.

Canvassing off trade premises

Traders are restricted in the way they can seek new credit or hire business by calling on people at home or stopping them in the street. Briefly, traders can now only call on people, to sell goods or services on credit or to hire out goods, if they possess a special licence. For example, a person going from door to door selling double-glazing will need a licensing authorisation if he arranges credit.

Under no circumstances can anyone call uninvited to offer loans or credit brokerage services, where there is no link with the supplier of goods or services.

The term 'canvassing' does not cover the use of the telephone or sending letters or circulars. It is illegal to send documents to people under eighteen inviting them to borrow money or obtain other credit facilities.

194

Equal liability

Under the Sale of Goods Act 1893, as amended by the Supply of Goods (Implied Terms) Act 1973—see Chapter 16—if the supplier does not fulfil his obligations, the customer can sue him for breach of contract—just as the supplier can sue a customer who refuses to pay. And if the supplier persuades a customer to enter a contract by making a false statement of fact, he may find himself in court for 'misrepresentation', and the customer's right to damages is governed in England, Wales and Northern Ireland principally by the Misrepresentation Act 1967, the Misrepresentation (Northern Ireland) Act 1967, and in Scotland by common law.

However, if credit is involved the provider of the credit is *equally liable with the seller* for any breach of contract or misrepresentation by the seller of goods or services. This applies to commercial credit agreements:

- made on or after 1 July 1977 (or earlier for HP agreements);
- for a cash price in excess of £30 and less than £10 000.

If a consumer has a complaint it is usually best to go back to the seller in the first instance, but if that fails he can now claim against the provider of credit as well. He can sue either or both, not only for faulty goods but also for consequential damages caused by faulty goods. The credit grantor may be a finance company, or a bank; or a credit card or trading check may have been accepted by the seller.

The aim is to protect customers, when a dealer cannot be traced or has gone out of business, and they are faced with having to pay off expensive credit agreements for defective, or even useless goods. Finance companies, credit card companies and the like will no doubt take great care to ensure that suppliers are of high standing, so as to avoid claims arising through no fault of their own. Many of the credit grantors are taking out insurance policies to cover themselves in the event of claims.

Credit reference agencies

When money is borrowed, or things hired or bought on credit, someone has to provide the cash. Before doing so they may consult a credit reference agency. This is an organisation which collects information about the financial standing of people (for example, how promptly they have paid their debts). Such information is collected from various sources, such as from local authorities, court reports and previous lenders, and is stored for future use.

Normally an agency does not give an opinion on whether the applicant is a suitable person to lend money to, but instead tells the trader what facts it has.

A credit reference agency is defined under the Consumer Credit Act 1974, as:

> a person carrying on a business comprising the furnishing of persons with information relevant to the financial standing of individuals, being information collected by the agency for that purpose.

Under the Act, credit reference agencies must be licensed by the Director General of Fair Trading and there are certain rights given to the consumer.

- As a result of a written request to a creditor, owner or negotiator, the consumer has a right to be supplied with the name and address of any credit reference agency approached for information about him.
- He can obtain a copy of any file kept on him by an agency, providing he makes a written request (enclosing a non-returnable fee of 25p). (Business consumers, such as sole traders and partnerships, have the right to receive only certain information—not the entire file.)
- The consumer can ask an agency to amend his file if he believes that it contains incorrect information and that he is likely to suffer as a result.

Disputes procedure is laid down, with time limits imposed but, if necessary, disagreements about the content of a file can be referred to the Director General for settlement.

The very existence of credit reference agencies, monitoring our financial transactions, means that we should not over commit ourselves since any debts unpaid will be recorded and may affect the availability of credit in the future.

It has already been seen that credit can be of great advantage in the modern consumer society, to the buyer, to the seller, to the manufacturer, and to the financier who supplies the money. Indeed, many financial institutions are anxious to participate, and credit is readily available to almost anyone with a reasonable and secure income. The Consumer Credit Act is designed to protect those wishing to take advantage of this, but purchasers must still remember that living on borrowed money means that one's income may become tied up for months or years ahead. Careful consideration of future needs and resources is still necessary.

Questions

1. A small company is offered some reconditioned machinery for £1250 cash or at a higher figure but on an instalment plan.
   (a) how much would the firm pay for the machinery on the basis of £1250 less 5 per cent cash discount?
   (b) the instalment plan requires a deposit of 8 per cent and 12 monthly repayments of £118. How much would the company pay in total for the machinery?
   (c) How much more would they pay by adopting the instalment plan rather than paying cash?

   (RSA)

2. Two of your friends, Joan and Stephen, will shortly be getting married. They have insufficient money to furnish their flat completely and have asked your advice as to whether they should buy the rest of their furniture on hire purchase. How would you advise them, commenting on the advantages and disadvantages?

   (SR)

3. (a) When buying goods on hire purchase the customer has—
   (i) the right to information
   (ii) the right to withdraw
   (iii) protection against repossession.
   Explain each of these.
   (b) How does the hire purchase system benefit
   (i) consumers
   (ii) retailers?
   (c) Mention *one* other way by which people can buy on credit.

   (MR)

4. If you wished to have a colour TV set you could buy it for cash, buy it on hire purchase or rent it.
   Explain the advantages of each of these methods and say, with reasons, which one you would choose.

   (YR)

5. (a) What is credit?
   (b) State one of the differences between a hire purchase agreement and a credit sale agreement.
   (c) What does the principle 'truth in lending' refer to in credit transactions under the Consumer Credit Act 1974?

6. Buy now—pay later. Explain briefly the various schemes *apart from hire purchase* which are available to enable people to do this.

   (YR)

13

Saving and investing

Today, so many items are bought on credit, using credit cards or deferred payment schemes (see Chapter 12), that it could be argued that there is no need to save.

However, it is still a wise precaution to save for 'a rainy day'. Provision must be made for the future; for getting married, for buying a house, for which a deposit will be required, for having a family and for retirement. There is also unplanned expenditure such as repairs to a car, to a house, or to equipment, or a journey to visit a sick relative, or even a fine for speeding. There are also predictable short-term needs, such as Christmas, birthdays and holidays. In general, then, it is still wise to have some money in reserve.

Sometimes people prefer to use their money to buy goods as investments. Antiques, pictures, gold, jewels, etc often appreciate in value, and can be sold when money is required, but there are drawbacks. Expert knowledge is needed when buying; valuable items have to be safeguarded and insured; and when the time comes to sell the goods may not bring as much as expected or needed. Buying property has been found to be a good investment, but houses, for instance, often take some time to sell.

No matter how little or how much we put by we want to be sure of two things:

that it is safe,
that it is readily available when required.

If it was put under a mattress it would be readily available; but it would not be safe from fire or burglary. Perhaps, too, it would be too accessible and would dwindle as we dipped into it! Another disadvantage would be that the amount of money stored away would stay exactly the same, but £100 hidden ten years' ago would not be worth the same today. So, therefore, we should look for a third aspect: that the amount saved should

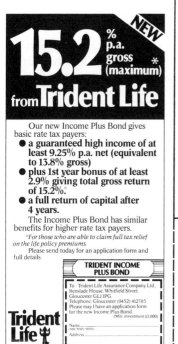
Newspaper advertisements of investment opportunities.

keep or, preferably, increase its value: ie *it should earn interest.*
Rather than let money lie idle it is wise to use it to gain
interest. The person concerned with quite small sums will find
it beneficial to invest sums not immediately required even

though it may be only for a short period, say a month. When very large sums are involved, however, it is possible to lend them to financial institutions for short periods, even overnight, to gain good and rapid interest. Experienced financiers are adept at making the most of the money they have at their disposal.

The amateur, though, can:

- study advertisements or announcements in the newspapers inviting investment;
- keep abreast of changes in savings schemes by reading the leaflets found in banks, post offices and building societies;
- consult *Money Which*, published by the Consumers' Association; or
- seek advice from an expert.

There are a number of institutions which will give interest on money deposited with them and, as mentioned in Chapter 9, they in turn re-invest the sums deposited with them (which will, of course, be very large in total). Generally speaking, the larger the amount available for investment the higher the rate of interest it will attract.

Income tax must be paid on most interest received and this should be remembered when comparing the rates of interest offered. Some institutions deduct tax, at the basic rate, before paying out. If they do not, the Inland Revenue regard this interest as 'unearned income', and investors paying income tax at the standard rate can expect to pay to the Inland Revenue about 30p for every £1 of interest received.

The main ways of saving money are through:

- National Savings Securities (National Savings Certificates, British Savings Bonds, Premium Savings Bonds)
- National Savings Bank
- National Girobank Deposit Account
- Contractual savings (Save As You Earn)
- Trustee Savings Banks
- Building Societies
- Clearing Banks
- Local Authority Bonds

In addition to these 'safe' ways of saving, which are really loans to the Government or to private enterprise, there are investments on the stock exchange and in unit trusts to consider. Both are discussed in detail in Chapter 9.

Buying **ordinary shares** is one of the riskiest forms of investment. It should not be undertaken lightly unless the buyer has other money not at risk, has reasonable financial knowledge and is able to study and understand market changes. Most daily newspapers include financial columns and the Financial Times is a specialist newspaper.

For persons wishing to invest in industry, in the hope of sharing profits, **unit trusts** carry less risk. This is a method of investment whereby money subscribed by many people is pooled in a fund, which is invested on behalf of the subscribers by the managers of the trust. Each subscriber acquires an interest in all the securities, and so receives interest on them all in proportion to his holding. Some unit trusts accept subscriptions as low as £10. Some trusts aim at obtaining a high income; others aim at growth in the value of the holdings. Some invest over a large range of ordinary shares, while others specialise in bank, insurance or investment trust shares, or put part of their money into manufacturing, commodities, mining or overseas companies.

Schemes are devised for regular monthly payments to the trust, and dividends can be paid at regular intervals or left in to accumulate capital.

A unit trust must be authorised by the Department of Trade under the Prevention of Fraud (Investments) Act of 1958, but it must be remembered that there is still an element of risk, since unit prices can fluctuate according to the state of the market.

Another form of saving is the **Endowment Assurance Policy** (see Chapter 14). By this the policyholder's life is insured for a sum which is payable after a certain number of years (usually not less than ten) or at his or her death, whichever is earlier.

Government savings schemes

As already stated, the Department for National Savings offers facilities for savings and investment through Savings Certificates, British Savings Bonds and Government Stock, through Premium Savings Bonds, National Savings Bank Accounts and Save As You Earn. Because Savings Department schemes have a fixed rate of interest, different issues are brought out from time to time offering new rates of interest. The previous issue is then withdrawn although deposits can remain intact and still earn interest.

National Savings Certificates

The National Savings Movement was started in 1916 to help finance the First World War by promoting savings. It also, of course, gained special importance during the Second World War

The symbol of the Department of National Savings.

when the Government was again needing money to provide arms. 'Save for Victory.'

It is perhaps one of the most widely known methods of saving because schools often form part of a local savings group. Children were once encouraged to get the savings habit by buying savings stamps which could be changed for cash or savings certificates. However, National Savings Stamps are no longer on sale.

Each savings certificate unit costs £1 but the minimum purchase is £5 (five units) and they can be bought from post offices, banks and through National Savings Groups. The maximum number that an individual may hold varies according to the Issue: the maximum holding for the fourteenth issue is 3000 units (£3000) but earlier and later issues will vary.

Savings certificates are intended primarily as an investment for individuals and cannot be held by registered companies, public bodies or firms.

National Savings Certificates are not available at post offices in Northern Ireland, but Ulster Savings Certificates and Index-Linked Savings Certificates are comparable investments.

To get full benefit from savings certificates they should be kept for the full term (which is usually four or five years), although they will continue to earn interest after that time. In order to cash certificates, an application form must be completed and at least eight clear working days' notice is required. If they are cashed within one year of purchase no interest is paid, but after one year interest is added to the cash price. The longer the certificates have been held, the greater the interest payable. Interest is completely free of income tax, and different rates of interest apply depending on which issue is held.

As an alternative to cashing the certificates the proceeds may be reinvested in the current Issue or deposited in a National Savings Bank Account, or used to purchase Premium Savings Bonds.

Index-linked National Savings Certificates

These certificates (popularly known as 'Granny Bonds') were first issued in 1975 and are meant to protect the 'nest egg' savings of elderly people, as the money deposited is linked to the *UK General Index of Retail Prices (RPI)*. This means that the money received for the certificates when cashed will be increased in proportion to the rise in prices.

Every month the Government collects the average prices paid for essentials, such as food, clothing, rents, transport, fuel, etc., and compares these with the prices paid in the previous month. If prices rise, RPI will rise, or fall if prices have fallen.

Anyone can now buy Index-linked National Savings Certificates, which are designed to protect savings from the effects of inflation. The certificates are £10 per unit, the maximum holding is £5000, and may be bought from post offices, Trustee Savings Banks and through some National Savings Groups.

Certificates that have been held for a minimum of one year will be revalued according to the RPI when cashed. All repayments are completely free of income tax.

British Savings Bonds

These can be bought at any bank, Savings Bank Post Office and through stockbrokers and may be bought by companies and organisations as well as by individuals.

Bonds are £5 each with a maximum holding (Jubilee Issue) of £10 000. Interest, which is taxable, is payable half-yearly and the amount varies according to the issue held. Bonds reach maturity after five years and a tax free bonus of 4 per cent is then due. One month's notice is required for encashment but no bonus is payable when bonds are cashed before maturity.

Government stock

The Department for National Savings undertakes the purchase of Government securities on the National Savings Stock Register.

Government stock may be held by almost anyone including children, societies and corporate bodies. Up to £5000 cash value of stock may be bought on any one day but there is no limit to the total amount held.

To buy stock, an investment application form (obtainable at post offices) is sent to the Bonds and Stock Office, Blackpool, together with the purchase money. To sell stock a sale application form enclosing the Investment Certificate is sent to the same office. Commission charges are payable on each transaction. Government stock can also be bought through a broker or bank, but it would then have to be sold through them, and not through the Bonds and Stock Office.

The price at which stock is bought or sold varies, but some indication of the current market price can usually be obtained from financial columns of the daily press.

Dividends are taxable and must be declared to the Inland Revenue.

Premium Savings Bonds

These are also a Government security but instead of earning interest the bonds carry, after a qualifying period of three months, a chance of winning a tax-free prize. The monthly jackpot prize is £250 000 with five prizes of £10 000 and fifty of £5000 each. In addition there are prizes ranging from £50 to £1000. The weekly jackpot prize is £100 000 and prizes of £50 000 and £25 000.

The winning numbers are generated by ERNIE (Electronic Random Number Indicator Equipment).

Premium Savings Bonds can be bought at post offices and banks by any person over the age of sixteen (Bonds may be bought for children under 16 by a parent or legal guardian), but cannot be held jointly or by corporate bodies, clubs, societies, etc. The Bonds are in units of £1, sold in multiples of £5, and the maximum holding is 10 000 units (£10 000).

Premium Bonds are repayable at face value and as such should not be regarded as a savings medium because unless the holder wins, the cash value of the Bond will be less than it was at the time of purchase. The National Savings Department puts the odds for a single bond winning at 10 800 to one.

The National Savings Bank (NSB)

This has branches at post offices all over the country and has two types of account: Ordinary Accounts, and Investment Accounts offering a higher rate of interest. Accounts may be held by individuals, joint holders, children, clubs, societies and other non-profit-making organisations, with a minimum deposit of 25p for an Ordinary Account and £1 for an Investment Account.

The Ordinary Account is designed for day-to-day needs, as withdrawals up to £50 can be made on demand at any Savings Bank Post Office on production of the Bank Book. Larger amounts can be withdrawn on application to headquarters. The maximum amount which a depositor may have in an Ordinary Account is £10 000. Interest is credited to the account and the first £70 of interest per annum is free of income tax.

Investment Accounts are designed for bigger, longer-term saving, with a limit of £200 000. The interest is taxable, and as it is not deducted at source it must be declared annually to the Inland Revenue. One month's notice is required for withdrawals, and forms for this are available at Savings Bank Post Offices.

Gift tokens

These may be purchased from post offices as presents and may be exchanged for or put towards the purchase of National (or Ulster) Savings Certificates, British Savings Bonds, Premium Savings Bonds, or deposited in a Savings Bank Account. They are £5 in value with a maximum of six on any one card.

The National Girobank deposit account

This was launched in April 1978 for customers of the National Girobank (see Chapter 11). Stationery is provided for:

- deposits to be made in cash at a post office;
- transferring money from a current account;
- posting cheques to the National Girobank at Bootle; or
- standing orders for regular deposits.

Withdrawals are made by transferring money back into the holder's current account. Interest is credited to the deposit account and is paid without deduction of tax.

The Save As You Earn Scheme (SAYE)

This is a contractual savings scheme. This means that the saver signs a contract to make sixty regular monthly contributions

DEPOSIT - NATIONAL SAVINGS BANK

| | cash | 1 | | cheque | 2 |

Please enter the Account Particulars EXACTLY AS PRINTED IN THE BANK BOOK

| Date | Month | Year 197 |

Office, code words, or letters (if any)

No.

AMOUNT DEPOSITED

POUNDS | PENCE

£

FOR POST OFFICE USE

Amount of Cheque £..................

BALANCE AFTER THIS DEPOSIT | POUNDS | PENCE

£

Deposit to account of (NAME and ADDRESS IN BLOCK LETTERS)

M..
(Mr., Mrs., Miss, etc., Initials and Surname)

Address ....
(including postcode)
....

SB 2CP ITEM CODE 620001   56-7905 1/79 Cr.P.C

1 Account parts checked.
2 Amount checked.
3 Entered in Bank book.
4 Balance (if in book) entered above.

Date Stamp

Initials ....

WITHDRAWAL ON DEMAND (LIMIT £50) NATIONAL SAVINGS BANK

Please enter the Account Particulars EXACTLY AS PRINTED IN THE BANK BOOK

| Date | Month | Year 197 |

Office, code words or letters (if any)

No.

AMOUNT OF WITHDRAWAL

POUNDS | PENCE

£

FOR POST OFFICE USE

3

BALANCE AFTER THIS WITHDRAWAL | POUNDS | PENCE

£

Address of depositor..
(including postcode)

TO BE WRITTEN IN THE PRESENCE OF THE PAYING OFFICER

I acknowledge receipt of the above amount.

Depositor's Signature.. (M.................)
SB10 ITEM CODE 620029   56-8238 3/79 QP   (Enter Mr., Mrs., or Miss)

1 Account parts and signature checked.
2 Entered in Bank book.
3 Bank book retained (if appropriate).
4 Balance (if in book) entered above.

Date Stamp

Initials....................

NSB deposit and withdrawal forms.

(maximum £20 a month) over five years. These contributions can be paid:

- in cash,
- by banker's standing order, or
- by deduction from pay if the employer runs a SAYE scheme.

Since SAYE is a regular savings scheme it is wise to start off with an amount that can be maintained from income; if more can be afforded later a further contract can be taken out, as long as it is within the upper limit allowed.

The saver may cancel the contract and apply for repayment before the five year period is complete. In this case, interest is payable after one year but at a lower rate than if the contract had run its full term.

If, after completion of the five year contract the sum is left in for a further two years, a bonus is paid without further contributions being made. Interest and bonuses are tax free and are paid when the whole sum is withdrawn.

The National Savings SAYE scheme, third issue, is index-linked, and may be started at any high street bank, Trustee Savings Bank or Post Office.

Building societies also offer SAYE schemes and, for the second issue the equivalent of fourteen months' savings is added after the five year period of contributions. If the completed savings are left with the society for a further two years the tax free bonus is doubled.

Trustee Savings Banks (TSB)

Most of the Trustee Savings Banks were founded in the nineteenth century to encourage small savings and were originally entirely for that purpose. They operate under their own trustees but are subject to the supervision of the Trustee Savings Bank Central Board and the Registrar of Friendly Societies. There has been a planned programme of amalgamations and in June 1977 there were nineteen individual banks compared with sixty-seven in 1975.

A recommendation that TSBs should be freed from Government control to develop full banking services for the personal sector was accepted by the Government in 1974. The Trustee Savings Bank Act 1976 gave TSBs the power to provide a full banking service including credit services. It also removed the requirement that deposits should be invested with the National Debt Commissioners (for investment in Government securities). However, the TSBs having been freed from Government control under the 1976 Act, the Treasury argued that they must compete on more equal terms with their competitors, and from November 1979 they lost one of their main advantages over the high street banks: that is, the tax exemption on the first £70 of interest on savings accounts.

Recent developments by TSBs are loans to householders for home improvements and to small businesses.

In addition to the current account service, the TSBs have two savings departments, known as Ordinary and Special Investment.

Deposits in the **Ordinary Department** are similar to deposits in the National Savings Bank, the first £70 of interest per annum being free of tax; except that interest on NSB and TSB ordinary accounts in the same name is added together in determining tax-free interest. (But see change from November 1979 mentioned above.) Most withdrawals from ordinary accounts are normally paid on demand.

Deposits in the **Special Investment Department** receive a

higher rate of interest and withdrawals may be subject to at least one month's notice. Interest on Investment Accounts is paid without deduction of tax and is, therefore, taxable. An Investment Account can be opened by any depositor who has an Ordinary Account.

The TSBs also offer a SAYE scheme, and in 1967 the TSB movement was authorised to set up its own Unit Trust, which also offers Life Assurance-linked monthly savings plans as well as various unit trust investments.

Building Societies

Building societies provide an important channel for the investment of small personal savings, and the major source of long-term loans for house purchase. The purchase of property is, in itself, regarded as a wise investment and is, therefore, a means of saving.

The first building societies were founded in industrial areas in the late eighteenth century and were small groups in which the members, by paying fixed monthly sums, gradually accumulated funds which were used to acquire land and build houses. These houses were then allotted to members and when every member had acquired his own house and every house had been paid for by members' subscriptions, the society was dissolved.

However, after about 1850 there came into existence a new type of society: funds were borrowed not only from those who were saving in order to buy a house but also from people who had savings to invest but had no intention of borrowing. In this way, the society had funds to make loans with less delay than before and it was no longer necessary to bring the society to an end when the original members' houses were paid for.

Today, all building societies are of the 'permanent' type and some societies still have 'permanent' in their name, eg the Leeds Permanent Building Society.

Investment facilities

Although no building society can guarantee mortgage facilities to an investor, it may well give special consideration and priority to those who have been saving with it for a reasonable period of time. In order to have funds to lend building societies must attract savings, and they do this by offering competitive and attractive rates of interest.

The interest offered is tax-paid; tax at the basic rate having been deducted by the society. This means that unless tax is

208

payable by the investor at a higher rate, further tax should not be deducted. On the other hand, non-tax payers might be wiser seeking a form of investment where tax is not deducted at source as the tax paid is not reclaimable.

Rates of interest, which are usually fixed by the directors of the society, may be varied from time to time in accordance with changes in monetary conditions.

The maximum amount that can be invested with a society is £15 000 (for joint accounts this would be £30 000).

There are two main investment facilities offered to the public: 'shares' and 'deposits' and about 95 per cent of all investors in building societies invest in shares.

A share account This is the simpler of the two and can be opened with as little as £1 (one fully paid share). Interest is paid twice yearly and can be credited to the account or paid out to the holder. Withdrawals are normally paid on demand except for substantial sums when short notice may be required.

Deposit accounts These can be opened with as little as 5p and added to as convenient. The money deposited is readily available and depositors have a prior claim over shareholders on the society's assets. The rate of interest is slightly less than that for share account holders.

Other forms of investment offered are:

Monthly savings plan This is designed for regular savings of an amount not less than £1 and not exceeding £40 and for any period of time to suit the investor. Interest is allowed up to the date of withdrawal and is higher than that for share and deposit accounts.

SAYE These schemes are offered by some societies. This is a five year term for regular monthly savings (maximum £20 a month) and has already been discussed above.

Term shares, or Bondshares These are for those seeking a higher return on their investment in return for a commitment to leave the savings intact for either two or three years. The minimum investment is £500; each investment is treated as a separate account and odd amounts cannot be paid in as they may with share and deposit accounts. No withdrawals are allowed until the end of the contract period.

The tax-paid interest offered is $\frac{1}{2}$ per cent above that for share accounts for a two year term and 1 per cent above for a three year term. Interest is calculated half-yearly and can either be credited to an account or paid to the investor.

Mortgage operations

The main business of building societies is to make advances on the security of freehold or leasehold property. For each advance a **mortgage deed** is drawn up which gives the society a legal interest in the property until the loan is repaid. Most loans are made on the security of private houses for owner-occupiers, although loans are occasionally made on the security of shops, blocks of flats, farms and commercial premises, etc.

The advances are usually repayable by fixed monthly instalments, which include both capital and interest, over periods ranging up to thirty years. Building societies will usually lend about 80 per cent either of the property's value or of its purchase price, *whichever is the lower*. (Sometimes they are prepared to lend up to 95 per cent depending on the circumstances.)

If, therefore, a house is for sale at £15 000 but is valued by an independent valuer at £14 000, this means that the prospective buyer would have to find £1000 in addition to that part of the purchase price not covered by the building society mortgage.

Interest rates fluctuate and the building societies usually offer a choice when they rise: either the monthly repayment figure is increased accordingly or the term of the loan is extended. To encourage home ownership interest paid on mortgage loans is subject to relief from income tax and is regarded as non-taxable income. In simple figures, if, say, a person's taxable income is £3000 and he has paid £500 interest on his mortgage loan, this reduces his taxable income to £2500 less personal allowances.

When considering an application for a mortgage, a building society is likely to consider the following (not necessarily in this order):

- whether the applicant is in a steady occupation
- whether the applicant has a steady income, sufficient to cope with mortgage repayments
- the size of the loan
- the age of the applicant in relation to the length of the loan
- how much the applicant is contributing towards the total cost
- whether the applicant has been a regular saver with the society
- the type of property (new property is viewed more favourably than old) and its condition, value and position
- whether the applicant is a first-time buyer (they often receive priority).

Houseowners often raise funds by taking a **second mortgage** usually from a finance company. Interest rates are higher than those charged by a building society on a first mortgage because in the event of the houseowner defaulting the second mortgages has second claim on the property.

In 1968 the Government introduced the **Option Mortgage Scheme**. This was designed to help those with insufficient income to take full advantage of tax reliefs on mortgage interest payments (ie, low wage-earners paying little or no tax). The scheme enables people to forgo tax relief in exchange for a Government subsidy of roughly equivalent value. Also under this scheme people may obtain a 100 per cent mortgage on cheaper properties, and loans granted by building societies are guaranteed jointly by the Government and by insurance companies.

More recent help by the Government is the **Homeloan Scheme** for first-time buyers, introduced in December 1978. This is a loan of £600 which will be interest-free for the first five years, and a grant of between £40 and £110 which does not have to be repaid. Both loan and grant will come from the Government but will be arranged by the organisation that is providing the mortgage. The conditions are that the applicant must have £600 to match it, £300 of which must have been on deposit for a year, and must have been saving under the scheme for at least two years with an approved savings organisation (such as a building society, bank or National Savings Bank).

To join the scheme does not, however, guarantee a mortgage and there are upper and lower limits with the Environment Secretary having the power to vary the figures.

The scheme should have the effect of encouraging saving, especially by the young, and there is competition between the savings media with bonuses and gift schemes being offered.

It is also possible to obtain mortgages from local authorities or by an endowment mortgage from an insurance company. In the latter case the amount of the loan for the property is the sum assured on which the policy holder pays premiums plus interest charges. At the end of the term, or at the policy holder's death, whichever is earlier, the sum assured is used to pay off the loan. A more expensive kind of endowment policy is 'with-profits' whereby, at the termination of the policy, a sum of money is paid to the policy holder in addition to the repayment of the loan.

Advice about mortgages can be obtained from building societies, from mortgage brokers, estate agents or banks.

Ways of saving
This table is for comparison only as interest rates are likely to be varied from time to time by the institutions concerned.

	Interest	Maximum holding	Withdrawal
National Savings Bank: Ordinary Accounts	5% pa (First £70 pa tax free, including any TSB interest.)	£10 000	Immediately for £50 or under. Within a few days for larger amounts.
Investment Accounts	12% pa, without deduction of tax.	£50 000	One month's notice.
Premium Savings Bonds	No interest: chance of winning fixed sums by electronic draw. Prizes tax free.	£3000	Within about a week.
National Savings Certificates: 18th Issue	None paid annually, but the Certificate grows in value over a fixed number of years. The 18th Issue gives about 8.4% pa interest if Certificates are not cashed for the five year term. Tax free.	£1500	At least eight clear working days.
Retirement Issue	Index-linked plus 4% bonus if held for five years. Tax free.	£700	ditto
£5 British Savings Bond	$9\frac{1}{2}$% pa without deduction of tax. Full term bonus of 4% tax free (ie after five years).	£10 000	One month's notice.
National Girobank Deposit Accounts	10% + 1% on minimum balance in the account over six months. Interest paid without deduction of tax.	No limit	Immediate transfer to current account.

Type	Interest / Return	Limit	Withdrawal terms
Save As You Earn 2nd issue (Building Societies)	8.5% pa after five years. 8.66% after seven years. Tax free.	£20 a month (minimum £1)	Short period of notice but no interest paid if under one year. 6% pa if between one and five years.
3rd issue (National Savings)	Index-linked with tax free bonus after seven years.	£20 a month (minimum £4)	ditto
Trustee Savings Banks: Savings Accounts	4% pa. No tax on first £70 of interest per annum—including NSB interest (until November 1979).	No limit	Less than £50 on demand: some banks need a few days for larger sums.
Investment Accounts	6–9% pa $\quad$ without		
Term or fixed Deposit Accounts	6–10% pa $\quad$ deduction of tax	No limit	At least one month's notice.
Building Societies	8 to $9\frac{1}{4}$% pa according to type of investment or deposit. Tax paid at basic rate.	£15 000	Within a few days but a certain amount on demand.
Deposits with Clearing Banks	10% pa without deduction of tax. May vary from bank to bank.	No limit	Seven days' notice.
Local Authority Bonds	10–$12\frac{3}{4}$% pa gross, depending on amount and term, but tax paid at basic rate.	No upper limit but minimum may be £100 to £5000.	Fixed term of investment.
Deposits with Finance Houses	Depends on term, eg one month $8\frac{1}{2}$%, one year $10\frac{1}{4}$%	No limit but minimum may be between £100 and £1000.	Withdrawal terms vary.
Unit Trust shares	Dividends vary depending if 'Income' or 'Growth' Trust. Taxable	Variable.	Can be sold back to the managers of the Trust.
Endowment Assurance Policy	Bonuses vary according to amount and the time for which the policy is taken out. Tax relief on premiums	No limit	Can be realised (sold for cash) before maturity but much of the benefit is lost.

Clearing bank deposits

Clearing banks and their services are discussed fully in Chapter 8. Because tax is not deducted at source the rate of interest for bank deposit and savings accounts is higher than that offered by the building societies. However, for tax payers this interest is part of their taxable income and, as such, is declarable to the Inland Revenue. But to non-tax payers the higher rate is beneficial.

Interest is credited to the account and payments and withdrawals are easy to make over the bank counter. Although the regulations state that seven days' notice is required for withdrawals, in practice amounts can be withdrawn or transferred on demand. The account holder, though, may suffer a loss of interest for seven days.

Savings account deposits below a specified limit may earn less interest from that paid on deposit accounts; over that limit the rate is the same.

Local authority bonds

Local authorities may raise loans to finance capital expenditure which may be by means of private mortgages; by issuing stock upon the Stock Exchange; and by bonds which may or may not be quoted on the Stock Exchange.

Investors wishing to lend money to a local authority should contact it direct or watch for advertisements in the newspapers. Bonds can also be bought through stockbrokers or banks. Interest is often quoted gross but basic rate tax (which is reclaimable by non-tax payers) is deducted at source.

The minimum investment is usually fairly substantial, eg, £250 for one authority, £1000 for another and £5000 for another, and is for a minimum period of time (perhaps one year to five years). Therefore this form of investment is for a lump sum which is not required in the immediate future.

Although at the beginning of this chapter savings were encouraged for personal reasons it should not be overlooked that savings are vital to government, industry and commerce, for without investment they would flounder. For this reason successive governments encourage savings:

- by special tax free savings scheme through the Post Office;
- by introducing the SAYE scheme so that savings can be deducted from pay;
- by introducing Premium Savings Bonds, giving the public a chance to gamble;

- by giving tax relief on life assurance premiums and on home loan interest (both forms of saving); and
- by giving concessions to first-time house buyers if they have savings of their own.

This illustrates the importance of saving to governments, to institutions and to individuals.

Questions

1. Give *three* reasons why a person might prefer to invest his money in shares rather than place it in a bank.

(RSA)

2. Suppose you had £1000 to invest in Local Corporation Loans or the National Savings Bank. How would each one compare with regard to:

(EM)

(a) safety; (b) rate of interest; (c) ease of withdrawal.

3. Describe one actual method of saving
   (a) through a clearing bank;
   (b) through the Post Office;
   (c) through the stock exchange.

(SRE)

4. Study the following advertisement and then answer the questions below.

$8\frac{1}{2}\%$ Interest per annum	BRITISH SAVINGS BONDS	Plus 3% maturity bonus after five years

(a) Where can the above bonds be purchased?
(b) In what amounts are they sold?
(c) Explain '3 per cent maturity bonus'.
(d) Give three disadvantages of investing in these securities.
(e) A boy was bought £100 of British Savings bonds to be cashed when he was twenty-one. How much interest would be accrued in the five year period?

(EM)

5. Describe the services provided by a building society for,
   (a) the saver   (b) the borrower

(NR)

6. What is a unit trust? What are the differences between a general and a specialised unit trust? What advantages does the purchase of units offer to the small investor?

(SW)

215

7. If you were saving money regularly, you could:
    (a) open a deposit account at a commercial bank,
    (b) open an account with a building society,
    (c) take out a life endowment assurance policy,
    (d) buy units in a unit trust,
    (e) buy stocks or shares on the Stock Exchange.

(YR)

Explain the advantages and disadvantages of *three* of these methods.

8. (i)   Give three reasons why people should save.
   (ii) What advantages do unit trusts offer to savers, over the facilities of the National Savings Bank or a building society?
   (iii) Name two types of savings organisations which offer the small short-term saver the most favourable terms and the most comprehensive facilities.

(NI)

9. Is buying your own house still a wise investment, or is it more profitable to employ your money elsewhere? If you were to decide to purchase a house explain in detail *two* types of mortgage and state from whom they were obtainable.

(SW)

10. You are a taxpayer wishing to save a regular sum of money each month over a period of time. There are several facilities available to you which will give you either income tax relief on your investment or tax free interest. Name *five* such facilities and explain in detail the advantages and disadvantages of *one* of the methods you select.

(SW)

14

Insurance

Insurance gives protection against certain risks. People take out insurance against many kinds of accidents and losses. They can insure against loss by fire, loss by theft, damages from accidents to their property, or to themselves. They must also insure against having to compensate other people whom they may injure, say in a road accident, or while on their premises. For this protection regular small payments, called premiums, are paid to the insurance company, so that if the calamity happens the company will make good the loss by paying out a sum in compensation.

An Act of Parliament dealing with insurance—the spreading of risk—in 1601 states: 'By means of which policies of assurance. . . the loss lighteth rather easily upon many, than heavily upon few.'

The premiums paid to the insurance company are paid into a pool and compensations for loss or damage are paid out of this 'Common Fund'. By 'pooling their risks' in this way, the insured gain some peace of mind, without fear of ruin should a fire, or other disaster, destroy their belongings or property.

The insurance company must make sure that the contributions to the Common Fund are adequate to cover claims made by those who have suffered loss, and premiums are calculated scientifically, in the case of life contracts by **actuaries** and for non-life contracts by underwriters, who calculate the risk involved by statistical records. The pool must also be looked after carefully and invested wisely so that the interest obtained can be used to swell the fund.

These investment departments are in the hands of very experienced people, with considerable knowledge of the selection of stocks and shares. Their resposibility is great because their shareholders and their policy-holders rely on their skill. Their investments cover all kinds of British Government and Commonwealth Government stocks, foreign government stocks, debentures, preference stocks and, increasingly, ordinary shares in industrial companies. (See Chapter 9, Finance for industry, for explanation of terms.) They also invest in property. Their aim is to achieve the best possible return consistent with security. The funds are held to meet future liabilities a long time ahead, and so they can be invested with an eye to long-term growth. On the other hand, non-life funds—the reserve behind the fire, accident and marine underwriting—must be readily available to meet sudden large losses caused by catastrophes such as floods and hurricanes. British insurance has won world-wide confidence by its ability to pay claims promptly and in full, and that is why so many people in other countries insure their risks in Britain.

People can insure themselves against many kinds of risk, but there are some risks which cannot be insured. These **uninsurable risks** are those which are not measurable by past experience. Normally the insurer is able to assess the size of the premium by the number of times that a particular event has occurred in a particular set of circumstances, over a past number of years. If an event is not so measurable, then it is uninsurable. A businessman, for example, cannot insure himself against the event of his business failing through his own incompetence; likewise a retailer cannot insure loss of money on stock which has gone out of fashion or out of date.

Principles of Insurance

There are three main principles of insurance:

- Insurable Interest
- Utmost Good Faith
- Indemnity

Insurable interest

means that the insured event would directly result in loss to the person taking out the policy. The insured property must be his own, or he must rent it: the insured life must be his own, or that of his wife. You cannot insure the life of an elderly person next door, just because you know he is very old and likely to die soon. This would be a gamble, and is prevented by law. It is possible, however, to insure the life of a partner in a business if his death were to result in financial difficulties by the remaining partner.

DEPARTMENTS IN LARGE GROUP OF INSURANCE COMPANIES

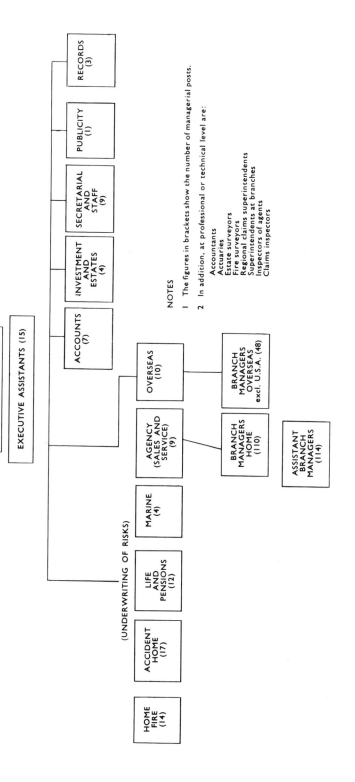

GENERAL MANAGER (I)

EXECUTIVE ASSISTANTS (15)

(UNDERWRITING OF RISKS)

HOME FIRE (14)

ACCIDENT HOME (17)

LIFE AND PENSIONS (12)

MARINE (4)

AGENCY (SALES AND SERVICE) (9)

OVERSEAS (10)

BRANCH MANAGERS HOME (110)

BRANCH MANAGERS OVERSEAS excl. U.S.A. (48)

ASSISTANT BRANCH MANAGERS (114)

ACCOUNTS (7)

INVESTMENT AND ESTATES (4)

SECRETARIAL AND STAFF (9)

PUBLICITY (1)

RECORDS (3)

NOTES

1 The figures in brackets show the number of managerial posts.

2 In addition, at professional or technical level are:

   Accountants
   Actuaries
   Estate surveyors
   Fire surveyors
   Regional claims superintendents
   Superintendents at branches
   Inspectors of agents
   Claims inspectors

Utmost good faith (uberrima fides)

When a person wishes to take out insurance he must be completely honest in stating absolutely everything that is relevant to the proposed risk: he must show utmost good faith. The insurer has to rely on the information given him by the client and it is obvious that if the proposer withholds information which would affect the willingness of the insurer to accept the risk, then the insurer is not bound by the contract of the insurance. If, for instance, a person suffering from a heart condition fails to disclose this on his proposal, and therefore is not required to have a medical examination, his death later from a heart attack may cause the insurance company to disclaim liability. Either the insurance might have been refused, or the premiums charged made much higher.

Utmost good faith continues throughout the term of the policy. If the person with a life policy or personal accident policy takes up a dangerous occupation or sport, he must inform the insurers. This would be the case if he gave up, say, an office job for work on an oil rig; or took up hang-gliding as a hobby.

Indemnity

This is the third principle of British insurance. It states that you are not allowed to make a profit out of a loss. The object of the principle of indemnity is to place the insured person as far as possible in the same position as he was before the event happened. For instance, if a second-hand car is stolen, the compensation will be assessed on its present-day worth and not its original cost. If compensation is paid out and then the car is recovered, the insurance company takes possession of the car and sells it to recover some of the money paid out to the owner. Also, if the owners of a wreck receive compensation, the wreck is inherited by the insurer, or insurers, and they then have the moneys received from salvage of the wreck. This is called **subrogation**, and also allows insurance companies the right to sue other parties for negligence causing the accident.

A further condition of indemnity is that the insurer is not allowed to profit from loss by double insuring; for instance insuring his house with two different companies and then claiming from each. However, a more usual case of double insurance is if two policies overlap. Claim forms require the claimant to state whether any other insurance company has any interest in the loss, and this must be honestly answered. If more than one company is involved, then the companies apportion the compensation paid.

It has become possible with some companies to insure on a 'new for old' basis, so that the cost of replacement is covered, and new items may be purchased. However, much higher premiums are charged, and it is essential to maintain insurance to cover rising values.

This question of indemnity does not, of course, apply to life policies, or to personal accident policies, because if a person loses a limb, he cannot be placed in the same position as he was before the accident. A fixed sum is therefore paid, depending on the sum assured. The assured sum can be as large as the proposer wishes and the premium is calculated accordingly, assuming that medical reports or examinations are satisfactory.

Procedure

Whatever type of insurance is required, the procedure is the same. Advice can be sought from **insurance brokers** who are not 'tied' to one insurance company, but can advise clients

TAKING OUT AN INSURANCE POLICY

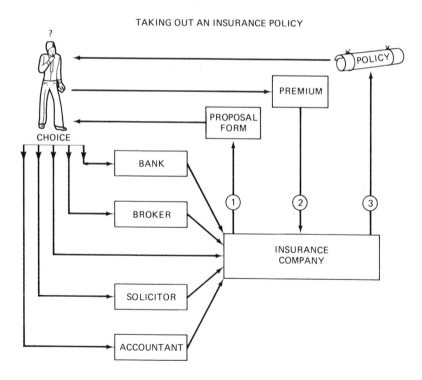

which insurance company offers the best terms and conditions for the type of policy they wish to take out. Banks, solicitors and accountants also give advice and will arrange insurances for their customers. The offices of insurance companies, or their agents, can also be approached, so that terms can be compared. Often, of course, the person wishing to take out an insurance goes to his usual, or his family's favourite insurance company without checking to find out if better terms can be found elsewhere.

When the insurance company has been chosen, a **proposal form** is completed and signed as being a true statement of the facts. The questions are quite searching and vary according to the type of insurance cover required. The form signed by the insured person is called the **declaration**, and is regarded as an important legal document, as it is a statement that he is telling the truth.

If the proposal is accepted by the insurance company, a **policy** is drawn up, which is a contract between the insured and the insurer. The policy has many clauses, conditions and exceptions and although it may be difficult for the layman to understand, it should be scrutinised very carefully to see that sufficient cover has been obtained.

The proposal form sets out all the details required to assess the **premium**—the sum paid weekly, monthly, quarterly or annually to the insurer for insurance cover. These premiums can be paid by banker's order, direct debit or by paying at the local insurance office, or to the insurance agent who calls on policy holders to collect premiums. Some insurance companies offer a reduction in the premium if it is paid direct through a bank account, as they are sure of getting their money on time.

In the event of a mishap requiring compensation, the insured notifies the insurance office at the very earliest opportunity and a **claim form** has to be completed. Companies usually set a time limit of twenty-eight days for claims to be made, and may reject them after this period. The police also have to be informed in cases of theft or burglary. Full details have to be stated when claiming and the circumstances and amount of the claim are then thoroughly scrutinised and investigated by the insurer. If the claim is justified, insurance companies take a pride in settling promptly. However, there are sometimes complications. If an article, or property is under-insured, the company may pay out only a proportion and, unless special provision has been made on a New for Old basis, claims for household articles, for example, are calculated on the cost of the article, less wear and tear depreciation. Remember that the insured should not be better off after the event. In cases of death or a fire under suspicious circumstances, insurance companies have experienced investigators to look into the affair before settling a claim. Likewise, if a valuable piece of jewellery is said to be lost, the insurers will try to make quite sure that it has not been sold or hidden. There are, also, cases from time to time when persons go 'missing' in order for their dependents to claim their life assurance.

Types of insurance

The main types of insurance are:

- marine, aviation and transport
- property, including fire and theft
- life assurance
- personal accident and sickness
- motor vehicle
- employer's liability
- public liability
- products liability

There is no real difference between the terms 'insurance' and 'assurance' but it is common usage to use 'assurance' to cover those events, such as death or retirement, that will assuredly happen, and 'insurance' to cover the risks of events which may or may not happen, such as road accidents, fire and burglary.

Marine insurance

Marine insurance is a complicated and costly business, the main sections being the hull of the vessel, the cargo, freight and ship-owner's liability. Freight, in insurance terms, is the charge for carrying cargo, not the cargo itself, and the ship-owner is not legally due to receive it until the cargo has been safely delivered. However, he often does, and therefore if the cargo goes overboard, he is liable for the cost of the cargo and its freight. A ship-owner's liability ranges from docks, wharves, beaches, and from fixed installations to crew and passengers. The amount of insurance cover required is so vast that the amount is underwritten by several underwriters, rather than being covered by one syndicate alone which might then be ruined should a disaster occur. (See details under the section on Lloyds.)

Similar conditions apply to aviation and other forms of transport.

Property insurance

Property insurance began as fire insurance, but the need arose for cover for a wider range of risks. It now includes not only fire, storm and tempest but damage caused by burst pipes, impacts, explosions, burglary, aircraft, collapse of television aerials and falling trees, as well as accidental damage to fittings and fixed glass, and householder's liabilities to the public, should they sustain injury on the premises. Insurance policies state, however, that the householder should take every precaution to take care of his property and some remission may be given on premiums for special precautions such as burglar alarms and fire sprinkling devices. Claims may be disallowed if the householder has been found to be negligent.

Contents can also be insured against the same perils and special cover can be arranged for frozen food, television sets, valuables, personal effects and credit cards.

As with all policies, the policyholder should read the small print very carefully to make sure what is and what is not covered. Some insurance companies offer a 'new for old' contents insurance policy, where replacement value is given for items lost or damaged. However, this form of insurance is more expensive and it is particularly important that the property is insured for its full value.

For especially valuable items that require 'all risks' cover, insurance companies may ask for valuation certificates or receipts. Most reputable jewellers, for example, will, for a fee, value jewellery, gold or silver. House contents insurance policies do not usually cover possessions and jewellery lost, damaged or stolen away from the address given. Extra cover for 'all risks' in respect of items carried about by the owner should, therefore, be specified by the proposer when taking out the insurance.

Because of the rise in prices and values caused by inflation, insurance companies are now offering **index-linked** insurance policies. This means that every year the sum insured will be reviewed against the cost of living index, and the sum insured increased if necessary. This has two effects—the policyholder's property remains fully insured, with the benefits and security that that brings, and the insurance company is ensured that the policyholders are playing fair (their premiums, of course, being increased accordingly). Insurance companies have been suffering because householders have not bothered over the years to increase the amount of their insurance cover to allow for inflation and to cover new and extra items bought in the home, or for improvements to the building, such as extensions and double glazing. Companies hope to encourage frequent revision of values by allowing policyholders to increase their cover during the year, but being charged no extra until the next premium is due for the following year.

There is a scale of charges for property insurance and the amount of the premium is decided by the value put upon the property by the householder. (Although the term 'householder' has been used throughout, it refers also to owners and occupiers of business premises.) Incidentally, the sum insured on a house or other building is not based on the market value but on the cost of rebuilding.

Clothing, money and personal possessions can also be insured when travelling or going on holiday and this can be arranged through either the travel agent or an insurance company.

Life assurance

Many people insure their lives so that if they should die prematurely their dependents are provided for. However, there are several different forms of life assurance which can also provide a means of saving and of providing pension or annuity payments on retirement.

Premiums are based on life expectancy, the sum assured and whether the policy is with or without profits. In order to estimate the life expectancy of the proposer he (or she) has to give his age, occupation, past illnesses and operations, whether his parents are alive and, if not, what they died of, and he has to state if he drinks, and if so, in what quantity; if he smokes and how much. He may be required, also, to undergo a medical examination.

The main types of life assurance are:

Whole life policies These are some of the simplest. Life is assured for a specific sum which goes to dependants on assured's death. It can be for a large sum or merely enough to cover funeral expenses.

Endowment policies These are very popular as they provide for long-term saving. The sum assured becomes payable after a fixed number of years, or at death if this is earlier. It is possible for new parents to take out an endowment policy on their young baby so that when it is, say, eighteen or twenty-one years of age, it will receive a lump sum of money. There is the danger that if the sum assured was £100, in seventeen or twenty years' time it would not be the substantial sum it was intended to be.

There is another form of policy that provides for profits on top of the sum assured.

With-profits policies The policyholder or beneficiary becomes entitled to a share of the profits earned by the insurance company on the money invested over the years. The premiums are obviously higher than for whole life or endowment policies without profits.

Family income policies These provide an income in regular payments, rather than a lump sum, on the death of the policyholder. This is useful for the young family man who wishes his family to be provided for in the event of his death. The income will continue for an agreed period which may be until the children reach a certain age, or for a specified number of years. It may cease on the remarriage of the wife.

Mortgage protection policies These are another way in which the family man can be assured of security for his wife and children. On his death the mortgage on his property is repaid, leaving no outstanding mortgage payments for his wife to find. This can work in two ways. It could be in the form of an endowment policy (with or without profits) for a stated sum, or on a sliding scale reducing over the years. Either way, the dependants are relieved of a financial burden on the death of the wage-earner.

Personal accident and sickness

These policies cover the insured for all manner of accidents, for partial or complete disablement, or for loss of limbs. There is a limit to the amount of benefit which can be obtained. This varies from company to company, but usually it is between 50 per cent and 75 per cent of the insured person's income. Policies can also be taken out to cover parties of people, for example a club outing, or sports teams. Automatic machine insurance is available at airports and railway terminals for short-term cover for journeys.

As well as compensation in the event of loss of luggage while on holiday or travelling, travel agents and insurance companies can arrange for insurance cover in the case of accident or sickness abroad, where there is no National Health Service to provide free medical attention. These special comprehensive insurance schemes also cover loss of deposit should the holiday have to be cancelled because of personal or family illness. The Foreign

Office has requested travel agents to make this comprehensive travel insurance compulsory because otherwise British tourists look to the British Consul abroad when they get into difficulty, and much of this could be avoided by insurance cover. The premium is only a matter of a few pounds.

There are, of course, National Insurance contributions which are compulsory deductions from the wages and salaries of employed persons and which provide for state retirement pensions, unemployment and sickness benefits, invalid and widows' benefits, maternity benefits, death grants, and industrial injury and disablement benefits. It is also possible to insure privately through insurance companies for benefit payments in the case of sickness.

To insure for private specialist and hospital treatment outside the National Health Service there are organisations such as BUPA (British United and Provident Association) and PPP (Private Patients' Plan). Members pay a subscription based on the amount of benefit cover required. Many companies, as a fringe benefit, subscribe on behalf of their employees. By providing prompt specialist medical attention the company hopes to lose the services of employees through sickness for a minimum of time and, in non-urgent cases, the employee can choose to go into hospital when it is least inconvenient for his employer.

The largest volume of accident insurance is the insurance of liability. Organisers of public functions insure against accidents to members of the public while attending an event. The premium will take into consideration the number of people likely to attend and what hazards there are. For instance, accidents are more likely to happen if there is a large attendance at a cross-country motor rally than at a local church garden fête. Employers by law must insure against accidents at work for all employees.

Motor vehicle

By law, all motorists are obliged to insure themselves against having to compensate anyone injured by their negligence or carelessness. Under the Road Traffic Act cover is compulsory for injury to a third party. In insurance terms, the first party is the insured, the second party the insurer and the third party is any other person affected by the contract; for example, passengers, pedestrians, cyclists or the occupants of other vehicles. Third party insurance can cover damage to property as well as injury and very few insurance companies will allow only the minimum cover required by the Act.

Many motorists wish to take out comprehensive cover for

more insurance than the minimum they are obliged by law to do, and they insure their vehicles against accidental damage, fire and theft, as well as against damage done to the property of third parties.

The proposal form requires the proposer to state the age of the vehicle, the make and model, the value, the age(s) of the driver(s) and whether the owner has been involved in any road accidents. Also taken into consideration are the age, sex and occupation of the owner, the area where he lives and the classification of use of the vehicle (private, for business, for hire, for competitions, etc).

The insurance company will consider all these facts and fix a premium accordingly. For instance, a school teacher of forty-five, living in rural England, who is the sole driver of a medium-sized saloon car and has had no accidents or endorsements to his driving licence, will pay a much less premium than a youth of twenty, owning a sports car, living in London who has had an endorsement to his driving licence for dangerous driving.

The insurance company will also vary its premiums according to the value of the car—the more expensive the car the higher the premiums—and some companies require to know for how long the driver has had a driving licence, or if he has a disability which may affect his driving, such as loss of an eye.

'No claim' discounts are allowed by insurance companies when no claim has been made upon them, and these can be quite substantial.

All road users, including those on foot, have a liability to others. For example, a pedestrian was ordered to pay £5200 to a passenger in a car who was hurt in an accident for which the walker was held largely responsible. It is possible to insure against claims arising out of one's personal liability towards others.

An insurance certificate for at least the minimum third party cover has to be produced when applying for a Motor Vehicle Road Licence.

Insurance for the businessman

In addition to insurance on property and motor vehicles, the chief types of insurance associated with business are as follows.

Burglary A company can insure against loss or damage resulting from burglary. The insurer, however, may stipulate special security arrangements, such as an approved safe and the installation of burglar alarms. Otherwise insurance may be refused, or premiums increased.

228

Cash in transit Wage snatches by armed bandits can be insured against. Provision can also be made against the injury or death of an employee who is the victim of such an attack.

Consequential loss A normal fire insurance policy does not include indemnity for loss of a company's profits, continuing overhead expenses, or increased working costs, directly resulting from a fire or other disaster; but these are covered by consequential loss insurance, which compensates all losses arising from the occurrence of the insured risk.

Death of a principal In a partnership, if a partner were to die, this could result in capital being withdrawn from the business to meet death duties. But insurance can enable the surviving principals, through a joint life policy, to replace any capital which may be withdrawn from the partnership. Similarly, a company can insure the life of an essential employee or principal who is not a partner.

Employer's liability National Insurance contributions cover employees against injuries suffered whilst at work. It does not, however, cover an employer's liability for injuries arising from the employer's negligence or that of a fellow-employee. These risks are covered by employer's liability insurance which is compulsory by law.

Fidelity guarantee This insures an employer against possible losses through the dishonesty of employees, although the money is unlikely to be reimbursed until the employee has been charged in the courts.

Goods in transit This is insurance against loss or damage either for single consignments or for all consignments.

Plant and equipment The Factory Act requires plant, such as boilers, lifts, cranes, etc to be examined periodically by a qualified person. Plant and equipment insurance includes the required inspection, and covers an employer against electrical or mechanical breakdowns or boiler explosions.

Products liability There is a legal liability to compensate a member of the public caused injury or illness by the product of one's business. This would include illness caused by a food product.

Public liability There is also a liability to pay the cost of injury or the damage to property of members of the public. For example, a building firm must compensate a passer-by who is injured by falling bricks or tiles.

Miscellaneous Items include: plate glass (such as shop windows and show cases); bad debts; contracts guarantee (insurance against agreed penalties due through failure to fulfil a contracted undertaking).

Contingency insurance

Almost everyone is familiar with the variety of insurance cover that can be obtained—a dancer's legs, a concert musician's fingers, etc. Other examples of contingency insurance are:

- protection against the untraceable beneficiary of a will who turns up after the estate has been shared out. This enables the estate to be paid out without having to wait indefinitely for someone who may never turn up
- a mother-to-be who insured herself for £10 000 against being paralysed by a spinal injection— it cost her £150
- last-minute cancellation or postponement of a wedding possibly because of death or illness
- local authorities who run lotteries, against criminal activity and human error—there might, through a printing error, be more than one ticket printed with the winning number, and there is always the danger of forgery
- loss of false teeth and contact lenses
- with the lesson of the 1976 drought in mind, a Midlands pleasure boat owner insured against the canals drying up
- the 'hole-in-one' golf shot is the perennial on which companies pay out regularly
- fête and gala day organisers insure against bad weather, and holidays can also be insured against this.

The possible list is endless.

The insurance market

Although a certain amount of insurance is provided by friendly societies and trade unions, most insurance services in Britain are in the hands of mutual or joint stock insurance companies, or of Lloyd's underwriters. Mutual societies have no shareholders to whom to pay profits—all the profits go to the members who are

230

policyholders.

The insurance market comprises the insurance companies, some 300 of which belong to the British Insurance Association, Lloyds (see below), Insurance Brokers, and International Insurance Services. Over 60 per cent of the general (non-life) business of members of the BIA is carried on overseas. The basic principle of this international business is that resources capable of meeting any potential loss are instantly available for use in any part of the world. Directives addressed to the government states of the European Economic Community are intended to regulate insurance and re-insurance, and bring the legislation of the member states in line with each other.

Reinsurance

This is used when very large risks are accepted, such as for an aircraft, which may involve several million pounds. The insurance company accepting the risk will split it by re-insuring with other companies, so that should there be a disaster, the compensation is covered by several companies instead of by one.

The underwriting room at Lloyds today.

Lloyd's

The Corporation of Lloyd's of London grew out of Edward Lloyd's coffee house where Elizabethan merchants met and made it their business to insure ships and cargoes. They promised to pay for losses at sea, and because they wrote their names under their promises, they were called '**underwriters**'.

Lloyd's today is an international market for the sale of insurance. There are some 8500 underwriting members, grouped into 360 syndicates for business purposes. Membership is open to men and women of any nationality but they must meet the most stringent financial regulations laid down by the Committee of Lloyd's before they are permitted to transact business there.

Lloyd's itself is not a company: it does not accept insurance but provides premises and other services. Therefore you cannot insure *with* Lloyd's, only *at* Lloyd's. Your contract is with the syndicate of underwriters.

The syndicate is represented by what is known as an underwriting agent. He spends his time in this market (known as 'the Room'), accepting or refusing offers to insure which are brought to him by Lloyd's brokers on behalf of their clients, working in much the same way as the Stock Exchange brokers approach the jobbers. Members of the public cannot themselves go direct to Lloyd's underwriters to arrange insurance cover, but must go through a broker.

Underwriters and their clerks sit at their 'boxes' in the Underwriting Room at Lloyd's, one of the largest commercial rooms in Europe. A broker wishing to place an insurance may go to numerous underwriters, if a large amount of cover is required, offering each a part of the risk until the full risk is covered. Thus the risk is spread among a number of underwriters.

Although in its earlier history the activities of Lloyd's were confined to marine insurance business, there has been built up a very considerable world-wide market for almost any type of insurance, such as aircraft, oil rigs, cargo, motor cars, civil engineering projects, personal accident and third party liability. All this brings in some £750 million of premiums to underwriters each year. Two-thirds of this business comes from overseas and makes a valuable contribution to the country's balance of payments. Cover at Lloyd's is regarded as the safest in the world.

Alongside its insurance business, Lloyd's has built up the most comprehensive shipping intelligence service in the world. Shipping information is collected and distributed to newspapers, radio and television. **Lloyd's List** is printed and published daily at Lloyd's and is sent all over the world; it gives not only ship-ping information but contains news of general commercial interest. **Lloyd's Shipping Index**, also published daily, lists some 28 000 ocean-going vessels in alphabetical order and gives the latest known report of each. **Lloyd's Register of Shipping** is a source of reference on ships throughout the world, almost every ship being registered at Lloyd's. This Register can be seen at most public libraries.

Questions

1. Insurance may be described as a 'pooling of risks'.
   (a) Explain what this statement means.
   (b) Describe *three* risks a businessman is likely to insure against and *one* which he must bear himself.
   (c) Explain the meaning of 'indemnity'.
   (d) If a person applied to an insurance company for life assurance, what details would the insurance company need to know before deciding the premium?   (NW)
2. Explain what you would do if you wanted to take out an insurance on some valuable thing you own such as a diamond ring or a motor cycle and what you would do to make a claim if it was lost, seriously damaged or stolen. What would happen to your claim if you had insured the article for less than it was really worth?   (YR)
3. Write a paragraph on *four* of the following:
   (a) Insurable Interest   (b) Insurance is a contract of
   Indemnity
   (c) Utmost Good Faith   (d) Underwriters
   (e) Statistical Basis of Insurance   (SR)
4. Insurance is important to industry and commerce, to the private individual and helps our balance of payments. Explain why this is so and explain the principles which must be observed for insurance to work satisfactorily.   (EA)
5. Mr Jones owns a small grocery shop and runs a car for business purposes. He is twenty-eight years old, married and has recently moved into a new house.
   (a) What types of insurance should Mr Jones take out?
   (b) Explain the stages in taking out one of these types of insurance from when Mr Jones makes his first inquiry until payment is made for a claim.   (EM)
6. A retail newsagent and stationer asks your advice on the insurance policies he should take out for his business. Describe

three risks which you think he might cover by insurance and *one* risk which he must bear himself. (NB. Life assurance and compulsory forms of insurance such as motor vehicle or National Insurance are *not* to be included in your choice.)

(RSA)

7. (a) What do we mean when we say that insurance is based upon a 'pooling of risks'?
   (b) Name and explain *two* of the principles of insurance.
   (c) Explain the difference between an insurance agent and an insurance broker.
   (d) A life assurance policy is often described as an investment. Why is this so?

15

Advertising and public relations

Advertising

Advertising affects everyone's life. At its simplest level advertising is a personal recommendation for a film or a brand of soap powder. But advertising is also business, in fact a whole industry, which could be as simple as paying a newsagent to put a card in his window or as complex as a plan for publicising a new product throughout Europe and America at the cost of hundreds of thousands of pounds. In 1975, advertisers spent £967 million in Britain.

In recent years advertising has come in for a great deal of criticism. Some people have claimed that billboard advertising is unattractive and spoils the look of an area. In fact, outdoor advertising is controlled by legislation, and the consent must be obtained of the local planning authority, whose duty it is to ensure that it will not threaten either the public safety or public amenity value. Others have felt that advertising both confuses and manipulates the public. A clear distinction can be drawn between **informative advertising**, which makes available the price, quality and terms of sale, and **persuasive advertising**, which is concerned only with making a product appear desirable. Critics point to the increasing amount of advertising directed at children who then ask Mummy to buy a particular product. And most critics believe that advertising is a costly business that must add to the price of a product.

The chief arguments against mass advertising fall mainly into two categories. One general category includes suggestions that advertising exaggerates and misleads; and that it plays on people's emotions, encourages snobbery and social competitiveness, and tempts people to spend unwisely, either by buying goods that they do not need or cannot afford, or by not investigating the advertised product's competitors. The second, and perhaps more serious criticism of advertising is that it offends against good taste, either in its use of sex, or by playing on the fears of people in medical matters, or by the exploitation of children in advertising. In fact, the Code of Advertising Practice of the Advertising Standards Authority makes special mention of unacceptable practices regarding medicinal products, and regarding young children, and also requires that advertisements should not contain material offensive to the standards of decency of those likely to see them.

In the free-enterprise economy, in fact, it could be said that advertising is often a helpful, and probably a necessary part of business. Many firms feel that they have to advertise because they face strong competition. Since most goods are made by mass production to keep their cost at a reasonable level, a manufacturer must sell his goods in large quantities to make a profit and this will increase as he sells more goods. Outselling the competition, therefore, is a condition for a successful manufacturer.

If the manufacturer can bring his product to the attention of the public and if he can explain why they should buy it, the public is more likely to choose that product than another brand about which they know nothing. **Brand names** and **trade marks** of well-known producers catch the eye and become recognised by the public. They know what to expect from products of that name. Some trade names become synonymous with a particular product; for example you may say you are going to hoover the living room when your vacuum cleaner is, in fact, of a different make. Likewise, writing with a biro now means using any ball-point pen.

Over 10 000 new trade marks are registered at the Patent Office each year, and once registered they may not be used by any other business. Possessing a trade mark or brand name makes it possible to advertise on a large scale.

A manufacturer will want to publicise a new product, or a new manufacturer will want to publicise himself to arouse people's interest and encourage them to try something new which they may find they like and continue to use. In all these cases the advertising, if successful, should pay for itself in increased sales. The same arguments for advertising apply in the case of firms with a service to offer, such as airlines or dry cleaning firms. If they can influence more people to use their services, their profits should increase.

Advertising supplies an important part of the income of most magazines and newspapers which would be prohibitively expensive and probably could not exist without the money from the advertisements they carry. Many publications also attract readers by their advertisements, from firms and individuals who want to buy or sell items, or employ someone or find employment.

236

Brand names and trademarks.

Some, such as *Exchange and Mart*, are devoted entirely to advertisements.

When a firm decides to advertise its product, it approaches an **advertising agency**. Most advertising is done on behalf of large businesses by agencies, who also will provide marketing and consumer research. Reputable agencies are members of the Institute of Practitioners in Advertising. The agency and the firm decide on a yearly advertising budget called an **appropriation**. The agency then begins to devise an advertising **campaign** which is the strategy of promoting the product. Details of the campaign include the *image* to be given the product, the areas for advertising (national or in certain areas only), and the places where the advertisements should be displayed. These may include television, the cinema, magazines and newspapers, hoardings, public transport, shop fronts and displays, trade journals, exhibitions and fairs, postal advertising and, more recently, sponsorship of major sporting events, especially those likely to be televised.

The **creative department** works out the product's image in the advertisements: for example, lightbulbs might be publicised as 'sophisticated lightbulbs', 'fun bulbs', 'long-lasting bulbs', 'the brightest lights', 'beautiful bulbs' or as any combination of these images. Once an image is chosen, the creative department devises advertisements that promote the bulb in that image. This may take the form of an easily remembered slogan, possibly mis-spelt or ungrammatical, eg, Beanz meanz Heinz, and Drinka pinta milka day.

Meanwhile, the **media department** is concentrating on finding the best **media** for lightbulb advertisements. The medium is the place where advertising will be displayed, and usually the department will use a combination of media. The skill of the department lies in the selection of the most effective media for a particular series of advertisements.

The space for advertising in magazines or on television is expensive and great sums of money are spent on producing the advertisements. A two-minute advertisement on commercial television could cost £30 000 to make. Models and photographers may sometimes be flown to exotic places to find the right setting for the advertisement. The client obviously wants his appropriation to be spent well and the most persuasive advertisement will fail if it is placed in the wrong medium. Obviously no one would place an advertisement for washing-up liquid in a men's magazine but the media department has to make more difficult decisions than that. An agency handling dog food advertisements, for example, wants to find the medium where the advertisements will be seen by the most dog owners. Information, such as how many dog lovers read *The Times* or watch independent television, is needed and must be discovered by careful research.

This specialised information necessary to a successful campaign can be supplied by a market research firm or by the market research department of the agency. **Market research** means what it says: research into the market; that is the people who buy, the consumers. Besides discovering factual information like statistics for the media men, market researchers also

238

employ science to discover facts, such as what colours are most pleasing to the eye or which is the best angle at which to place a billboard. The psychology of the customer is also researched in great detail; agencies want to know, for example, if people are softened when they see a baby or a fluffy kitten in an advertisement or whether housewives prefer to see a man or a woman sell them a packet of soap powder. Psychological research is carried further to discover what makes people behave in a certain way. Agencies can use this information to decide how people will react to an advertisement.

Agencies also carry out **test marketing** in selected areas. They choose an area which has a cross-section of the population and see how well a new product sells there. This also presents an opportunity to test an advertising campaign for the product in a small way before spending money on a national campaign. The information gained from testing the product and the campaign helps the agency and the manufacturer to decide whether or not to go ahead on a national basis. These decisions must be backed by knowledge and experience since a number of factors have to be considered; for example, the regional differences in Britain can mean that a campaign is successful in the south-east of England but a failure in Scotland.

With the increase in international trade through the Common Market, for example, and advances in technology, new products are bound to come on to the British market. This means more competition and therefore the need for more advertising. Greater affluence is creating new customers for more expensive goods which must be publicised to a greater extent. One example of this is the boom in foreign travel which has brought tour operators, transportation companies, such as airlines and shipping lines, and government tourist authorities into the advertising business in a big way.

This increase in goods and services and the greater wealth of the general public has been reflected in the new methods of advertising.

Provision has been made by the government for commercial radio broadcasting supported by advertising on a local level under the auspices of the Independent Broadcasting Authority. This allows firms to bring radio advertising into the home in the same way as television commercials.

The Independent Broadcasting Authority receives all its income through advertising. It is financed by annual rental payments by the fifteen TV programme companies, who in turn get their income from the sale of advertising time. Unlike American television practice, advertisers are not allowed to sponsor programmes, but are allowed a limited time (only seven minutes in any one hour) between and during programmes. The IBA has a code of practice which prohibits advertising on religion, politics, cigarettes and gambling, and a total ban during broadcasts to schools.

An advertising hoarding.

In many areas of Britain newspapers have been published which are given away and are completely supported by advertising revenue. These are delivered to every household in a particular area and carry items of local news and features of general interest as well as local and national advertising. Both commercial radio and giveaway newspapers may take advertising from the established media but when the economy is strong and business is doing well, competition provides enough advertising for all.

Agencies, advertisers and media are members of the Advertising Association, which has set up its own Advertising Standards Authority. This independent body promotes and enforces the highest standards of advertising, in particular through the British Code of Advertising Practice.

The Government produces a deal of publicity material, for instance on safety, health, fuel economy, new pension schemes, changes in contributions, etc and supplies it through the **Central Office of Information**. The COI conducts press, TV, film and poster advertising, for exhibitions at home and at British Information posts abroad. It also organises tours for official visitors to Britain.

Public relations

In addition to advertising, a firm may publicise its product

240

through public relations. Advertising and public relations do different jobs but are related by their common aim of drawing the public's attention to a product or service.

In one sense anyone in a firm who deals with the public is concerned with public relations. A friendly and helpful sales girl in a store makes customers want to return because it is a pleasant place to shop. She is, therefore, increasing her firm's profits by bringing in more business. In the same way, if a manufacturer deals efficiently and fairly with complaints about its product, customers will feel confident about buying that brand and will recommend it to others. A less helpful firm will have far less prestige with the consumer. Many companies believe that good relations with the public are worth the cost of replacing apparently faulty goods without question. The good-will gained will bring in valuable sales in the future.

Like advertising, public relations can be a business in its own right. Many firms hire their own public relations staff or employ a public relations consultant to make their goods more widely known. For example, a fashion display in a magazine gives publicity to the clothes manufacturer, as well as to the accessories manufacturer and the maker of the cosmetics, as all the brand names are usually listed. In another instance, an article on skin care includes an editorial mention of various products. The manufacturer does not have to pay the magazine for printing his brand name, but he has to pay the public relations firm for making contacts with journalists and persuading them to mention the product in appropriate features. The skilled public relations man or woman has the ability to assess the editorial possibilities of a product and to present these properly to journalists in that field. The skate-board 'craze' succeeded in getting free publicity from BBC and independent television, as well as extensive cover in national and local newspapers and magazines.

A public relations firm uses other methods besides **editorial publicity** to publicise the products of its clients. They may send out to the newspapers any information about a client's firm, such as the opening of a new factory, a new management appointment or record profits for the year. Information sent out to the papers in this way is called a **press release** and may be accompanied by a photograph or a profits chart. Press releases come under the category of news and might be reported in a short article. Local newspapers will be particularly interested in news items related to a local firm or a well-known local personality who has received a promotion or been appointed director of a company.

Other ways of bringing a product to the attention of the public are free demonstrations, such as fashion shows and beauty treatments, to women's organisations or in large department stores, visits to the client's factory by school children or any interested group, contests connected with buying a product and the sponsorship of events, such as car races or exhibitions. Although most people would not consider these methods as advertising they are carefully planned to publicise a product or firm and in certain cases, such as a holiday competition are usually linked to a major advertising campaign.

The man or woman in a public relations firm who deals directly with a client is called an **account executive** because he is the firm's link with the client, known as the account (not to be confused with the book-keeping term). The account executive looks after the day to day running of his accounts. Each account executive may have several accounts to handle or, in the case of an important client, he may be responsible for that account only. Advertising agencies also employ account executives who must understand fully the work of the creative and media departments, as the account executive is the link between the client or account and these other departments. As publicity plays such an important part in the manufacturing and selling processes, many large firms have their own advertising and public relations department. They still employ an advertising agency to implement the advertising campaign since this is a specialised business requiring skilled people with different types of knowledge and experience.

Today when people are bombarded on all sides by advertising and public relations promotions, it is important that this publicity is not misused. Laws have been passed to prevent false claims being made about products or services. (See Chapter 16 Consumer protection). The Institute of Public Relations established in 1948, has over 3000 members from commerce industry, the professions, national associations and central and local government, and it is associated with other organisations in administering the British Code of Advertising Practice to stop misleading or unscrupulous advertising. In this way advertising by keeping its own house in order, hopes to show that further government regulation, such as the Trades Descriptions Act (see page 249) is unnecessary.

Ways of Advertising

Medium	Target audience	Examples	Basis of cost
commercial television	national and some-times regional	*national:* household goods, food, drink, cosmetics, medicines, holidays, fuel, etc. *regional:* do-it-yourself, caravans, furniture and carpet stores, local sales, and special offers.	Expensive but often memorable. Cost of film and screen time. The cost of time varies according to the time of day.
national newspapers and magazines	national	*display advertisements:* as for television, mail order items, finance and banking, office equipment, tobacco, job vacancies requiring nationwide search. *classified advertisements:* items for sale or exchange, situations vacant, accommodation, births, marriages, deaths, of national interest.	according to space. according to number of words or lines.
local and regional newspapers and magazines	local and regional	*display:* by local traders, hoteliers, estate agents, local events, entertainment, local job vacancies. *classified:* as above but with local appeal	as national newspapers, but cheaper rates.
trade journals	national	commodities relating to trade—food, household goods, shop fittings, hairdressing products, salon fittings and equipment, hotel, restaurant, public house fittings etc exhibitions, businesses for sale	according to space or number of words or lines.

medium	scope	description	cost
hoardings, posters, public transport	national and local	*national:* products of all kinds. *local:* events, sales, department stores. Underground and escalator displays aim to catch the eye—food, drink, clothing, entertainment, employment bureaux.	variable, depending on charge by owner of space.
cinema	local	advertisements by local traders including jewellers and car salesmen who often share cost with manufacturers; also national advertisers.	depends on length and cost of film.
commercial radio	national and regional	products of all kinds.	cost according to time.
direct mail (either to every household in certain areas or to selected households)	national, regional or local campaigns (by post or hand delivery by agents)	leaflets advertising branded goods, local special offers, double-glazing, insulation; literature on book or record clubs with introductory offers; catalogues, competitions, free samples.	P.O. allows postage rebate on items posted in bulk; agencies employ local residents to deliver in area.
shop counter and window displays (point of sale)	local campaigns	to introduce new product or to boost existing one—free samples, cut prices, competitions, vouchers.	negotiable with retailer.
yellow pages (classified telephone directories)	regional	all types of sales and services available within the area of the directory.	one free entry but advertising space is sold for heavy print and display entries.
paper bags, wrappings and carrier bags	local	branded goods or name of shop or store.	printing and materials costs.

Advertising

Advantages	Disadvantages
Informative advertising	
• gives information, details, cost, uses, quality, performance and stockists. • Public may compare a product with its competitors.	• no real disadvantages.

Persuasive advertising	
• introduces new product, • encourages demand which increases productivity, • increased productivity leads to cut prices. • use of brand names gives confidence to consumer. • provides entertainment and pays for independent television. • claimed to improve the standard of living. • keeps down cost of newspapers and magazines. • provides income for sporting events. • keeps mail order firms in business. • provides employment for artists, designers, models, actors and film makers.	• appeals almost entirely to the emotions, such as sex, snobbery and ambition. • product taken on trust because very little information given. • irrelevant information put in to catch the eye. • sameness of various brands is concealed. • public is victim of continuous exaggeration and suggestion. • overspending is encouraged. • encourages bad habits such as unwise eating, drinking and smoking. • wasteful—competitiveness encourages rival firms to over-spend.

Questions

1. State concisely *two* good reasons why manufacturers use advertising. Describe *four* different methods of advertising and say for which kind of products they are most suited.

(EM)

2. What do you understand by the term Market Research? Apart from the Government who else is likely to conduct market research and for what reasons?

(SW)

3. What are 'branded goods'? What are the advantages to manufacturers of branding and advertising, and how does this benefit the retailer?

(SW)

4. Describe:
    (a) the work of an advertising agency and its organisation;
    (b) methods used by Public Relations to publicise a firm's products.
5. The following are means of advertising:
    (a) leaflet (b) poster (c) newspaper advertisement
    (d) catalogues
In *each* case, indicate a product or service which might be advertised by the above means. Give reasons for your choice.

(NR)

16

Consumer protection

At one time the attitude of the law towards buying and selling was summed up in the phrase *caveat emptor* (let the buyer beware), and no protection was given to consumers, the persons who buy goods or services, if they were deceived by traders. However, although shoppers should still exercise care in their purchases, in recent years the interests of the consumers have become guarded by a number of organisations, some of which are set up by law, and others by voluntary bodies.

Legislation

In 1972 a Minister of Trade and Consumer Affairs was appointed, and his duties were taken over in 1974 by the new post of Secretary of State for Prices and Consumer Protection. This Department became responsible for a wide range of laws to protect customers, consumer credit and consumer safety. In addition to prices, it deals with weights and measures, metrication, quality control, and monopolies, mergers and restrictive practices. It is concerned with the Price Commission, the Monopolies and Mergers Commission, the Consumer Protection Advisory Council and the Consumer Councils of the Nationalised Industries. It sponsors the National Consumer Council and the British Standards Institution.

The Consumer Councils of the nationalised industries were set up initially by the ministers responsible for each industry (gas, electricity, coal, the Post Office, etc), since they are required by law to protect the interests of their customers. Each consumer or consultative council is an independent body: it considers the complaints and suggestions of customers, and makes recommendations to the Minister in charge.

The Monopolies and Mergers Commission

This commission investigates monopoly situations. These occur

Consultative councils of nationalised industries

Service	Organisation	Where to find out
Airlines	Airline Users' Committee	From the Civil Aviation Authority, Aviation House, 129 Kingsway, London WC2B 6NN
Airport facilities	Heathrow/Gatwick/Stansted/Prestwick/Aberdeen/Edinburgh/Glasgow Consultative Committee	From British Airports Authority at the appropriate airport. Complaints about facilities at other airports should be addressed to the airport manager.
British Rail	Transport Users' Consultative Committee	From notices at railway stations, or telephone directory
Coal and other solid fuels	Regional Secretary, Approved Coal Merchants' Scheme	From your coal merchant, a Citizens' Advice Bureau, or Consumer Advice Centre (see telephone directory)
Electricity	Electricity Consultative Council	From your Electricity Board shop or telephone directory
Gas	Regional Gas Consumers' Council	From your local gas showroom or telephone directory
Post Office	Post Office Advisory Committee	From the Post Office Users' National Council, Waterloo Bridge House, Waterloo Road, London SE1 8UA, or your telephone directory

The consultative councils are set up by Parliament and are independent of their nationalised industry. They will take up complaints for consumers about the services supplied.

when one company or group of companies takes control of the production or sale of goods or services to the extent that it has as much as one quarter of the market. All of the nationalised industries are monopolies, but government control should prevent this being against the public interest. The Commission investigates proposed mergers of large companies, on behalf of the Prices and Consumer Protection Department, which can take action to prevent them if they are against the public interest. For example, the Commission investigated the take-over by Boots the Chemist of Timothy Whites and Taylor when it was first proposed, to make sure that the combination, by providing more than a quarter of the chemist shop services in the country, did not become a threat to the public interest. Similarly, under the **Fair Trading Act (1973)**, the **Restrictive Practices Court** has power to stop agreements between companies to limit production in order to keep up prices.

The Office of Fair Trading

This Act also established a **Director General of Fair Trading** to be responsible for a continual review of consumer affairs. One of his functions is to prevent unfair trading, for example by deceptive advertising, or by misleading price tickets; and he proposes new laws to stop such methods. He can bring court action against traders who commit offences or break their civil obligations to their customers. He also encourages trade organisations to set up voluntary codes of practice which all their members accept.

The Prices and Consumer Protection Department is helped in its work by several Acts of Parliament.

The Consumer Protection Acts (1961 and 1971)   These acts enable regulations to be made preventing the sale of unsafe goods. These include electrical appliance wiring colour codes, carrycot stands, oil and electrical heaters, flame-resistant nightwear for children and cooking utensils. It is a criminal offence to break these regulations.

The Trade Descriptions Acts (1968 and 1972)   These acts make it a criminal offence for traders to describe their goods inaccurately or make false statements about the services they provide, so that they can be fined or imprisoned for doing so. False statements could include those on size or quantity, how made ('hand-made'), material ('pure wool'), strength or per-

249

formance ('thirty-five miles to the gallon'), distance ('five minutes walk from beach') and where made ('Sheffield made'). It is also illegal to claim falsely that goods have the approval of a person or organisation, such as a local authority. Facilities must be maintained as advertised, so that 'twenty-four hour service' at a garage must mean that petrol is always available for sale. A spoken false description is just as much an offence as a written one. Customers may end a contract entered into through deception by a trader, whether it is intentional or accidental. The Act also makes it an offence for a trader to advertise a reduction in price unless the goods have been offered at the former price for twenty-eight consecutive days in the previous six months. This sign would be illegal if the trader had not been selling the goods at £12.50 for the required period of time.

```
┌─────────────────────────────────┐
│                                  │
│        PRICES SLASHED            │
│                                  │
│           £ 12.50                │
│                  £ 9.95          │
│        SALE OFFER                │
│                                  │
└─────────────────────────────────┘
```

Under the **Passenger Car Fuel Consumption Order, 1977,** car dealers are required to display the petrol consumption on all new cars for sale, and in all advertisements and brochures. It is an offence not to show consumption in 'urban driving', at 56 mph and 75 mph.

The Supply of Goods (Implied Terms) Act 1973 This act amends and brings up to date the Sale of Goods Act (1893), and is concerned with the consumer's rights in civil law. The trader has three obligations:

- the goods must be of **merchantable quality**. This means that, for instance, if a consumer unpacks a blanket he or she has bought and finds a hole in it, it can be returned. The same would be true of an electric toaster which would only burn toast.
- The goods must be **fit for the purpose** for which that type of goods is normally used. For example, a bucket must not leak. Glue which is sold as suitable for mending china must serve that purpose.

250

- The goods must be **as described**. If the customer buys a pink blanket, he should not find that a blue one has been wrapped for him. A down continental quilt should not contain feathers.

Under all these circumstances, the consumer is entitled to ask for the return of his money. If offered a credit note, or exchange, he may accept, but should bear in mind that having accepted, he can not change his mind later and ask for his money.

These rights cannot be taken away, and do not depend upon a guarantee offered with the goods. If there is a guarantee to be returned to the manufacturer, it should be signed and sent. It cannot take away the above rights, but may add others, such as a free replacement for a major part up to, say, five years. The consumer should not be persuaded by a shopkeeper that a fault should be referred to the manufacturer. It is the responsibility of the seller to put things right if he supplies faulty goods, and if necessary he can be taken to court.

Where the consumer should still exercise care is if he examines the goods before buying, and should have seen faults, or if he had faults pointed out. For example, a girl who has tried on a dress before buying cannot later ask for money back on the grounds that the hem is uneven, or the dress does not fit. Under those circumstances no refund can be demanded, nor is the consumer entitled to a refund if he has ignored the advice of the seller, as, for instance if the seller had said that the glue on sale might not be suitable for broken china, or even if the seller said that he did not know if it was suitable.

Again the buyer must still beware when buying privately. The above rules only apply when buying from a trader in his normal business. They would not cover a man buying a second-hand car from the owner, if he was not a car dealer.

The buyer must be especially careful in buying second-hand goods, because he must expect to buy the faults as well as the virtues of the goods. However, the trader must still describe the goods accurately, and if he does not, the buyer can ask for his money back, or enquire if there is a case for prosecution under the Trade Descriptions Act. For example, a table lamp made in the 1930's should not be described as a 'genuine Victorian lamp'. It is as well to have a witness present when buying second-hand goods.

A customer has normal rights when buying in a sale. If the goods are marked 'seconds' the buyer must accept that the goods are not perfect, but if an appliance fails to work, needless of any notices to the contrary, the buyer is entitled to a refund.

It should be remembered that a trader does not have to sell an article to a potential customer. If he wishes, he may refuse the customer's offer to buy. However, if he agrees to sell, and the article has a price on it, he must not sell it at any higher price, or again he can be prosecuted under the Trade Descriptions Act. For instance if, by mistake, a furrier had a ticket £50 on a fur coat in the window, and it should have read £500, he is not bound to sell that coat, but if he does it must be for £50.

The Prices Act (1974) This act is intended to permit government subsidies on food and regulation of food prices. It requires traders to mark the prices (or unit prices) on all goods for sale. Unit pricing is the system of showing the price for a specified quantity (55p per kilo, £1.60 per lb), and helps customers to compare prices when there is a variety of different sized packages.

The Consumer Credit Act (1974) This act is aimed at 'truth in lending', and has been introduced to give greater protection to consumers buying on credit, including hire purchase. Licences are required by firms engaged in selling by hire purchase, owners of hired equipment, debt collectors and credit reference agencies, and these people are required to supply full information about their transactions, including the true annual percentage rate of interest charged.

The Act also provides a remedy for a consumer who is refused credit, because of a credit reference agency report. The agency, on payment of 25p, will hand a copy of its file on him to the customer, who can then check the information and, if it is incorrect, require the agency to put it right. The customer should ask the shop refusing credit for the name and address of its credit reference agency. The Director General of Fair Trading superintends the working of the Act.

The Weights and Measures Act (1968) This provides for inspectors, employed by local authorities to check the accuracy of all measures used by traders, such as butchers' scales, petrol pump meters and public house spirit measures. This protects the public against short measures. However, many goods, especially groceries, are now pre-packed instead of being weighed out for the customer. Under the Act it is a criminal offence if the weight or other measurement of quantity is not shown on the packet, tin or bottle. This includes packed meat as well as cheese and other groceries. There are some exceptions, such as well-known measures (a pint bottle of milk), or small packets. It is an offence under the Act to give short weight or mark goods with a wrong amount, and traders can be prosecuted for these offences.

The Unsolicited Goods and Services Act (1971) This forbids traders to demand payment for goods sent through the post (Christmas cards or stickers, or books) when they have not been ordered by the consumer. If they are unwanted, the sender can reclaim them up to six months after sending them. If the consumer has not agreed to keep them or send them back, the goods become his property at the end of the six months. The six months can be cut short by the consumer if he sends his name and address to the trader, stating that he has received unsolicited goods. If the sender does not then collect them within thirty days, the goods become the consumer's property.

The Food and Drugs Act (1955) This act controls the description of food by a trader. Local authorities, through their public health departments, enforce regulations on food hygiene in shops, abattoirs and restaurants, food labelling, and food content such as the amount of meat in a sausage. The Ministry of Agriculture, Fisheries and Food also has some responsibilities in consumer protection. They include measures regarding food quality and safety, including its labelling and advertising, and the hygienic handling of milk, and of meat in slaughter-houses. These measures are being brought into line with the legislation of the EEC.

Under all these Acts of Parliament, the consumer should take any complaint in the first place to the council-run **Trading Standards Department** (sometimes called the **Consumer Protection Department** or **Consumer Advice Centre**). This department is generally responsible for enforcing the Acts and many local authorities have set up these advice centres in shopping areas. As already mentioned, each nationalised industry has an independent consumer council to consider the complaints of customers.

Independent organisations

Outside the public sector, there are many independent trading associations which have set up **codes of practice** to protect their customers and to investigate complaints. The **Retail Trading Standards Association (RTSA)** is supported by voluntary contributions from retailers and trade organisations, and it will investigate and if necessary prosecute dishonest traders. It also supports a laboratory to examine and report on textile products.

253

such as children's blazer-cloth, for reliability.

The **Association of Manufacturers of Domestic Electrical Appliances (AMDEA)** provides an arbitration service to settle disputes between traders and consumers, as does the **Radio and Television Retailers' Association (RTRA)**, which will also expel a firm for misconduct. Other associations cover almost every branch of retail selling of goods and services. Membership of such an association indicates that a firm can be regarded as reliable and trustworthy. The **Periodical Publishers' Association** has also given an undertaking to refund money sent in by readers of magazines in response to mail order advertisements, when the traders fail to deliver the goods owing to bankruptcy or liquidation.

Private associations include the **Consumers' Association**. This is the largest private consumer organisation, with over 700 000 subscription-paying members. It carries out extensive investigations of services and testing of a wide range of goods, ranging from cameras to cars and from concrete mixers to convenience meals. For most products they recommend a 'best buy', basing it on cost, performance, reliability and safety. Its views and reports are published each month in its magazine *Which?*, which itself is widely reported in the national press and on radio and television. It receives no money from advertising, industry, or any source apart from its subscribers. The CA has frequently caused manufacturers to rectify faults and initiate improvements. Besides the monthly *Which?*, there are also magazines with special interests: *Handyman Which, Holiday Which, Money Which* and *Motoring Which*. The CA also publish many booklets giving advice on a wide range of topics from *The Newborn Baby, Slimming Guide*, and *The Legal Side of Buying a House*, to *Living Through Middle Age* and *Claiming on Insurance. Which?* magazines are available at most public libraries.

The **British Standards Institution (BSI)** is a voluntary non-profit making organisation financed by subscription from members (British manufacturers) and government grants. It has the task of preparing documents setting out standards of dimension, quality and performance at an acceptable and safe level for a variety of goods. These include windscreens, crash helmets, pressure cookers, light bulbs and fire-proofed nightdresses for children. Manufacturers are asked to accept and use these standards, and many do so voluntarily. Their products can then carry the BSI 'kite mark'. Decorative items are not standardised. Standardisation of electric light bulbs means, for example, that we can buy any make knowing that it will fit our sockets. Specifications of all goods carrying the BSI kite mark are pub-

KITEMARK of
the BSI–on
goods which
comply with
standards
laid down.
Goods are
continually
tested

Approval of
the DESIGN
COUNCIL for
goods which
are well-made,
attractive and
practical in
use

Mark of BEAB
(British
Electro-technical
Approvals Board)
on tested
electrical goods

Mark of
NICEIC
(National
Inspection
Council for
Electrical
Installation
Contracting)
– reliable
electrical
contractors

HOME
LAUNDERING
CONSULTATIVE
COUNCIL–
Care Labelling
Code now
accepted
internationally

255

lished and copies of these manuals are in most public libraries.

The Design Council assesses all aspects of design—whether the item is fit for its purpose, is of good appearance, of satisfactory quality and easy to maintain. Goods carrying the Design Centre label are, therefore, of reputable quality. The Design Council is a government sponsored body and members are appointed by the Secretary of State for Industry. At the Council's Design Centres in London, Glasgow and Cardiff there are permanent displays of well-designed modern British goods. The products displayed are chosen for their high standards of design, safety and performance.

The Citizens' Advice Bureaux, of which there are nearly seven hundred, give independent, confidential and free help and guidance to the citizen who is in doubt about his rights or who does not know about the State or voluntary services which could help him. They deal with any sort of enquiry such as health, housing, legal, social and consumer queries. Local bureaux rely on voluntary help but in busy centres there may be trained, professional workers. They rely on local councils for financial assistance, and the Department of Prices and Consumer Protection provides a grant for CAB's central services.

The National Consumer Council, sponsored by the Department of Prices and Consumer Protection, was established in 1975 and, together with the Scottish and Welsh Consumer Councils, ensures that the consumer's view is made known to those in Government and industry whose decisions affect consumers.

Although the consumer is protected by a number of organisations, to whom he or she may turn for advice, there are still occasions when legal action becomes necessary. Many people will prefer to make a civil claim for damages by using a solicitor, who will present their case. The Citizens' Advice Bureaux or Consumer Advice Centre will advise the consumer on how to obtain a solicitor. However, since 1973 a simplified procedure has been in use in county courts (in England and Wales) and sheriff courts (in Scotland) for small claims up to £100 involving consumers. All that is needed is to go to the County Court Office and fill up a form, and court officials will help with this. The plaintiff will have to explain his case in court, but County Courts are well used to this. For claims under £100, it is possible to ask for arbitration, and the case will be heard informally in private. County courts also deal with hire purchase and the Rent Acts. **Legal aid** is available to people of limited means for civil actions in magistrates' courts and county courts but it would not be approved if it appeared that the applicant would gain only trivial advantage from the case.

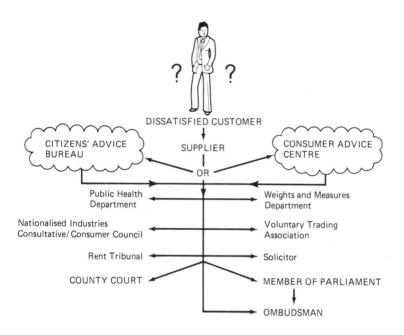

The Parliamentary Commissioner for Administration, popularly known as the **Ombudsman**, will investigate complaints of maladministration by government departments, if these are brought to his notice either by a Member of Parliament, or by a member of the public.

Consumer protection in the United Kingdom is now complicated by legislation by the EEC. For example, it has directed member States to ban unsafe substances from cosmetics. This was brought about by the deaths, in France, of 22 babies through talcum powder containing too much hexachlorophane. There is also legislation regarding the safety of children's toys. However, much of the EEC's requirements is already dealt with by Britain's laws. Where this is not so, the EEC sends either a **directive** or a **regulation**. A regulation automatically becomes law in this country without reference to Parliament. For example, a new egg grading scheme was introduced by EEC regulation. A directive is sent to the Government which has to alter UK law if necessary to give effect to the directive, as it did

257

to make textile manufacturers label their goods to show what type of fibres they contained.

Making contracts

Most people make contracts all day and every day—when buying a newspaper or clothes, or a ticket for a bus or train. A contract is made every time we buy anything, so it is obvious that a contract need not be in writing. It can be by word of mouth or even by implication, as when a man selling papers accepts money and hands over a paper without a word being spoken. The protection of the consumer is based on contracts, because there is a law of contract, and a contract is binding on both parties to it, no matter how it is made, as long as they are both qualified to make it.

A contract is an offer and an acceptance of that offer. If conditions are made at the time, and these are accepted, they become binding. It is possible to withdraw right up to the time of acceptance, and the withdrawal of the person offering the contract (the seller) is effective from the moment the receiver (the buyer) is informed of it. The withdrawal of the buyer becomes effective from the moment it is made or is put in the post.

When goods are sent on approval, acceptance of the offer takes effect from the time acceptance is written or spoken (for example, on the telephone). On the other hand, as already stated goods sent unordered, as a form of advertisement, do not put the receiver under any obligation, if he does not wish to buy them.

It is obvious that care should be taken before signing any form of agreement. If it is not easily understood, advice should be obtained from a Citizen's Advice Bureau, or, in the case of a legal document, from a solicitor. If, when the terms are understood, they are not all fully acceptable, it may be possible to have one or more erased, but equally possibly the trader may refuse to sell the goods or supply the services without the full terms.

The implementation of the **Unfair Contract Terms Act (1977)** has had far-reaching effects. Under it, much of the small print in contracts, limiting the liability of the person offering the contract will be ineffective unless it can pass the test of 'reasonableness' in Court. This applies to all types of contracts.

In trading, a **guarantee** usually means that the manufacturer will supply replacement parts, or the whole, for a certain period after sale, but this does not limit the liability of the trader in

258

the event of faults or damage (see the 1973 Supply of Goods Act). This is not a guarantee in any legal sense. A **legal guarantee** is one which a person signs as an agreement to pay a sum of money on behalf of a relative or friend who fails to do so. He agrees to act as 'guarantor'. This is a separate contract, and binds the person who signs it, who becomes legally bound to pay the money if the relative or friend disappears, or even if he or she cannot or will not pay the money for some reason.

Employment

Although the protection of a person in his or her employment is not the same as protection of a person buying goods or services, probably the most important contract that most people will sign is in connection with employment. Recent legislation has provided considerable protection for employees. both in terms of employment and in working conditions.

The Contracts of Employment Act (1972)

This act requires that an employer shall provide written terms of employment to each employee. This includes methods of making complaints against grievances, and the rights of employer and employee to minimum periods of notice.

Employers have a duty at common law to take reasonable care of their employees and provide a safe system of working, while employees have a duty of care towards each other and also to take care for their own safety. In addition, minimum required standards of safety in certain kinds of workplaces or work are laid down under a number of statutes and some of these also deal with health and welfare. For example, special precautions and safeguards are required when working with asbestos and dangerous liquids, gases and chemicals. **The Health and Safety at Work Act (1974)** reorganised, safeguarded and extended aspects of safety, health and working conditions at work including the protection of the general public from industrial hazards.

The Redundancy Payments Acts (1965 and 1969)

These acts entitle an employee who has worked for a firm for at least 104 weeks to a lump sum as a redundancy payment if his job ceases to exist.

259

Trade unions

Trade unions exist not only to negotiate rates of pay but to improve working conditions and hours of work. Trade union officials will advise a member whether he has a just grievance and will, if necessary, take it up on his behalf. Should a member become involved in a law suit concerning his employment, the trade union will also advise and assist.

The **Trade Union and Labour Relations Act (1974)** enables an employee to bring an action through an industrial tribunal if he considers himself to have been dismissed unfairly, and the **Employment Protection Act (1975)** established an Appeal Tribunal to hear appeals against decisions made by tribunals. The industrial tribunals also hear complaints regarding sex discrimination and equal pay under the **Sex Discrimination Act (1976)**, the Equal Opportunities Act (1974) and the Employment Protection (Consolidation) Act (1978) which gave equal status to women employees on matters of promotion, pay, training, transfer, dismissal and benefits, as well as job opportunities.

The Race Relations Act (1977)

This act brings legislation on racial discrimination in line with the law on sex discrimination; so that industrial tribunals may consider complaints of unfair treatment in employment on account of race or colour.

The individual employee is also subject to agreements arrived at by 'collective bargaining' between employers and the trade unions.

Housing

Another important contract is that entered into when buying or renting a house. The transfer of a house to a new owner is often a slow process, to which there are usually two stages: the agreement to make the transfer, and the process leading up to the formal signing of the deeds of transfer, or conveyance. Before this, full enquiries must be made on behalf of the buyer, so that his full rights are known on what he is buying. This enquiry, or 'search' is normally made by the solicitor acting for the buyer. A building society is usually involved in lending money on mortgage, and the relationship between buyer and building society is clearly laid down. The **National House Building Council (NHBC)** sets standards for private houses, and enforces them on its members by inspection, prior to issuing certificates which carry a ten-year guarantee against structural defects and a two-year guarantee against bad workmanship. Most building societies will not give loans on a new house unless it is covered by a NHBC certificate.

Rented accommodation is subject to various kinds of rent restriction. **Rent control** is available for some tenants who have lived in a property continuously since 1957, especially in low-rated buildings. **Rent regulation** was introduced by the **Rent Act (1965)** for unfurnished dwellings with certain rateable values; and the **Rent Act (1974)** extended the system to furnished accommodation where the landlord did not live on the premises. Tenants in accommodation with landlords living in the same building may ask a **rent tribunal** to determine a fair rent, with security of tenure for up to six months, which may be extended.

Holidays

A recent aspect of consumer protection is its extension to holidays, especially those abroad. In 1975, following the failure of several travel firms which left holidaymakers stranded, and an increasing number of complaints, the Association of British Travel Agents (ABTA) introduced its own code of conduct. Complaints regarding accommodation, and failure to provide a holiday in line with the details in the brochure are investigated. Clauses in the contract which exclude liability or allow last-minute surcharges, are forbidden to members. The Unfair Contracts Act 1977 now gives greater protection against exclusion clauses. In addition, all ABTA members have deposited money which is available to make sure that holidaymakers can complete their holidays and return home if their tour operator goes out of business.

Reputable holiday firms, builders, traders and magazines, etc belong to their specialist associations and by such membership the consumer is assured of receiving a fair deal.

Thus in this country, the consumer is protected in almost everything for which he pays, from food to houses and from electric heaters to holidays abroad. The Law no longer permits the exploitation of the buyer.

Questions

1. (a) A trader who deliberately sold low grade grass seed from a container marked for a higher grade could be prosecuted under the:
   (i) Weights and Measures Act (ii) Sale of Goods Act
   (iii) Allotment Association rules (iv) Trade Descriptions Act
   (b) Mr South buys a new car, which proves to be useless for the purpose for which it was intended. His rights to compensation depend upon:
   (i) Sale of Goods Act (ii) Road Traffic Act
   (iii) Common Law (iv) Trade Descriptions Act
   (c) The sale of goods is subject to the basic principle of:
   (i) utmost good faith (ii) indemnity
   (iii) let the buyer beware (iv) unconditional guarantee
   (d) The enforcement of the Trade Descriptions Act is the responsibility of:
   (i) local Chamber of Commerce (ii) Weights and Measures inspectors
   (iii) local authorities (iv) British Standards Institute
   (SW)

2. Who would the consumer be advised to contact in each of the following cases?
   (a) Repeated complaints to your local Gas Board about very low gas pressure have not been dealt with
   (b) An elderly widow is in difficulties because her pension has been stopped through an error at the local Department of Health and Social Security
   (c) A firm has gone bankrupt after you have sent it money in response to an advertisement in a magazine
   (d) Bad cracks have appeared in your house six months after completion
   (e) A travel agent fails to supply the holiday abroad you have paid for
   (f) A new dress comes apart at the seams, and the shop refuses to refund your money
   (g) The landlord living on the floor below your flat puts up the rent unfairly

3. Show how *two* of the following help the consumer.
   (a) The Design Council (b) British Standards Institution
   (c) Consumers' Association (d) Retail Trading Standards Association

4. (a) Describe the work of the Consumers' Association.
   (b) Explain with examples the ways in which the consumer is
       helped by the operation of
       (i) The Trade Descriptions Act
       (ii) Weights and Measures Act
   (c) Give *two* examples of distinctive labels which we might
       find on goods we buy, which show that the goods are of
       an approved quality.

                                                        (NI)

5. (a) Consider the following cases and indicate which Act of
       Parliament will provide the customer with a remedy
       (i)   A holiday brochure giving an inaccurate description
             of the facilities and location of a hotel on the Costa
             Brava
       (ii) A young child is given short weight when buying a
             quarter pound of sweets
       (iii) An old age pensioner buys an electric fire not fitted
             with a fireguard
       (iv) A transport cafe suspected of having dirty kitchens
   (b) For each Act of Parliament mentioned, describe how it is
       designed to protect the consumers' interests.

                                                        (EMR)

6. Which of the following Acts would protect or help you under
   these circumstances?
       (a) Your job ceases to exist at the firm where you have
           worked for 3 years
       (b) You have been, in your opinion, dismissed unfairly
       (c) As a woman you feel that men less qualified than you
           are being promoted in your place
       (d) You are dismissed without notice

           Sex Discrimination Act 1976
           Trade Union and Labour Relations Act 1974
           Redundancy Payments Acts 1965, 1969
           Contracts of Employment Act 1972

17

Budgeting and money management

How to buy, and how to spend wisely should be learned by everyone with money to spend; and this knowledge is used by every adult, every trader and businessman, and by the country itself. Each of us has a limited income, and we have to decide which of the goods or services we need have the highest priority, and how much we can afford to spend on each. We must learn to **budget**.

As soon as a child is given pocket money, he has decisions to make; and with money from part-time jobs the choices become wider. For a girl they range from cosmetics to clothes and from jewellery to records; for a boy they may include sports gear and motor-cycle accessories; and a choice has to be made.

Wage-earners find that careful budgeting is even more necessary. Some of their earnings are deducted by their employers before they receive their pay packet or cheque. **Gross pay** is the amount they have actually earned, but **net pay** is the amount actually received. The difference is made up of various deductions. **Statutory deductions** are required by law, and these include income tax and National Insurance contributions, which the employer forwards to the Inland Revenue. Some employers may also deduct **voluntary deductions** with the permission of the employee, and these may include a variety of payments, to such things as company pension schemes, sports clubs, hospital or medical benefit funds, and savings schemes.

Most employees pay income tax under the **PAYE (Pay As You Earn)** scheme. Instead of paying a large sum once a year at the end of the tax year (5th April), the employee has an amount deducted each pay day according to the tax tables which the Inland Revenue supplies to the employer. The amount actually paid depends upon a code number which is based upon personal details such as the number of dependants and mortgage interest. This information is required by the Inland Revenue on the employee's annual tax return. The code number arrived at decides how much of the pay is free of tax. Money earned in excess of this free pay is taxable. If the tax free pay is higher than the gross pay, no income tax is paid.

Under the *Social Security Act, 1973*, every person over school-leaving age who earns over a certain amount is liable for **National Insurance contributions.** Class 1 contributions are paid by an employed person and is a fixed percentage of that person's gross pay over the lower earnings limit. Contributions are not paid on earnings above a certain limit. In 1982, the employee's standard rate for Class 1 contributions is 8.75 per cent, the employer's rate is 11.70 per cent and the lower the upper earnings limits are £29.50 and £220 a week.

Self-employed persons must also make contributions, partly on a flat-rate basis (Class 2), and partly as a percentage of net profits (Class 4).

From what remains in the wage packet after deductions, contributions to housekeeping expenses are usually expected, and money has to be allocated for clothes, fares, holidays and other expenses. Saving becomes necessary for more expensive items and for unforeseen needs.

For people with the full responsibility of running and maintaining a home, balancing income against outgoing money is a constant and permanent problem. Changes in taxation rates, and the difficulty of predicting changing prices add to the difficulties, as do unpredictable expenses, such as the repair or replacement of necessary household equipment and increases in rent, rate and mortgage payments. It often means a difficult time for young married couples building up a home and raising a family, and careful budgeting and saving play a very important part in a rising standard of living.

Statistics showing the pattern of consumer spending show the ways in which, on average, each £1 was spent in 1966 and in 1976.

	1966 (in pence)	1976
Food (household expenditure)	22	19
Housing, fuel and light	16	20
Clothing	9	8
Durable and other goods	14	14
Tobacco	6	4
Travel (including motoring)	11	12
Alcoholic drink	7	8
Catering (meals and accommodation)	5	4
Various	10	11

It will be noted that the average person does not spend money on education or on medical services. This is because these are largely provided by the welfare state, and are paid out of tax revenue and National Insurance contributions. In addition a variety of payments are made out of money paid by taxation, including family allowances, old persons' pensions, and supplementary benefits. Other social security benefits, such as sickness and unemployment benefits, maternity and widows' benefits and retirement pensions are paid in return for contributions to the National Insurance scheme made during one's working life. All of these help people in difficulties or who are no longer earning to 'balance their budget', that is to meet necessary expenditure out of income.

Most people realise that, to budget carefully, they must know their probable income over a period of time (a week, a month or a year) and then, preferably allowing for emergencies, make a choice between various essential and desirable items. Items regarded as essential may vary from household to household. A family living in an isolated area may regard a car as essential; a household with an invalid member may think a television set a necessity. A house with no cold larder may need a refrigerator. With today's higher standards of living these things are now no longer regarded by many people as luxuries.

Expensive items may be saved for, but buying on credit has become more popular, and this has led to a great increase in the importance of credit facilities (see Chapter 12). It has also made it much more easy to indulge in **impulse buying**. When living on a budget, almost all spending is **planned spending**, with decisions carefully made on the relative merits of various desirable items, and priority given to the most essential. Sensible housewives make a shopping list and stick to it. Impulse buying is the reverse of this, when an article for sale is so appealing that it is bought immediately without consideration of the consequences. It may well lead to inability to buy necessary items. On the other hand, something may be bought comparatively cheaply, for example in a sale or on special offer, and in the long run it could be more expensive to postpone purchase.

The Government makes a budget annually. Every Government department sends its estimated annual expenditure for the following financial year to the Treasury for approval, and Treasury officials advise the Chancellor of the Exchequer on taxation to cover the approved expenditure. Budget Day is in early April when the Chancellor tells the House of Commons of his tax proposals, including both direct and indirect taxation. **Direct taxes** are those paid by the individual or company direct to the Government through the Board of Inland Revenue, and include income tax, capital gains tax, profits tax and estate

National Westminster Bank Limited ♺

Bank Copy

Budget Account

Schedule of Estimated Annual Commitments

Nature of Payment	Estimated Maximum Annual Expenditure £	p	Month(s) when payment(s) become due
General Rates and Water Rate	90	—	May, November
Telephone			
Electricity	80	—	Feb, May, Aug, Nov
Gas	70	—	Jan, Apr, Jul, Oct
Fuel (including Oil and Coal)			
School Fees			
Life Insurance	80	—	May
House and Contents Insurance	14	—	April
Car Insurance	63	—	March
Car Licence	60	—	March
Season Ticket			
Television Licence	21	—	April
Holidays			
Annual Subscriptions			
Clothing			
Christmas Expenses			
Mortgage	722	—	Every month
Total Estimated Annual Expenditure	1200	—	
Deduct credit balance brought forward	—	—	
Sub Total	1200	—	
Add: Service Charge of £10 to cover first £200 thereafter £1 per £50 of expenditure or any part thereof NB Minimum charge £10	30	—	
Add: Savings	—	—	
Total	1230	—	
Amount, hereby authorised, of monthly transfer from Current Account, being 1/12th of the total	102	50	

NWB 1406

Date **7th August 1982** Signature(s) *A Saunton*

Most banks operate a budget account whereby one-twelfth of annual out-goings is transferred from the customer's current account to their budget account each month. Payments are then drawn from their budget account even though it may be overdrawn on occasions. This helps those with limited incomes to spread their expenditure over the year. There may be a small service charge and, in addition, interest is charged on an overdrawn budget account.

267

		Total Payments	Receipts	Balance
SPECIMEN				
Budget Account				
January				
Gas	24			
Rent	32	56	70	14
February				
Electricity	25			
Rent	32	57	70	27
March				
Car Ins.	63			
Car Licence	50			
Rent	32	145	70	48 overdrawn
April				
Gas	24			
Fire Ins.	14			
TV licence	9			
Rent	32	79	70	57 overdrawn
May				
Life Ass.	80			
Rates	45			
Electricity	25			
Rent	32	182	70	169 overdrawn
June				
Rent	32	32	70	131 overdrawn
July				
Gas	12			
Rent	32	44	70	105 overdrawn
August				
Electricity	15			
Rent	32	47	70	82 overdrawn
September				
Rent	32	32	70	44 overdrawn
October				
Gas	10			
Rent	32	42	70	16 overdrawn
November				
Rates	45			
Electricity	15			
Rent	32	92	70	38 overdrawn
December				
Rent	32	32	70	nil
Totals		£840	£840	

This statement shows what a budget account might look like at the end of the year.

duty. **Indirect tax** is that collected by other bodies acting as agents for the Inland Revenue and the principal indirect tax is Value Added Tax (VAT). This is collected at each stage of the production and distribution of goods, with the final tax borne by the consumer. Thus it is a broadly-based tax falling on final customer expenditure. (VAT is discussed more fully in Chapter 4). The Chancellor of the Exchequer has the use of the 'regulator'; that is, the power to vary VAT rates by up to 25 per cent between budgets. Other indirect taxes include car tax and duties on betting and gaming, alcoholic drinks and tobacco. More than three-quarters of the money spent on tobacco goes

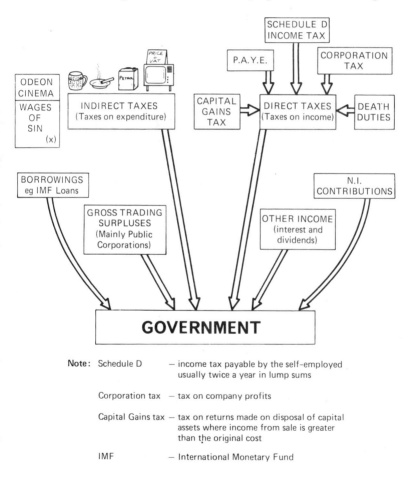

Note: Schedule D   — income tax payable by the self-employed usually twice a year in lump sums

        Corporation tax   — tax on company profits

        Capital Gains tax — tax on returns made on disposal of capital assets where income from sale is greater than the original cost

        IMF   — International Monetary Fund

Sources of government income.

to the Government. Internal indirect taxes have taken the place of the former customs revenue duties in line with the Common Market's common external tariff.

Recently there has been a tendency to have supplementary budgetary measures, usually called 'mini-budgets'. Nowadays the practice has grown of using the Budget to increase or reduce demand on economic resources, and for a review of the economy.

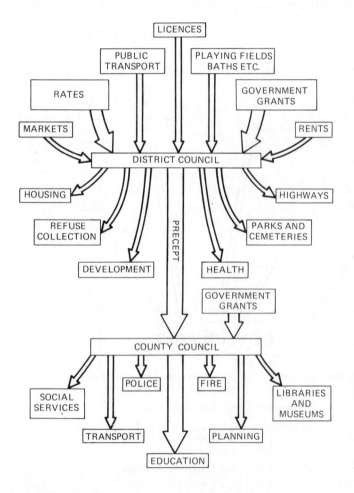

Local government income and expenditure.

The Government also raises money through the sale of Government stock and National Savings Bonds and Certificates. The House of Commons controls government expenditure through the Committee of Ways and Means, the Comptroller and Auditor-General, and the Public Accounts Committee, which ensure that public monies are only spent as authorised. Similarly, local authorities can spend their money, raised largely from rates, on authorised services, and subject to audit by central government.

For business firms, budgeting is an intricate task including deciding on what to produce, estimating costs and sales returns at different levels of output and forecasting the profit from a new product or new market. Market research today is a continuously developing aid to business planning, and rapid and precise answers to forecasting problems are provided by computers. Corporate or long-term planning is regarded as normal management practice by all large and medium firms.

The state of the economy

All budgets, whether national, business, family or personal, are relatively easy in a period of stable prices and income. We expect the Government to maintain this, and avoid both inflation (when prices in general keep rising) and deflation (when prices in general keep falling). This difficult task they try to do by methods which include the issue of money, and creating credit, while encouraging more efficient methods and new products.

Inflation

Inflation can only be understood by considering it with the opposite condition, **deflation**. Inflation is a marked and disagreeable rise in prices, while deflation is the decline of prices accompanied by a fall in business activity. Until comparatively recently, inflation and deflation occurred separately. Inflation happened when people had plenty of money, but there was not a corresponding increase in the amount of goods available. It was a simple matter of too much money chasing too few goods, and naturally the prices of those goods rose sharply. Deflation was recognised as a period of industrial depression ('slump'), resulting often from a lack of capital investment, leading to less production and the closing down of industrial plant, with resultant high employment.

More recently it has been recognised that the situation is

271

more complicated, and that inflation and deflation have a complex relationship with boom and depression, and are linked with the level of employment. Deflationary measures by the Government after the Second World War seemed likely to reduce the production of goods and cause unemployment. Businesses objected to lowering prices, and trade unions objected to the wage cuts which would have followed. Political pressure led to the Government permitting a constant increase in prices, and it was believed that this inflation would stimulate business, thus providing more employment, and so expanding the economy.

By the 1970's a situation combining the worst features of inflation and of deflation had arisen. Increases in the cost of imported food and raw materials (especially oil) had made prices rise very quickly, and workers demanded higher wages to keep up with them. Production was not increasing enough to cover increased costs of materials and wages, and prices were further increased to pay the higher wage bill, resulting in even higher wage demands. This 'inflationary spiral' meant that businesses had insufficient money for new factories or equipment, and unemployment grew as workers became redundant. Thus, an inflationary rise in prices and wages was accompanied by a deflationary fall in business activity and large-scale unemployment.

The difficult problem of controlling economic activity is now accepted as a duty by governments of Western countries with a capitalist free enterprise system.

Former prices and incomes policies

In 1965 the Government set up the National Board for Prices and Incomes to investigate all questions of productivity, prices and incomes referred to it. It had no statutory authority to enforce its recommendations, but relied on persuasion and public opinion. In July 1966 a 'stand still' on prices and incomes was announced to allow industrial productivity to 'catch up' with the excessive increases in incomes which had taken place. In August 1966, the Prices and Incomes Act gave the Government power to refuse increases in wages and prices. The Prices and Incomes Board was abolished in November 1970. In 1972, a pay and prices freeze was announced, which extended to 1973, and a Price Commission and Pay Board were set up to enforce a Price and Pay Code to regulate pay, prices, dividends and rents. The controls were set out in a Price Code, drawn up by the Government and amended from time to time as appropriate.

The Conservative government, after the 1979 General Election, no longer applied a prices and incomes policy.

Control of wage increases

In 1973 a 'social contract' was devised. This is an agreement between the TUC (Trades Union Congress) and the Government by which the latter agreed to control prices, maintain free collective wage bargaining, help the lower paid and pensioners, and aim at full employment; and the former acknowledged that trade unions should aim to keep pay rises in step with the cost of living.

Various methods were devised during the 1970's to keep pay rises within limits and the study of this control is part of the subject Economics. Another branch deals with relative price determination: why are some prices higher than others?

The simple answer is that the price of an article depends upon the **supply** of it, and the **demand** for it. Generally speaking, rare and desirable goods command a high price; common and easily acquired goods command only a low price. If the supply of the common goods become limited, and the demand for them rose, the price would increase. Similarly, if rare goods such as diamonds became plentiful, the price would fall.

The more successful the Government is in finding solutions to problems of prices and incomes, the easier it is for personal budgeting. In turn, the Government's task is easier if individuals budget wisely, keeping within their incomes and setting aside savings. These can be used by Government, and by businessmen, for financing for example, new roads and new factories.

Good money management will enable the country to expand production, which will lead to increased exports and imports, thus contributing to international trade and international prosperity.

Questions

1. (a) What is the difference between Direct and Indirect Taxation? Give examples of each.
   (b) Which tax would be deducted from an employee's gross pay by his employer?
2. (a) Who pays National Insurance contributions and how are the contributions calculated?
   (b) Give an account of the benefits paid under the National Insurance scheme.

3. (a) What do you understand by 'inflation' and 'deflation'?
   (b) What is an 'inflationary spiral'?
4. (a) What is the difference between planned buying and impulse buying?
   (b) Why is budgeting particularly important to young people setting up and running a home? What outside factors may affect the budget, and how should these be provided for?
5. The following may be deducted from an employee's wages. Sort them into 2 columns under the headings 'Statutory Deductions' and 'Voluntary Deductions'.

   Social Club,   pension scheme,   PAYE,   hospital benefit, holiday club,   SAYE   NI contribution,   drum draw, charity contribution,   Christmas club.
6. (a) How can the Government raise money?
   (b) Give an account of how VAT is raised.
7. Your take-home pay is £40 a week, you are still living at home and give some of this to your parents. Draw up an imaginary budget of your expenditure.
8. (a) Clearly explain what you understand by personal budgeting.
   (b) Show how each of the following could affect a person's budget.
      (i)   Advertising.   (ii) Hire purchase. (iii) Inflation.
      (iv) Changes in taxes.   (v) Reduction in overtime
                                    working.
      (vi) Reduction in mortgage interest rates.
      (vii) Increase in Local Government expenditure.

                                                        (EM)

18

The role of the State

The State has always assumed responsibility for certain functions, in particular for management of the national budget, defence, foreign relations and the maintenance of law and order. In comparatively modern times it has added to its responsibilities the welfare of children, including education: the safeguarding and improvement of health, and of working conditions and the relief of distress of various kinds. However, the twentieth century has seen a great expansion in the State's interests and influence, not only in the fields of health, education, and social security, but in fuel and power supplies, transport, agriculture, technological development, economic planning and the protection of the individual and the environment.

This growth of interests has led to a corresponding growth in the size of government organisations and staff. A hundred years ago, a Prime Minister would appoint about thirty ministers: Mr James Callaghan's 1976 ministry included exactly 101 ministerial appointments. However, the chief expansion has been not so much in the creation of new government departments, but in the growth of those already existing, so that for instance there are ten times as many non-industrial civil servants as there were in 1900. Total government expenditure also increased, from about 9 per cent of national income in 1870 to nearly 52 per cent in 1974.

Government income

It is perhaps in the field of finance, the taking away and giving away of money, that the majority of people are most aware of the presence of Government.

Income Tax, which for most is deducted as PAYE (see Chapter 17) may be varied each year at the Chancellor of the Exchequer's April budget. In the 1970's it became a weapon in the prices and incomes war on inflation, lower taxation being offered in return for wage claims being kept within the limits thought reasonable by the Government.

In April 1982, income tax on taxable income up to £15 000 (i.e., after personal allowances and deductions) was fixed at a rate of 30p in the pound, so that a person earning a taxable income of £6000 would expect to pay £1800 of it in income tax.

Above £15 100 bands of higher tax rates commence, at 40 per cent increasing to 60 per cent above £31 500. These figures tend to be altered by successive Budgets.

Another **direct tax** (see Chapter 17) is **Corporation Tax**, which is a levy on the profits of companies and commercial organisations. For the financial year of 1976-77 this was at the rate of 52 per cent for large companies, and 42 per cent for small companies. In 1977-78, Corporation Tax provided an income for the Government of £2500 million, compared with £19 000 million from income tax and surtax.

Further income from direct taxation is provided by the **Capital Transfer Tax**, which is essentially a tax on gifts over £15 000. It was introduced in 1975 to prevent people avoiding death duties on estates by giving them away (to their heirs) in their lifetime. A **Capital Gains Tax** has also been introduced, and this is a 30 per cent surcharge on gains added to capital on the sale of the assets which are worth £1000 per year or more. Homes, private motor cars and National Savings Certificates are exempt from this tax, which brings in about £300 million per year to the Government.

All the above are direct taxes in that they are paid by the person or organisation directly to the Inland Revenue. **Indirect taxes** are those paid on money spent (expenditure), and are collected by Customs and Excise. The largest is VAT (see Chapters 4 and 17), which had a tax yield of £4240 million in 1978. Most people are aware of VAT as an addition to the price of goods in shops, but it is also added to the price of services, including entertainment (eg cinemas, football matches). There are further duties on cars, tobacco, spirits, beer and wine.

Other sources of income to the Government include TV and radio licences (£275 million), motor vehicle licences (£1068 million), and gambling (£315 million), and duties on oil and petrol (£2400 million), and tobacco (£2150 million). The total income to Government in 1977-78 was £37 608 million.

The public also has access to services provided by the Government to facilitate saving which are, in effect, loans to the

Government. A variety of savings methods are available through the Department of National Savings (see Chapter 13). The post offices are used to make easy the purchase of savings certificates, bonds, etc as well as payments into National Girobank; this is in addition to the remittance services by post or telegraph (see Chapter 11). The Post Office has, of course, a full service of postal and communication systems available to commerce, industry and the public (see Chapter 7).

Public expenditure

Taxation was originated to pay for public expenditure, thus providing the public with a range of public services and goods, and this remains the most important reason for taxation. Other reasons include:

- the control of the economy. The Government can put money into people's pockets or take it out, by altering taxation. This it does according to whether it wants people to spend on consumer goods to boost production, or wishes to curb over-spending.
- encouragement of growth and investment. Using tax allowances as incentives, Government can channel the resources of industry into areas it considers desirable.
- equality. Taxation redistributes wealth by taking it away from the well-to-do and using it for providing allowances and social services for the needy.

Public spending in 1976-77 totalled £53 698 million. As shown, the greatest proportion of this spending was on Social Services, including Social Security (see Chapter 17), Education and Health (see Chapter 3). The Environment, including Housing, Law and Order, and also Roads and Transport (see Chapter 6) accounted for 22 per cent of Government spending.

Commerce and Industry received 7.5 per cent of the Government's spending (see Chapter 9). This included grants for companies setting up or modernising factories, help in development areas, and finance for special projects in key industries and for research and training, especially re-training. A number of Finance Acts made provision for this assistance. Regional Development grants, plus low interest loans are available for the purpose of creating employment, and for improving and modernising equipment.

The **National Enterprise Board (NEB)** is particularly concerned with the use of public money to develop industrial efficiency and international competitiveness, and also any aspect of the provision, maintenance and safeguarding of employment. Other organisations supported by public funds include the National Economic Development Council (NEDC),

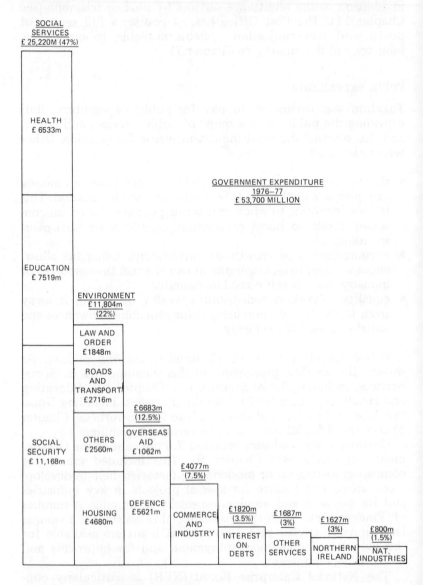

SOCIAL SERVICES
£ 25,220M (47%)

HEALTH
£ 6533m

EDUCATION
£ 7519m

GOVERNMENT EXPENDITURE
1976–77
£ 53,700 MILLION

ENVIRONMENT
£11,804m
(22%)

LAW AND ORDER
£1848m

ROADS AND TRANSPORT
£2716m

£6683m
(12.5%)

SOCIAL SECURITY
£ 11,168m

OTHERS
£2560m

OVERSEAS AID
£ 1062m

£4077m
(7.5%)

HOUSING
£4680m

DEFENCE
£5621m

COMMERCE AND INDUSTRY

INTEREST ON DEBTS
£1820m
(3.5%)

OTHER SERVICES
£1687m
(3%)

NORTHERN IRELAND
£1627m
(3%)

NAT. INDUSTRIES
£800m
(1.5%)

Government Expenditure 1976-77.

278

and the National Research Development Corporation (NRDC). (See Chapters 3 and 9.)

The nationalised industries receive about 1.5 per cent of national spending, plus a further 5 per cent for roads and public transport. Public corporations were set up to run the national-ised industries and services (see Chapter 3) and this constituted a heavy initial outlay, and a number of industries required to be subsidised out of the public purse, especially during periods of extensive modernisation. In addition, public money has enabled the NEB to buy shares, sometimes with a control-ling interest, in a number of public companies which were in difficulties.

It should be remembered that local authorities also use public money, either from rates or from government grants for the provision of services, including housing, public health, public protection and education (see Chapter 3).

Protection of the individual

One area which has developed considerably in recent years is the protection of the public, both in employment and as consumers (see Chapter 16). A range of Acts of Parliament enable the Prices and Consumer Protection Department to prevent goods being inaccurately described, or sold with a false or misleading price reduction; to ensure that goods sold are of a merchantable quality, and are fit for the purpose for which they are being sold; to protect people buying by hire purchase; to take action over traders who send unsolicited goods; to prevent 'price-fixing'; and to take action over unsafe goods. In addition, action has been taken to ensure that prices are clearly marked on goods.

Further consumer protection is provided by local authorities, who have Inspectors of Weights and Measures, and Trading Standards Departments to investigate complaints by the public. Complaints against the nationalised industries are heard by Consumer Councils.

In the area of unemployment, too, Acts of Parliament protect those who are made redundant, those who feel that they have been dismissed unfairly and those who feel that they have been discriminated against either on account of their sex or on account of their colour.

All employees now must have a written contract of employ-ment, clearly stating their rights as to notice, or to make complaints. The Government is also concerned with working conditions and provides factory inspectors under the terms of the Health and Safety at Work Act. (See Chapter 16).

Protection is also given, by various Rent Acts (see Chapter 16) to those who rent accommodation. The Acts introduced rent regulation and access to Rent Tribunals. For those buying their first home, the Government has introduced mortgage schemes, together with loans and grants (see Chapter 13). Mortgages are also affected, of course, by implementation of Government monetary policy since this has often been effected by variation of the Bank Rate. This influences the rate of interest paid by home-owners on loans from building societies (see Chapters 8 and 13). Housing accommodation is provided by local authorities for rental.

Industrial relations

Legislation has been passed with the intention of improving industrial relations by setting up an **Advisory Conciliation and Arbitration Service (ACAS)** under the Employment Protection Act (1976). ACAS encourages collective bargaining between unions and employers, and may offer to intervene in an industrial dispute in order to conciliate or arbitrate. It may, at the joint request of union *and* employer, appoint an arbitrator, or a board of arbitrators, or refer the case to the Central Arbitration Committee (CAC). This is the permanent body for settling disputes.

Public health

The Health Service is the responsibility of the health ministers of the four home countries, and their departments are responsible for overall planning, although the pattern of organisation is largely in the hands of area organisations, and day-to-day running is carried out by management teams (see Chapter 3). The service is largely subsidised by the Treasury, as National Insurance contributions and charges only bring in one-fifth of the cost. Charges include those for prescriptions, dental treatment, spectacles and some other articles. Some of these services have exemptions from charges for some categories of people, such as old-age pensioners and expectant mothers.

Medical care includes not only treatment by general practitioners, opticians and dentists, and hospital treatment, but the facilities of clinics, including family planning, vaccination and immunisation, district nurses, midwives and health visitors. Health inspections for children are provided at schools.

Transport

Nationalisation of transport facilities has led to Government control, through various public corporations, of all transport of goods and passengers by rail, and much of that by road, air and canal. The Government intends to bring all commercial ports and cargo-handling facilities under public ownership and control, establishing for the purpose a National Ports Authority, but already one-quarter of all port capacity is nationalised under the ownership of the British Transport Docks Board or of the British Railways Board. Others are owned by local authorities. The National Dock Labour Board (NDLB), with which 30 000 dockers are registered, is a statutory corporation.

Under a Merchant Shipping Act, the Department of Trade is responsible for regulations regarding the safety of ships, including certification of the Plimsoll line (which ensures the safe loading of a ship) and ensuring the provision of live-saving and fire-fighting equipment. It also deals with the discipline, health and accommodation of the crews. Some ships are operated by British Rail. (See also Chapters 3 and 6.)

There is, in addition, control over private road users through licensing, tests, safety requirements, traffic law and road worthiness of vehicles.

Overseas trading

The Government also has influence in areas of which the general public is less aware. Companies trading overseas know that the Government can affect imports by imposing tariffs and import quotas, and by devaluation of the pound. Devaluation may also increase exports, and so may the introduction of a bounty scheme. The Government in fact provides a good deal of help for exporting companies through the Overseas Trade Board and the Department of Trade. It includes insurance against non-payment by a foreign buyer, and guarantees to banks which finance exporting companies. The Government is also represented in the policy making of the European Economic Community. (See also Chapter 5).

Finance

The Bank of England, as already stated, is an instrument of Government monetary policy. It controls the supply of money through the printing (or minting) and issue of notes and coins, and the regulation of bank credit. In addition it is agent for the issue of Government bonds, and controls their interest payments. It is also concerned with the weekly issue of Treasury Bills to cover short-term Government borrowing (see Chapter 8).

The aim of the state

It will have been seen that the State, in some way, is concerned in some aspect of every chapter in this book; and that it has some influence on every aspect of our lives.

In general, the aim of the State must be to raise the national standard of living, secure stable prices and protect the consumers, while effecting a reasonable balance of trade, and the running of commerce and industry for the benefit of the country and the whole community.

Every decision in these interests, therefore, must be made by those answerable to the whole community, as the Government is through Parliament.

Glossary of transport and delivery terms

Bill of Lading (B/L) A receipt given by the shipper for goods received from consignor (sender) promising delivery in return for payment of freight. This, or an *Airway Bill* for goods being transported by air, fulfills the same purpose as a Consignment Note.

Bonded goods These are imported goods which are liable to duty and have been deposited in a Government or bonded warehouse until the duty has been paid. Such goods are said to be 'In Bond', because the owner of the warehouse has signed a Bond to guarantee that the duty will be paid before the goods are removed (eg, tobacco, wines, spirits).

Carriage forward (cge fwd) Carriage costs to be paid for by the consignee (receiver). Seller will pay the cost but will include this on his invoice to the buyer.

Carriage paid (cge pd) Carriage costs paid for by the sender.

Charter party (C/P) This is an agreement in which a shipowner, or plane owner, leases the whole ship, or aircraft, or part of it, at a fixed rate or for a fixed period.

Company's risk (CR): owner's risk (OR) The carrier's charges will vary according to the quantity, value, size, etc of the goods he is asked to carry, but he offers two rates:—at company's risk the Company (the carrier) is responsible for losses, delays, or damage through the negligence of its servants. At owner's risk the owner can claim against the Company for injury, loss and delay only when negligence by the carrier can be proved. Goods sent at OR will incur a lower charge than those sent at CR.

Consign The forwarding of goods from one place to another.

Consignee The person to whom the goods are sent or consigned.

Consignment The goods themselves. The term also means the sending or delivering of goods by one person to another.

Consignment note Forms which are completed when goods are sent by road or rail: the form gives information for the benefit of haulier and consignee. A consignment note forms the basis of contract for the carriage of goods. Information includes:

collection date
name and address of sender (consignor)
name and address of consignee
description of goods, number of packages, any marks or
    numbers, weight
vehicle number
signature of consignee obtained upon delivery

Cost, insurance and freight (cif) To the price of the goods, the following are added: cost of transport to the ship, cost of loading, cost of carriage of goods by ship, and the cost of marine insurance.

Customs declaration When a postal packet is sent to an address outside the country, the sender is required to complete a Customs Declaration form, on which he states the nature and value of the parcel, the date of postage, the country where the goods were made and the weight of each separately described goods.

Customs entry A list given to the Customs Officer by the importer or shipper, which shows the weight, value and description of the goods to be landed or shipped.

Customs export value The cost of the goods to the purchaser abroad, including packing, inland and coastal transport in the UK, dock dues, loading charges and all other costs, charges and expense (for example, insurance and commission) up to the point where the goods are deposited on the exporting vessel. Sea freight and marine insurance should not be included, and cash and trade discounts allowed to the purchaser should be deducted.

Delivery sheet Used by firms which deliver their own goods in their own vehicles. It sets out deliveries for the day on a particular journey. Signature obtained upon delivery of goods as proof of delivery.

Drawback The sum returned by the Government upon certain classes of goods exported on which duty has already been paid. This helps the exporter to compete in foreign markets.

Ex site The purchaser pays for the cost of transport from the site at which the goods are lying: this term is often used in connection with the sale of machinery, builders' equipment, etc.

Ex stock From stock, implying immediate delivery.

284

Ex warehouse The purchaser pays for the cost of transport from the warehouse where the goods are stored. Many commodities are stored in public warehouses which may be many miles from the offices of the owner of the goods where the sale takes place.

Ex works The purchaser pays for the cost of transport from the factory where the goods are made. The price quoted for a new motor car is often 'ex works' and this means that the purchaser will have to pay for the delivery from the factory to the showroom.

Franco In addition to paying all carriage and insurance costs, the seller will pay Customs duties.

Free alongside ship (fas) The price of the goods includes the cost of transport as far as the ship's side—this may be on the quay or by barge alongside the ship.

Free on board (fob) The seller pays all expenses until the goods have been loaded on to the ship.

Free on rail (for) The price of the goods includes the cost of transport to the railway; this term is often used by firms which have a private siding at their works.

Gross weight, net weight, and tare Gross weight is the total weight of the package; the weight of the goods is net weight; and the weight of the packaging is tare.

Loco The buyer takes the goods from their site and pays all subsequent charges.

Shippers Persons who place goods on ships for transportation abroad.

Shipping notes Documents which are addressed to the superintendent of the dock where a ship is lying, requesting him to receive and ship certain goods which are described on the note.

Stowage orders These are needed for dangerous or harmful substances, refrigerated shipments and particularly valuable goods.

Index

Index

British Transport
  Docks Board, *31*, 88, 281
  Hotels Ltd, 82
British United and Provident
    Association (BUPA), 227
British Waterways Board, 86
Broker
  Baltic Exchange, 91
  commission, 142
  credit, 190
    canvassing, 194
  export, 60
  insurance, 221, 231
  Lloyd's, 231, 232
  mortgage, 211
  stock, 120, 135-6, 142, 203,
    204, 214
Budget account
  bank, 121, *267-8*
  department store, 39, 187
  National Girobank, 177
Budgets
  advertising, 237
  Budget Day, 266, 275
  business, 271
  government, **266 et seq.**, 275
  personal, 264 et seq.
Building societies, *9*, **20-21**, 113,
    208 et seq.
  computerised records, 106
  investment by, 138
  savings accounts, 200, 207, 208
    et seq., *213*
  also see mortgages
Bulk buying, 34, 37, 44-5
Bulk posting, 96, 99, 102
'Bulls', 136-7, 142
Bus services, 85
Business reply service, 98, *99*
  for parcels, 102
Buy now — pay later, — also see
    credit cards, 173
Buying
  department, *16*
  documentation, 47 et seq.

impulse, 44, 175, 266
legislation, 247 et seq.
methods, 45 et seq.
procedure, 47 et seq.
sale goods or seconds, 251
second-hand goods, 251

Cable transfer — see bank air mail
Callers' services, 101
Canals, 76, 78, **86-7**, 281
Canvassing, 194
Caveat emptor, 247
Capital, 1, 128 et seq., *142*, 147
    et seq.
  appreciation, 137
  authorised, 12, 142, 148 et seq.
  circulating or working, 12, *147*,
    148, 151
  fixed, 147, 148, 150
  floating, 138
  insurance of, 229
  issued, 149
  liquid, *147*, 148
  market, 132
  share, 144, 151
Capital Gains tax, 266, *269*, 276
Capital transfer tax, 276
Capitalist investment, 140
Car ownership — also see motor
    vehicle, 76, **84-5**, 184, 266
Care labelling code, *255*
Carriage forward, 50
Carriage paid, 50
Cash and carry
  discount stores, 37, 44-5
  wholesale, 33, *34*, 35
Cash on delivery (COD), 41, **102**,
    176
Cash discount, 50
Cash with order (CWO), 41, 102
Cash payments, 47, **157-8**, 192
Cashless society, 188
Central Arbitration Committee
    (CAC), 280

Daily list, 143
Datapost, 100-101
Datel, 106-8
Debenture, 138, 143, 144, 217
Debit note, 49, 50
Debtor, 147, 150, 166, 167, 190, *192*, 193, 194
Deferred shares, 143, 150
Deflation, 271-2
Delivery — see also Post Office services
department, 78, 83
note, 48
Department stores, 39-40
credit facilities, 39, 186-8
public relations, 241-2
Deposit account — see bank, building societies, finance houses, National Girobank
Deposit bank — see banking
Design Council, *255*, 256
Despatch note, 48
Devaluation, 59, 73, 281
Development areas and organisations, 128 et seq., 277
Diners' Club, 169-70
Direct debit — see bank, National Girobank
Direct mail, 244
Direct selling, *34*, 40-41
Direct services, 2-3
Direct tax, 266, *269*, 275-6
Director General of Fair Trading, 189, 196, 249, 252
Directors — see Board of
Discount House, 61, 131, 132, *141*, 145
Discount market, 132
Discount store, 44-5
Distribution
see chain of
Distributor, *76*, see Wholesale trade
District Councils, 82, 85, *270*

Dividend, 13, 133, 136 et seq., 143, 144, 145, 151, 154, 272
Co-operative society, 19, 154
Government stock, 204
Unit Trust, 201
Divisions of labour, 3-4
Dock warrant, 64
Docks, *76*, 87, 281
Documentary credit, 61
Documents
commercial, 47 et seq.
export, 62-3
of title, 63
Dutch auction, 46
Duty, 63-4, 269, 276

ERNIE, 204
Economic Development Committee (EDC), 130
Economy
EEC policy, 73
mixed, 8, *9*
the state of the, 271 et seq.
Editorial publicity, 241
Electricity Council, *9*, 25, *31*, 154, *248*
Emergency dialling service, 105
Employer's liability insurance, 227, **229**
Employment — also see trade unions
and the economy, 272
collective bargaining, 260, 273, 280
contract, 259-60, 279-80
creation, 128-9
Endowment policies, 201, 211, *213*, 225, 226
Enquiry, 47, 48, 103
Entrepôt trade, 63
Entrepreneur, 140
Environment, Department of the, 76, 82, 211, *278*
Equal liability, 195

Equal pay, 260
Equities, 137, 139, *142*, *143-4*, **150**, 201, 217
Equity Bank (Equity Capital for Industry Ltd), 139, 142
Errors and Omissions Excepted (E & OE), 50
Estate duty, 266
Euro-currency market, 140, 142
European Atomic Energy Community (Euratom), 66
European Coal and Steel Community (ECAS), 66
European Council, *71*
European Economic Community — see Common Market (EEC)
European Free Trade Association (EFTA), **67**, 68
European Monetary System (EMS), 72 et seq.
European Parliament, *71*
Exchange Equalisation Account (EEA), 113
Exports and exporting, 2, *3*, **57** et seq., *67*, *76*, 133, 281
    agent, 60
    bounties, 59, 281
    documentation, 62-3
    documents and terms, 283-4
    houses, 60
    invisible, 57 et seq., 87
    merchants, 60
Export Credits Guarantee Department (ECGD), 62, 281
Extractive industry, 2-3

Facsimile transceiver, 106
Factor, 61
Family income policy, 226
Ferries, 82, 84, 88
Fidelity guarantee insurance, 229
Fiduciary issue, 111-12
Finance Houses, 113, 131-2, **134-5**, *142*, 183, 185, 190, 191, 195, *213*

Association, 135
consumer credit licence, 190
equal liability, 195
second mortgage, 211
Finance corporations, 132, 138 et seq., *142*
Finance Corporation for Industry Ltd (FCI), 139, *142*
Finance for Industry Ltd (FFI), 139, *142*
Financial Times, 201
First class post, 97 et seq.
Fixed assets — see capital, fixed
Fixed expenses, 152
Fixed time calls, 105
Food labelling and hygiene, 253
Foreign currency and exchange, 120, 133, 178
Founders' shares — see deferred shares
Franco, 284
Franking machine, 96
Free alongside ship (fas), on board (fob), on rail (for), 284
Free enterprise — see private enterprise
Freefone, 104
Freepost, 98-9
Freight containers — see container traffic
Freightliners Ltd, 80, 83
Friendly Societies, *9*, 20-21, 207
    insurance by, 230
Fringe benefit, 227
Fuel and power, *9*, 24-5, *31*, 275
Futures contract, 46-7

Gilts, 137, 143 — also see Government or local authority stock
Girocheques, 178
Giro credit — see bank
Gold standard, 111-12
Goods received note (GRN), 48-9
Government — also see Common

303

Public corporations — see nationalisation and corporations by
name
Public expenditure — see government and local authority
expenditure
Public health — see National Health
Service, social services
Public liability, 223, 224, 227, 228,
230, 232
Public limited company, *9*, 11-13,
14-18, *20*, 114
advantages and disadvantages,
11-12, 14
capital, 11 et seq., 136 et seq.,
148 et seq.
organisation chart, *16*
profit sharing, 15-16
responsibilities, *17*
Public relations, 240-2
Public sector — see Nationalisation
Public transport — see Passenger
transport
advertising on, *244*
Public Works Loan Board (PWLB),
28
Purchase order, 47, 48, 103

Quantity discount, 50
Quota, import, 59, 281
Quotation, 48, 50, 190

Rail transport, 76, 78-82, 101, 281
advantages and disadvantages, 81
containers, 78, 80-1, 83-4
underground, 85, 244
Rates, 28, 168, *270*, 271, 279
water, 93
Raw materials, 1-2, 57, 75, *76*
Receipt, 49, 158, 224
Recorded delivery, 100
Redundancy, 259, 279
Refer to drawer (R/D), 124
Referendum, 67

Registered capital — see capital,
authorised
Registered post, 99-100, 102, 176
Registrar of Business Names, 9
Registrar of Companies, 12 et seq.
Registrar of Friendly Societies, see
Friendly Societies
Regulation Agreements, 191 et seq.
Re-insurance, 231
Remittances, 49
advice note, 49
bank, 158 et seq.
see National Girobank
see Post Office
Rent
control, 261, 272
regulation, 261, 280
Tribunal, *257*, 261, 280
see also Hire
Reply coupons, 101
Restrictive practices, 247, 249
Retail trade, 2, 3, 33, *34*, 37 et seq.,
76
advertising, *243-4*
associations, 253-4, 261
legislation, 247 et seq.
public relations, 240-2
River transport, 76, 78, **86**
containers, 78
Road licence — see motor vehicle
Roadline UK, 83, *84*
Road transport, 75, 76-8, 82 **et**
seq., 101
advantages and disadvantages, 85
containers, 78, 82, 83-4
documents and delivery terms,
283-4
haulage, 82-4
legal conditions, 84, 281
passenger, 84-5
versus rail, 79
Roads, 76, *82*, *270*, *278*, 281
bridges and tunnels, 82, *83*
Rome Treaty, 66, 68
Royal Mint, *9*, 26-7, 112, 281